The Mexican American

The Mexican American

SPANISH-AMERICANS
AS A POLITICAL FACTOR
IN NEW MEXICO ⊐ ₀ 1974
1912-1950

E. B. Fincher

ARNO PRESS
A New York Times Company
New York — 1974

Reprint Edition 1974 by Arno Press Inc.

Copyright © , 1974, by E. B. Fincher
Reprinted by permission of E. B. Fincher

THE MEXICAN AMERICAN
ISBN for complete set: 0-405-05670-2
See last pages of this volume for titles.

Publisher's Note: This dissertation was
reprinted from the only available copy.

Manufactured in the United States of America

Library of Congress Cataloging in Publication Data

Fincher, Ernest Barksdale, 1910-
   Spanish-Americans as a political factor in New
Mexico, 1912-1950.

   (The Mexican American)
   Originally presented as the author's thesis, New
York University, 1950.
   Bibliography: p.
   1. Mexican Americans--New Mexico. 2. New Mexico--
Politics and government--1848-1950. I. Title.
II. Series.
F805.M5F56 1974   320.9'789'05   73-14202
ISBN 0-405-05676-1

Sponsoring Committee: Associate Professor Jesse J.
Dossick, Chairman; Professor H. H. Giles;
and Professor Theodore D. Rice

SPANISH-AMERICANS AS A POLITICAL FACTOR IN NEW MEXICO

1912-1950

E. B. FINCHER

Submitted in partial fulfillment of the

requirements for the degree of Doctor of

Philosophy in the School of Education of

New York University

1950

State of New Jersey
STATE TEACHERS COLLEGE
AT MONTCLAIR
25 October, 1950

Graduate Committee
School of Education
New York University
New York, N.Y.

Gentlemen:

I hereby guarantee that no part of the dissertation which I
have submitted for publication has been heretofore published
and (Or) copyrighted in the United States of America, except
in the case of passages quoted from other published sources;
that I am the sole author and proprietor of said dissertation;
that the dissertation contains no matter which, if published,
will be libelous or otherwise injurious, or infringe in any
way the copyright of any other party; and that I will defend,
indemnify and hold harmless New York University against all
suits and proceedings which may be brought and against all
claims which may be made against New York University by reason
of the publication of said dissertation or document.

Yours very truly,

E.B. Fincher
Ass't. Professor,
Social Studies

EBF: nl

TABLE OF CONTENTS

TABLES

Tables (Continued)

CHARTS

v

DIAGRAMS

MAPS

THE NATURE OF THIS STUDY

Composers sometimes make their music more meaningful by explaining what inspired their composition and under what circumstances the work was completed. Likewise novelists may describe the actual situation upon which they have contrived a plot, and may go so far as to explain the purpose for which a particular book was written.

Although operating at what many consider a less creative level, the writer of a thesis may describe the inception of his idea and the manner in which it was developed. This in an effort to make his finished work more comprehensible.

An Important But Neglected Minority

Study of the Spanish-Americans of New Mexico as a political factor has certain peculiar attractions for the social scientist. The composition of the population of New Mexico is unique, and in itself makes for marked political differences. The once finely adjusted balance between Anglo-American and Hispanic-American is undergoing change. To those concerned with majority-minority adjustment in a democratic society, changes now taking place in New Mexico should be of considerable interest. Moreover, the role which the Spanish-speaking people play in politics is highly controversial, as succeeding pages will indicate, and for that reason an evaluation seems imperative to an interested student of public affairs.

The political problem posed by the Hispanic-Americans of New Mexico has national, as well as local, implications. For as Carey McWilliams recently pointed out, our Hispanic-American population is the farthest removed from general recognition, despite the fact that it numbers between three and four million people, thus constituting one of the largest ethnic minorities in the United States.[1] The social scientist's neglect of this large minority likewise is attested by scholars of Spanish descent. Ignacio L. Lopez, California newspaper publisher, observed that "There has been an appalling dearth of information concerning the Mexican immigrant and the American of Mexican descent."[2] According to Ortiz Hernan, Consul-General of Mexico for the Southwest, "The shelves of the Library of Congress . . .bulge with studies of all types about. . .the 'melting pot of the world.' Perhaps the Ibero-Americans of the southwestern United States rate only a frying pan; but as a matter of fact very little has been written about them one way or another."[3]

The Spanish-Americans of New Mexico also are of international importance, particularly in connection with the Good Neighbor Policy. As Ruth D. Tuck writes, "That (the Spanish-American) furnishes an important key to our relations with the southern half of this hemisphere is a fact of which the country at large, including the Southwest, is not yet aware.. . .When

---

1. "Mexican Bundle of Myths," Saturday Review of Literature, (Dec. 25, 1948), p. 13.
2. Preface, Ruth D. Tuck, Not With the Fist, p. ix.
3. Preface, Pauline R. Kibbe, Latin Americans in Texas, p. xiii.

we are greeted with polite mistrust below the border, we might
remember that a key to part of the puzzle is kicking around at
home."[1] This statement is corroborated by Joaquin Ortega, former
director of the School of Inter-American Affairs, who says that
"New Mexico is the shortest route to Mexican good will."[2]

Finally, the Hispanic-Americans of New Mexico are of
importance from the educational point of view. In the first
place, inter-group relationships always are of prime importance
to the educator. Moreover, an analysis of the political status
of the Spanish-Americans of New Mexico involves consideration
of educational problems which arise wherever large minorities
become established. (To cite a specific example, bilingualism
has become an educational problem of national scope, affecting
the school program not only in the Southwest, but also in the
City of New York and in the industrial centers of the Midwest.)
More important, any study of politics calls for treatment of
the relationship between educational advantage and political
opportunity in a tension area.

Despite the attractions which the Hispanic-Americans
of New Mexico should hold for the student of political science,
little has been done in the field. A check of two exhaustive
bibliographies of printed and unprinted materials dealing with
the Spanish-Americans of the United States,[3] Doctoral Disserta-

---

1. Tuck, op. cit., p. xv.
2. Quoted, Carey McWilliams, North from Mexico, p. 184.
3. Lyle Saunders, Guide to Materials Bearing on Cultural Relations in New Mexico, (1944-1949).
   _____, Spanish-Speaking Americans and
   Mexican-Americans in the United States, (1944).

x

<u>tions</u> <u>Accepted</u> <u>by</u> <u>American</u> <u>Universities</u>,[1] the catalog of the
Library of Congress, and other available sources reveals no
investigation in the field of politics which may be considered
comparable to any of the socio-economic documents noted in the
bibliography which accompanies this study. As a final check,
there have been statements from several members of the Department
of Government at the University of New Mexico that a project of
this nature has not been undertaken before.[2]

<u>Boundary</u> <u>Lines</u>

In order to confine this study within reasonable scope,
several delimitations have been established. Thus, the years
1912-1950 will be used as boundaries of this study because the
period represents the entire history of statehood in New Mexico.

When dealing with direct political action, the proposed
study is confined to gubernatorial campaigns and elections. This
decision has been made for two reasons: (1) whereas congres-
sional and presidential elections involve both state and national issues, gubernatorial elections tend to reflect local
differences alone. The influence which minority groups exert
on politics is more visible when local offices are at stake.
(2) Rather than give surface consideration to all elective offices, considerable stress has been given to the most important
state offices--the governorship and the lieutenant-governorship.

In drawing comparisons between Spanish-Americans and

1. 1934-1947.
2. France V. Scholes, Dean of the Graduate School, and Joaquin
Ortega, onetime Director of the School of Inter-American
Affairs, made similar statements in August, 1949.

other major elements in the population of New Mexico, the political status of the American Indian will not be considered. Since Indians received the franchise so recently, and since they have not as yet been drawn into politics,[1] their activities are not valid for purposes of comparison.

Consideration of Negroes has been excluded, for as the succeeding section indicates, they constitute a politically insignificant portion of the total population. "Wetbacks"-- i. e. Mexicans who illegally enter the southwestern states in great numbers--also have been excluded. As yet they have played no discernible role in the politics of New Mexico: they have no legal status; they are migrants; and, as R. L. Chambers points out, "Few of the wetbacks remain in New Mexico after the crops. They are paid off and return south of the border. The farmers keep them on the farms during the (cotton) picking season and then dump them. There is little reason for any of the wetbacks to stay on unless they can be given steady employment."[2]

Basic Terminology

Many of the quotations cited in succeeding pages indicate that the Spanish-Americans of New Mexico consider themselves members of a distinct race, and that they are so regarded by their Anglo-American neighbors. Some of the apparent barriers between the two groups are based upon this misapprehension. For the truth is that no ethnologist would classify the Spanish-

---

1. Interview, Thomas J. Mabry, Governor of New Mexico, Dec. 29, 1949.
2. "The New Mexico Pattern," Common Ground, (Summer, 1949), p. 22.

Americans as a race--"a division of mankind possessing constant
traits, transmissible by descent, sufficient to characterize it
as a distinct human type."[1] On the contrary, the Spanish-
Americans, like the Anglo-Americans, are described as but one
of the numerous sub-subdivisions of the Caucasian race.

One uses more accurate terminology when he designates
the Spanish-Americans of New Mexico as a culture-group. In
the pages which follow, it will be noted that social scientists
generally place the Spanish-Americans of New Mexico in this
category. Certainly if one uses Alpenfels' definition of culture as "certain common experiences all people in the group
share as they grow up,"[2] he can classify the Spanish-Americans
more adequately than if he attempts to attach the label "race"
to this group.

One might narrow the definition yet further by classi-
fication along linguistic lines: that is, the Spanish-Americans
of New Mexico are those whose home language is Spanish. It is
on this basis that Anglo-American and Spanish-American have been
differentiated when state or federal censuses have been taken.

But it should be emphasized that this study is political, rather than anthropological, in nature. Its purpose is
not to demonstrate that the Spanish-Americans of New Mexico are
a race, a culture-group, or members of a linguistic family.
Instead, it is an attempt to discover whether or not group consciousness exists, and, if it exists, to observe its political
manifestations.

---

1. Webster's Intercollegiate Dictionary
2. Ethel J. Alpenfels, Sense and Nonsense About Race, p. 27.

One indication of the status of the Hispanic-American of New Mexico is the evolution of popular terminology. Until recent years, the Spanish-speaking New Mexican usually referred to himself as a "Mexican" and was given that cognomen by his Anglo-American neighbor.[1] The term "native people" also was widely employed in designating the descendants of the early Spanish and Mexican settlers as opposed to newcomers of other national backgrounds.

In the last 20 years, however, the Hispanic-American people have come to resent the word "Mexican" when applied to them. Newcomers to the state, particularly Texans who have settled in the eastern section, have used "Mexican" in a derogatory sense to the point that Hispanic-Americans throughout the state have become highly sensitive to the word. That explains why the terms "Spanish-speaking," "Spanish-American," "Latin-American," "Ibero-American," and "Hispanic-American" have developed in recent years as descriptive of persons of Spanish or Mexican descent. The term "Anglo-American" is loosely defined as a New Mexican of Caucasian but non-Spanish stock.

As far as common parlance goes, however, such high-sounding terms are unnecessary. A New Mexican of Spanish or Mexican extraction is generally referred to as an "Hispano" without meaning or giving offense, while a New Mexican of any other "white" stock will be labeled an "Anglo." In this paper,

---

1. The statement, based upon observation over a period of years, has been checked with such long-term residents as Erna Fergusson, the writer, and Thomas J. Mabry, member of the constitutional convention of 1910.

both the popular terminology and the higher-sounding "Spanish-American and Hispanic-American" are employed.

The Scope of the Project

This study is a consideration of four basic questions:
(1) Is there evidence that Spanish-Americans constitute a recognizable minority in New Mexico? (2) Are there issues which divide the Anglo-Americans and the Spanish-Americans of New Mexico? (3) If such issues exist, do they visibly affect politics? (4) To what extent do the Spanish-Americans participate in political affairs?

In considering the possible minority status of the Spanish-Americans of New Mexico, the distribution of population, the nature of ethnic groups, the character of statistical evidence, and the recognition of minorities by constitutional, statutory, and administrative law have been treated.

The identification of issues which possibly may divide New Mexicans into Anglo-American and Spanish-American categories has been sought by an analysis of the socio-economic status of the two groups, an examination of religious affiliations, a consideration of linguistic differences and educational opportunity, a study of organizations based upon group consciousness, and a commentary on the historical basis of conflicting legal, economic, and political concepts.

Where issues which divide voters along linguistic or cultural lines have been found to exist, an attempt has been made to ascertain the possible influence on politics. First, an effort has been made to discover whether or not Anglo-

Americans and Spanish-Americans gravitate into opposing political parties, whether or not gubernatorial candidates and other political leaders have made appeals based on group differences, and whether or not such appeals have had visible effect.

An effort to ascertain the extent to which Spanish-Americans participate in New Mexican politics has been attempted by a study of voting qualifications to discover whether or not they bear equally upon Anglo-Americans and Spanish-Americans; an analysis of the voting habits of the two major groups; a study of party leadership; a consideration of party machinery, with particular regard to its financing; a study of pressure groups; a study of the balance of political power; and an appraisal of the part played by group affiliation.

Factual Basis

This study is based upon several types of data. Standard histories of New Mexico have been drawn upon for background material; where possible, controversial political incidents described by historians have been checked with contemporary newspaper accounts. Socio-economic treatises, many of them unpublished theses, have been used in seeking the roots of political behavior. Treatises and statutes have been examined for references to Hispanic-Americans, and statistical material has been widely employed, particularly in plotting the distribution of population and in comparing the socio-economic status of the major groups. Examination of election returns and the roster of party leaders throughout the period of statehood has been a major consideration.

The two most important sources of information, however, have been newspaper files and interviews. Three English-language newspapers: the <u>Santa Fe New Mexican</u>, the <u>Albuquerque Journal</u>, and the <u>Clovis News-Journal</u>, as well as two Spanish-language papers: <u>El Nuevo Mexicano</u> and <u>El Crepusculo</u>, have been followed for extended periods, while other newspapers have been checked for their differing points of view on specific political crises.

Facts and opinions gleaned from interviews with gubernatorial candidates, state and federal legislators, major and minor party chieftains, educators, political commentators, church officials, and free-lance writers are freely quoted in these pages. More rewarding, and, in the end, more significant, were countless informal conversations engaged in with "little people" over a period of years and in many parts of the writer's native state.

ACKNOWLEDGMENTS

Any study of this kind is by its very nature a cooperative enterprise. Certainly a great number of people have contributed to the compilation, interpretation and presentation of the data contained in this dissertation. Foremost among them is Dr. Jesse J. Dossick of New York University, whose ability to provide incisive analysis was equaled only by his expendability in behalf of this investigator. To Dr. H. H. Giles and Dr. Theodore D. Rice, also of New York University, another debt is owed, for as members of the candidate's committee each offered penetrating comment which corrected a number of misconceptions and clarified obscurities. Dr. Joaquin Ortega of the University of New Mexico gave freely of his time and offered invaluable suggestions. Professors Jack Holmes and Dorothy Cline, likewise of the University of New Mexico, and Ernest Lucero, graduate student, supplied information on contemporary politics which was of inestimable value. To Daniel T. Valdes of the League of United Latin American Citizens and Alfredo Montoya of the Asociacion Nacional Mexicana-Americana the writer is indebted for hours of background conversation. In this catagory also comes Melvin Mencher of the Santa Fe office of United Press, who not only gave background material via conversation but also supplied an extensive newspaper file.

It would be impossible to cite the names of librarians in New York, Albuquerque, Santa Fe and Washington who were so tireless in ferreting out dusty manuscripts and reports, much less to list the many public figures and private citizens who freely offered their views on the politics of New Mexico. Many of these are quoted in the body of this study; to others a blanket acknowledgment gratefully is given. Finally and importantly should come the names of those who sought to make this manuscript a creditable production. Immediately there come to mind the Misses Marie Frazee and Gene Haring of the New Jersey State Teachers College at Montclair, each of them an artist.

CHAPTER I

SPANISH-AMERICANS AS A RECOGNIZED GROUP

In crossing New Mexico, the traveler passes from one
sharply defined geographical zone to another. Eastern New
Mexico is but a continuation of the Great Plains of Texas; in
the northern section, high, forested mountains dominate; while,
in general, the remainder of the state is an extension of the
vast, arid tableland of Mexico. This semi-desert is cut from
north to south by two roughly parallel grooves--the narrow
valleys of the Rio Grande and Pecos rivers.

The traveler not only becomes conscious of the sharply
contrasting geography of New Mexico, but he also becomes aware
of linguistic and cultural boundaries. For when one leaves the
plains behind and crosses the Pecos, he enters a somewhat alien
land. The highway map, hitherto marked by such Anglo-Saxon
place names as Clayton, Clovis, Lovington, and Hobbs, now bears
a succession of Spanish names: Mora, Las Vegas, Santa Rosa, and
Carrizozo. More revealing, adobe replaces wood as the common
building material; isolated ranch houses give way to clustered
dwellings; soon the traveler gains the impression that he has
been set down in a foreign land, perhaps Mexico or Peru. The
belief is reinforced when the motorist turns from the highway
onto a country road. If he asks directions, as likely as not
he will be answered in Spanish, and only after some minutes does

a bilingual New Mexican come forward to offer his assistance.

In this fashion even the casual traveler discovers that marked linguistic and cultural differences exist in New Mexico. Should curiosity lead him further afield, he learns that such differences are almost universally recognized, although they are not always understood. He discovers the widespread use of the term "Hispano" to describe native or naturalized New Mexicans of Hispanic descent, with the word "Anglo" as the popular name of the other group. The would-be investigator perhaps becomes aware of group consciousness: a common bond which sometimes loosely, sometimes closely unites those of the same language, religion, and culture.

But to discover whether or not distinct and potentially antagonistic groups actually exist in New Mexico, one must turn from the impressions of the casual observer to the conclusions of trained investigators. Immediately one asks whether anthropologists, sociologists, economists, and historians accept the classifications "Hispanic-American" and "Anglo-American" so commonly employed.

To this question social scientists have given a rather conclusive answer. Examination of a wealth of material dealing with all aspects of the population of New Mexico indicates almost universal recognition of distinct groups. Thus, one of the most comprehensive bibliographies ever compiled--A Guide to Materials Bearing on Cultural Relations in New Mexico,[1]--contains an entire section dealing exclusively with Hispanic-Americans.

---

1. Lyle Saunders, (comp.), University of New Mexico Press, 1944.

Examination of the 433 separate titles in this division of the
bibliography can only lead one to conclude that social scientists
recognize the Hispanic-Americans of New Mexico as a group distin-
guishable from the Anglo-Americans, Indians, Negroes, and Asiatics
who also reside in the state.

An examination of the published and unpublished writings
of southwestern social scientists bears out the impression created
by this definitive bibliography. For almost without exception,
social scientists dealing with New Mexico pay tribute to the importance of the Hispano as a distinct type. A recent statement by
Carey McWilliams is typical: "No matter how sharply the Spanish-
speaking may differ among themselves over the question of nomen-
clatures, the sense of cleavage from or opposition to the Anglos
has always been an important factor in their lives and it is
this feeling which gives cohesion to the group."[1]

Joaquin Ortega, onetime director of the School of Inter-
American Affairs of the University of New Mexico, asserts that
"New Mexico has the most homogeneous Spanish-speaking community
in the United States, along with a typical cross section of Anglo-
Americans and other groups."[2]

"There is a racial division of the state between Spanish
and 'Anglos'", writes Swayne.[3]

In the words of Sanchez, "The New Mexican (Hispano) is
not yet an American culturally, the Treaty of Guadalupe not-

1. North from Mexico, p. 8.
2. Interview, July 15, 1949.
3. James B. Swayne, A Survey of the Economic, Political and Legal
   Aspects of the Labor Problem in New Mexico, p. 5.

withstanding."[1] Also "Almost a hundred years after becoming
American citizens, a broad gap still separates them from the
culture which surrounds them."[2], and ". . .the descendants of
the colonizers of New Mexico constitute an underprivileged socio-
economic minority in the state."[3]

Calvin, one of the most astute students of New Mexican
culture, writes that the Hispanic-Americans "have been denied the
privilege commonly accorded to conquered peoples of mixing their
blood with that of the conquerors. Accordingly one finds today
in New Mexico three perfectly distinct people, Indian, Mexican,
and American, lying side by side like the sharp strands in a
Navaho blanket."[4]

Manuel Gamio states:

In New Mexico the Americans of Mexican descent are a case apart. The great majority are descendants of the first Spanish or indigenous colonists of the
state; they have been American citizens for three quarters of a century, and yet they still have marked Mexican characteristics.. . .This group has been isolated,
as much because of its own characteristic aloofness as
because the whites, officially and personally, draw
apart from it.[5]

Somewhat similar statements are made by Fergusson,[6]
Chavez,[7] Hammond,[8] Johansen,[9] and other social scientists.

---

1. George I. Sanchez, Forgotten People, p. 13.
2. Ibid., p. 28.
3. Ibid., p. 34.
4. Ross Calvin, Sky Determines, p. 215.
5. Manuel Gamio, Mexican Immigration to the United States, pp. 130-1.
6. Harvey Fergusson, Rio Grande.
7. A. B. Chavez, Use of the Personal Interview to Study the Subjective Impact of Culture Contacts.
8. George P. Hammond and T. C. Donnelly, Story of New Mexico.
9. Sigurd Johansen, "Social Organization of Spanish-American Villages".

That educators consider the Spanish-Americans of New
Mexico as a distinct group is indicated by the school census of
1935, which classified pupils according to the language of the
home, and by the numerous studies of bilingualism as an educational problem.[1] Even those educators who are striving to bridge
the gap between Anglo and Hispano do not minimize differences
between the two groups.[2] Moreover, the organization of the
school system itself betrays differences between Anglo-American
and Spanish-American. For instance, a unique feature of the
public schools in most counties is the pre-first grade. This is
not to be confused with the kindergartens found elsewhere. Rather,
it is a special grade made necessary by the fact that the state
constitution requires that all instruction be in English.[3] Since
thousands of young Hispanos come from homes where English is
rarely if ever spoken, they must be taught the language before
they enter the first grade. Where the pre-first grade does not
exist, most Spanish-speaking children are kept in the first grade
for two years.[4] The fact that so many young Hispanos must be
considered as an instructional problem underlines differences
between the two major groups in New Mexico. This cleavage tends

1. Including: George I. Sanchez, Education of Bilinguals in a
   State School System; Annie Reynolds, Education of Spanish-
   Speaking Children in Five Southwestern States; School of
   Inter-American Affairs, Conference on the Problems of Education Among Spanish-Speaking Populations of Our Southwest;
   and others.
2. Interviews with R. J. Mullins, Executive Secretary, New Mexico
   Education Association; Gail Barber, supervisor elementary
   education, State of New Mexico; Patrick Sweeny, supervisor
   secondary education; Bernadine Kelly, supervisor teacher
   training.
3. New Mexico School Code, 1941 Supplement, 1938 Compilation, p. 9.
4. Thomas C. Donnelly, The State Educational System, p. 29.

to persist, for Spanish-speaking children ordinarily remain
retarded throughout their school career.[1]

Legal recognition of the Hispanic-Americans of New
Mexico must be added to this citation of evidence that a cleavage exists. In fact, stringent measures designed to protect
Hispanic-Americans were incorporated into the constitution of
New Mexico at the insistence of Hispano statesmen.[2] Thus, Article 2, Section 5, states that "The rights, privileges and
immunities, civil, political and religious guaranteed to the
people of New Mexico by the Treaty of Guadalupe Hidalgo shall be
preserved inviolate."[3] Article 7, Section 3, offers protection
as ironclad as it is specific. After stating that rights "shall
never be restricted, abridged or impaired on account of religion,
race, language or color," it extends protection to the illiterate.
Moreover, the provision for amending this section of the constitution is so worded that it cannot be changed without the consent of Hispanic-Americans: "and the provisions of this section
. . .shall never be amended except upon a vote of the people of
this state in an election at which at least three fourths of the
electors voting in the whole state, and at least two thirds of
those voting in each county of the state shall vote for such
amendment."[4]

Further recognition of Hispanic-Americans as a distinct
group is given in Article 12. Thus, in Section 8 provision is
made for training teachers to instruct "Spanish-speaking pupils

---

1. Loc. cit.
2. Reuben W. Heflin, "New Mexico Constitutional Convention," p. 66.
3. New Mexico Statutes, Annotated 1941.
4. Ibid.

and students in the public schools and educational institutions
of the state." More forceful in language is Section 10 of the
same article:

> Children of Spanish descent in the state of
> New Mexico shall never be denied the right and privilege
> of admission and attendance in the public schools or
> other public educational institutions of the state, and
> they shall never be classed in separate schools, but
> shall forever enjoy perfect equality with other children
> in all public schools and educational institutions of the
> state, and the legislature shall provide penalties for
> the violation of this section.[1]

Like Article 7, Section 3, this provision can be
amended only with the consent of Hispanic-Americans because of
the stipulations cited above.

Legal cognizance of the existence of a distinct Hispanic-
American group is indicated in the proviso that the assistant
superintendent of schools must speak Spanish[2] and by the establishment in 1909 of the Spanish-American Normal School for the
purpose of "educating Spanish-speaking natives of New Mexico for
the vocation of teachers in the public schools of the counties
where the Spanish language is prevalent."[3] Furthermore, the state
of New Mexico is officially bilingual, for Spanish remains on
par with English in many areas of government. According to the
Secretary of State,

> The laws of this State provide for all laws
> passed by the Legislature to be printed in both the
> English language as well as the Spanish language. All
> legal notices are published in English; however, if
> within the county where such legal notice is being
> printed and a newspaper is published in Spanish then
> again the law provides that all legal notices must also

---

1. Ibid.
2. New Mexico Statutes, Annotated 1941, V. 6, p. 980.
3. New Mexico Blue Book, 1921, p. 74.

be printed in Spanish. Election ballots are also required to be published in both languages. Courts pre-
side in English. The only Spanish used in courts is
when the witness can only speak Spanish, then a trans-
lator translates the Spanish into English, as the
testimony is given.[1]

Summary

In the same manner that the surface of New Mexico is
divided into distinct geographical zones, its population is
divided into recognizable human groupings, among which the
Spanish-Americans are conspicuous. Educators and social scientists have called attention to this group in a consistent manner. Furthermore, both constitutional and statutory law recognize the existence of the Spanish-Americans of New Mexico as
an entity.

---

1. Alicia Romero, letter to writer, September 29, 1949.

CHAPTER II

POPULATION DISTRIBUTION AS A POLITICAL FACTOR

The foregoing chapter indicates that social scientists, educators, and lawmakers recognize the Hispanic-Americans of New Mexico as an entity. The demographer not only recognizes the existence of distinct linguistic and cultural groups, but he approximates their number and describes their distribution.

The unique character of the population of New Mexico is revealed by census returns. It is essentially native, for less than three per cent of the people are foreign born; it is essentially white, for 92.6 per cent of the population is so listed. (Negroes constitute less than one per cent of the total, and Indians less than 6.5 per cent.)[1] Further study of population statistics reveals that this overwhelming majority of native whites is divided somewhat evenly between Hispanic-Americans and Anglo-Americans.

Writing in 1940, Sigurd Johansen of New Mexico State College set the number of Hispanos at 49.66 per cent of the total non-Indian population.[2] This estimate was corroborated by James I. Culbert whose study of population distribution[3] indicates that

1. United States Census, Population, V. II, part 4, p. 956.
2. Sigurd Johansen, Population of New Mexico: Its Composition and Change, Table 9.
3. "Distribution of Spanish-American Population in New Mexico," pp. 171-6.

approximately one half of the white population is Hispanic-American. More recent studies, including Paul Walter's Popula-tion Trends in New Mexico[1] and the George Peabody College Sur-vey,[2] likewise state that the native white population of the state is divided almost evenly between Hispano and Anglo. In August, 1949, officials of the State Department of Education estimated that Hispanos constitute between 40 and 50 per cent of the total white population of New Mexico.[3] The latter figure is confirmed by the office of United States Senator Dennis Chavez.[4]

The presence of two distinct and numerically equal groups gives a peculiar stamp to New Mexico politics at the out-set. Furthermore, the very distribution of Anglos and Hispanos must be considered a political factor of considerable importance. For the English-speaking and the Spanish-speaking peoples tend to be concentrated in specific areas, thus dividing the state into recognizable zones.

Boundaries between the two groups are projected in Map 1 and in Map 2. It will be noted that the Hispanic-American population "is concentrated along the middle reaches of the Rio Grande in a rather narrow strip somewhat like the trunk of a tree. Between Albuquerque and Santa Fe the trunk begins to branch out, and in the mountainous area in the north central part of the state, the Spanish population is dispersed in the little valleys of the

1. Paul Walter and Ross Calvin, Population of New Mexico, p. 16.
2. Public Education in New Mexico, pp. 3-4.
3. Interviews with Gail Barber, supervisor elementary education, State of New Mexico; Bernadine Kelly, supervisor teacher training; Patrick Sweeny, supervisor secondary education.
4. Interview, David B. Keleher, confidential secretary, United States Senator Dennis Chavez, December 28, 1949.

Map 1
DISTRIBUTION OF HISPANIC-AMERICANS
BY COUNTY, 1940

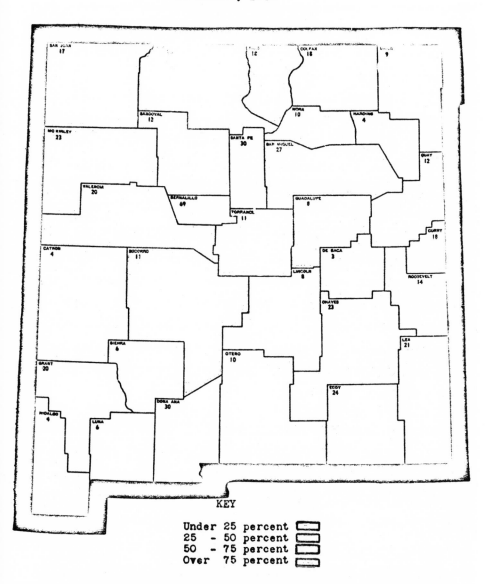

KEY

Under 25 percent
25 - 50 percent
50 - 75 percent
Over 75 percent

Source of data: Johansen, Sigurd, Population of New Mexico: Its Composition and Change, New Mexico Agricultural Experiment Station, State College, New Mexico, 1940, pp. 56.

Rio's tributary streams, which fork like the boughs of a tree top."[1] On the other hand, the English-speaking population is concentrated at the peripheries, particularly in the southern and eastern counties which border Texas.

Boundaries between Anglo and Hispano zones are best indicated by means of maps. For instance, Map 1 shows that of the 31 counties of New Mexico, seven are overwhelmingly Anglo, while seven have a predominantly Anglo population. On the other hand, eight counties are overwhelmingly Hispano, while seven are predominantly Hispano.[2]

This division of New Mexico into recognizable Anglo and Hispano counties has a profound influence on politics. "Were the Spanish-Americans scattered equally among the various counties of the state, they would long ago have ceased to be of the importance politically that they are today. However, since they are settled in a compact region--the Rio Grande valley, they either dominate the counties therein, or are of sufficient importance numerically to be a bloc with which to reckon."[3]

The Political Aspects of Population Change

If the present ratio between Anglo-American and Hispanic-American always had existed and if it could be guaranteed in the future, the political structure of New Mexico would be more stable than it is today. Certainly the leaders of the Hispanic-American

---

1. Paul Walter and Ross Calvin, op. cit., p. 23.
2. San Juan and McKinley counties have not been considered in this connection because of their heavy concentration of Indians. However, the population studies cited above would indicate that Hispanos outnumber Anglos in these counties.
3. Thomas C. Donnelly, Rocky Mountain Politics, p. 232.

people would feel more secure. For there is a belief among them
that the Hispano population gradually is being engulfed, and that
the political consequences of this development already are apparent.

This fear was expressed by a nationally known figure,
the late Senator Bronson Cutting who "from the very first foresaw the effects of immigration from the eastern states and feared
that the Spanish-American people would become a minority group,
relegated to an inferior position and deprived of their cultural
and political heritage."[1] More recently United States Senator
Dennis Chavez has voiced the same misgivings. A similar position has been taken by some members of the Catholic hierarchy,
who regard the rise of the Anglo population with concern.[2] Perhaps more significant, it is a view held by certain social scientists who have been influential in New Mexico politics, although
they have not held elective office.[3]

Local political figures frequently say that the Hispano
is being outmaneuvered because he is being outnumbered; this
attitude partly explains the bitterness of the debate which
marked the passage of the Fair Employment Practices bill in 1949.
And fear of the rising tide of Anglos crops out in the publications of those organizations which Hispanic-Americans have

1. Jonathan R. Cunningham, Bronson Cutting, A Political Biog-
   raphy, p. 220.
2. Interview, Monsignor William Bradley, Superintendent of
   Schools, Archdiocese of Santa Fe, July 21, 1949.
3. Notably George I. Sanchez, author of Forgotten People;
   Joaquin Ortega, formerly director of the School of Inter-
   American Affairs of the University of New Mexico; and Daniel
   T. Valdes, presently state president of the League of United
   Latin American Citizens.

established to protect their interests.[1]

Since the trend of population has assumed political significance, it may be well to examine the Anglo-Hispano ratio over a period of years. Unfortunately, statistical information is somewhat limited, for there are few census reports which differentiate between Hispanic-American and Anglo-American. This much is certain, however: in the century that New Mexico has been part of the United States, its population steadily has become more Anglo-American in composition.

A census taken shortly after the American occupation showed a population of 61,525, of whom only 772 were born in the United States.[2] Further indication that New Mexico was overwhelmingly Hispanic lies in the fact that nine out of ten members of the first constitutional convention of New Mexico (1850) were Hispanic-Americans.[3]

But the territory was on the threshold of a new era. The building of transcontinental railroads and the discovery of gold in Colorado stimulated the demand for cattle, while the suppression of the Indians made possible the occupation of the vast, hitherto deserted grasslands of eastern New Mexico. The population of New Mexico rose from 80,000 in 1860 to 91,000 in 1870, and by 1880 it had reached 110,000.[4] The increase was chiefly due to immigration from other parts of the United States,

---

1. Such organizations will be considered in the section which follows.
2. James I. Culbert, "Distribution of Spanish-American Population in New Mexico," p. 175.
3. LeBaron B. Prince, A Concise History of New Mexico, p. 229.
4. Helen Haines, A History of New Mexico, p. 243.

and the great majority of the newcomers were Anglo-Americans.[1]
It became increasingly evident that the composition of the population
of New Mexico was undergoing a major change.

Beginning in 1879, a network of railroads was built
across the territory, and great irrigation projects were developed
on the Rio Grande and Pecos. Another wave of settlers was
attracted to New Mexico. The year 1879 also saw silver displace
gold as the most valuable mineral resource of the territory.
Texas mine operators took possession of Socorro, while Silver
City also became a predominantly Anglo town. Cattle raising,
silver mining, lumbering, wheat farming, oil production, potash
mining--each new industry which developed brought more Anglo-
Americans to New Mexico. While the birthrate of the Hispano was
higher than that of the Anglo,[2] this was offset by immigration
from other states, particularly from Texas and Oklahoma.[3]

The changing ratio between the two major groups was
revealed in 1914, the only year when the voters were classified
according to descent. At that time 26,563 voters of Spanish-
American descent were reported, while 20,150 were of Anglo-
American extraction.[4] Moreover, Anglo-Americans already exercised
more political power than their numbers warranted, if representation in constitutional conventions is used as an index. It will
be remembered that in 1850 approximately 90 per cent of the membership of the territorial constituent assembly was Hispanic.

1. John C. Russell, "State Regionalism in New Mexico," p. 270.
2. Paul Walter and Ross Calvin, Population of New Mexico, p. 17.
3. John C. Russell, State Regionalism in New Mexico, Map IV,
   p. 53.
4. Blue Book of New Mexico (1915), p. 142.

Sixty years later only 32 per cent of the membership of the constitutional convention was Hispanic-American.[1] Distrust of
Anglo influence caused the Hispanic-American delegates to form
"a comparatively solid block welded by a common interest, i. e.,
the preservation of their traditional way of life and the language of their fathers."[2] The result was the inclusion in the
state constitution of those rigid protections cited in earlier
pages of this study.

Comprehensive socio-economic surveys of particular
regions also provide foundation for the Hispano's belief that he
is being crowded out. Thus, a study of the Spanish-American
villages of the Tewa Basin made by the United States Soil Conservation Service noted the presence of numerous Anglo families
in the Chimayo irrigation district. "Most of the newcomers are
from Texas and Oklahoma, and if they continue coming as fast
during the next 10 years as during the last 2, the natives will
be crowded out.. . .Very definitely there are appearing economic
rivalries and racial friction, which appear to be on the increase."[3]

A study of the human and natural resources of the Rio
Grande Valley of New Mexico, made by Harper, Oberg, and Cordova
in 1943, indicates that "because of the in-migration of Anglo-
Americans from outside the valley, this element is increasing more
rapidly than the other elements [Hispanos and Indians] combined."[4]

---

1. Blue Book of New Mexico (1947-48), p. 28.
2. Reuben W. Heflin, "New Mexico Constitutional Convention," p. 28.
3. Division of Economic Surveys, Soil Conservation Service, Tewa
    Basin Study, V. II, p. 71.
4. Allen G. Harper and others, Man and Resources in the Middle
    Rio Grande Valley, p. 16.

Perhaps the most significant statistics which bear on Anglo-Hispano ratios are those given by Thomas C. Donnelly in Rocky Mountain Politics: "Between 1850 and 1930 the 'native' (i. e. Hispanic-American) population increased 153 per cent, while the Anglo-American population increased 3,543 per cent."[1] According to Donnelly, interstate migration was responsible for this tremendous increase in the Anglo population.

The great depression of 1929-39 checked in-migration, but the period 1939-49 saw another influx of people from other states. In the latter year, an Hispanic-American political leader in Santa Fe pointed out that the "native" population of New Mexico, approximately 100 per cent of the total white population in 1830, had been reduced to less than half that percentage in 1940. Since the latter date, he argued, the Anglos had greatly increased their numerical advantage over the Hispanic-Americans.[2] Such statements frequently are made by Hispano leaders.

There are no completely valid data on which to base such generalizations. The annual reports of population changes made by the Bureau of Business Research of the University of New Mexico make no distinction between Anglo and Hispano. Perhaps the nearest that one can come to approximating relative changes in the Anglo-Hispano ratio since 1940 is to compare counties which long have been considered Anglo-American with those commonly regarded as Hispanic-American.

---

1. Rocky Mountain Politics, p. 231.
2. Interview, Sam Sosa, Chairman, Democratic Party, City of Santa Fe, Santa Fe, July 19, 1949.

Statistics compiled by the Bureau of Business Research in 1948 are projected in Map 2. It will be seen that 11 of the 15 Anglo counties made population gains in the period 1940-48, the average being 17.6 per cent. In the same period, 10 of the 15 Hispano counties showed population gains, the average being 16.46 per cent. Examination of population gains in so-called Hispano counties lends some credence to statements that even in these areas it is an influx of Anglos which accounts for the major gains.

For instance, the mushroom growth of Los Alamos, "the atomic city," changed the complexion of Sandoval county, since the new settlement was peopled almost exclusively by Anglo-Americans.[1] The creation of this center for atomic research likewise stimulated the migration of Anglos into the adjoining Hispano county of Santa Fe, which served as commercial and transportation outlet. In fact, the observer who returns to Santa Fe year after year can only be impressed with the increasing Anglo character of this most Spanish of all cities in the United States.

Sandia Base near Albuquerque also is associated with the development of atomic energy. This vast establishment, along with Kirtland Field and other federal military and civilian agencies accounts for much of the growth of Bernalillo County, according to Chamber of Commerce officials. Albuquerque, the county seat, is the largest city in the state and one of the largest urban centers in the Southwest. In the opinion of the

1. Interview, Robert Wegner, Superintendent of Public Schools, Los Alamos, July 20, 1949.

CHAPTER III

THE HISTORICAL BASIS OF THE ANGLO-HISPANO CLEAVAGE

Those who travel in New Mexico quickly discover that
a large portion of the population lives in isolation. Sometimes
that isolation is physical, for there are many villages which
are more than 100 miles from a railroad, and are remote from
telephone, telegraph, and postal service. Half forgotten by
the world, entire villages separately wheel through their cycles
of life and death.

But the isolation so noticeable in New Mexico is more
often cultural than physical. People living in the same community dwell behind social and economic barriers which separate
as effectively as mountain passes or hidden valleys. Thus, the
resident of the "Mexican" quarter of Carlsbad or Clovis drinks
the same water and enjoys the same sunshine as his "American"
neighbor, but that is about the extent of common experience.
For the Hispanic-American lives in a separate part of town; he
speaks a different language, attends a different church, and
goes to different movies, if at all. His children attend a
different school. He usually performs more menial work and re-
ceives less pay than the Anglo member of the community. His
food and his folkways set him apart, and almost invariably he
marries within the Hispano community.

The cultural isolation which the social scientist

ordinary Hispano citizen, much, if not most, of Albuquerque's growth has resulted from an influx of Anglos.

That such statements cannot be proved conclusively is indicated in the foregoing paragraphs. But lack of incontrovertible evidence does not lessen the Hispano's belief that New Mexico is becoming Anglo at an alarming rate. And it is feelings, not facts, which ordinarily influence politics.

Summary

Available population data indicate that the Spanish-Americans and the Anglo-Americans of New Mexico are numerically somewhat evenly balanced. However, the English-speaking and the Spanish-speaking peoples tend to be concentrated in specific areas. Thus, the state is divided into recognizable zones, with the south and eastern zones distinctly Anglo in character, and the central and northern sections of the state distinctly Hispano in character. This division of New Mexico into recognizable Anglo and Hispano counties has a profound effect on politics, for each group is able to operate as a bloc.

In recent years, the Anglo-American population of New Mexico apparently has increased more rapidly than the Spanish-American population. This has resulted in a feeling on the part of the Hispano element that it is being overwhelmed by a rising tide of Anglos.

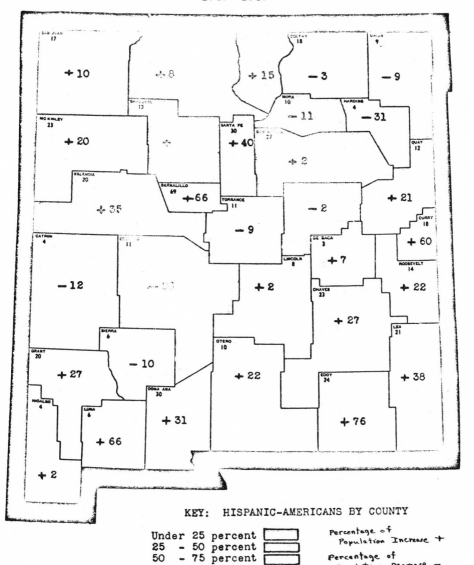

MAP 2
POPULATION CHANGE BY COUNTY

1940--1948

KEY: HISPANIC-AMERICANS BY COUNTY

Under 25 percent [   ]   Percentage of
25 - 50 percent [   ]   Population Increase +
50 - 75 percent [   ]   Percentage of
Over 75 percent [   ]   Population Decrease —

Source of data: Population of New Mexico Counties-1948, Bureau of
Business Research, University of New Mexico, 1948.

immediately notices in eastern New Mexico perhaps is less obvious
in other parts of the state. In Albuquerque and Santa Fe, the
visitor meets aristocratic, caste-conscious Hispanos who move in
the highest Anglo circles, and he learns of millionaires and
successful professional men of Hispanic stock. The student of
political science hears both Anglos and Hispanos argue as to
whether group consciousness is on the increase, and he talks with
educators, editors, and writers who foster cooperation between the
two groups.

But in Hispanic New Mexico, as in the Anglo region,
the social scientist observes what he considers cultural isolation.
For that reason it becomes the purpose of this paper to examine
socio-economic relationships which may lead to cultural isolation
and political differences.

Conflicting Principles of Ownership

In dealing with socio-economic differences which may
divide the people of New Mexico along political lines, it is
necessary to glance backward. For when it is remembered that
New Mexico was an Hispanic possession for more than 300 years,
and that it has been part of the United States only a third that
long, it becomes apparent that vestiges of the Spanish-Mexican
heritage must remain. The clash of the Hispanic and the Anglo-
Saxon cultures which marked the conquest of New Mexico was
violent, and its repercussions are heard today, many of them in
the arena of politics.

In the first place, the very settlement of New Mexico
followed an ecological pattern which has influenced history to

this day. Emigrants from Spain and Mexico settled almost exclusively in the Rio Grande valley, and almost without exception,
these early colonies were in the upper Sonoran life and crop zone.
Significantly, the most thickly settled area was the area of
least rainfall.[1] From the outset, a subsistence economy based
upon irrigation was established. People survived only by accom-
modating themselves to the delicate balance between soil, water,
temperature, and altitude. In many respects, it was a hostile
land, full of risks. Yet that part of New Mexico settled by
the ancestors of the present Hispanos closely resembled much of
Spain and Mexico; it was a simple matter to transplant the social
and economic organization of those lands to the new province.

Essentially the institutions of Spanish New Mexico were
feudal in character. This was nowhere more evident than in the
system of land holding--a form of tenure so alien to Anglo-Saxon
concepts that grave misunderstandings quickly developed when
New Mexico was annexed by the United States.

Under the Spanish system, occupancy and use of the
land were the important considerations; ownership was of secondary
importance.[2] Even where land grant boundaries overlapped, there
seldom was friction because of adherence to the principle that
to be possessed, land must be occupied and used. Under the
Spanish system, exact boundaries were not considered important.

Land measurements were as wide as the prairies
and as far away as a river or mountain. Inadequate des-

---

1. United States Department of Agriculture, Climate and Man,
   pp. 1011-16.
2. Allan G. Harper and others, Man and Resources in the Middle
   Rio Grande Valley, p. 18.

criptions proved to be one of the principal contentions
involved in land grant litigation after the American
occupation. At the end of the Mexican War and under
the Treaty of Guadalupe Hidalgo, claimants to various
grants had been assured of protection of titles by the
United States. Land-grant problems would have been
comparatively simple had there existed proper supporting
documents and correct surveys.[1]

The above would indicate that with American sovereignty

came a totally different concept of land tenure. Ownership, not

use, was the prime consideration. Exact titles were considered

necessary. Moreover, American occupation brought the land tax

for production of revenue, a device rarely employed under Spanish

and Mexican rule. Americans who migrated to the territory after

the Mexican War also brought with them a money economy. To a

people who had lived in a self-contained community having a sub-

sistence economy, the American system was a destructive innovation.

Insistence upon exact boundaries, imposition of land

taxes, and the introduction of a money economy quickly changed the

pattern of land ownership in New Mexico. The history of almost

any New Mexican land grant will reveal that titles largely passed

from the descendants of the original Hispano owners to individual

Anglos or to corporations controlled by them. The record of the

Anton Chico grant is typical, and it explains in part why many

New Mexicans of Hispanic descent are convinced that they have

been robbed of their heritage.

> The Anton Chico Grant was originally made to
> a community of 36 persons by the Mexican Government in
> 1822. As confirmed by the United States Government in
> 1860 it contained 278,000 acres. At the present time.
> . .The grant is owned in community by the heirs. . .

---

1. W. A. Keleher, "Law of the New Mexico Land Grant," p. 356.

Land contained within the grant is subject to the
regular property taxes of the State of New Mexico.
At a very early date delinquency in payment of taxes
became very serious.[1]

In 1926, lands became subject to foreclosure by the

state for taxes delinquent more than three years. This neces-

sitated sale of great tracts of the Anton Chico grant. In 1938,

only 85,000 of the 278,000 original acres remained in community

ownership.[2]

Not only did individual Hispanic-Americans and entire

native villages lose title to their land because it became

necessary to pay taxes, but they were also dispossessed by fraud.

The sordid details are told in most histories of New Mexico, but

the testimony of a territorial governor of the state gives the

story in a nutshell:

> . . .charges of fraud and crime are made as to some grants
> that have been confirmed, such as forgery of papers, per-
> jury, subornation of witnesses and false and erroneous
> surveys.. . .
>
> Success in securing confirmation of grants of a doubtful
> character so encouraged and emboldened the covetous that
> it is alleged the manufacture of grant papers became an
> occupation, and surveys have been so erroneously made as
> to lead to a belief that these grants are endowed with
> india rubber qualities.[3]

There is considerable evidence to prove that certain

Hispanic-Americans were as guilty of land frauds as any of the

Anglo culprits. And there is even more evidence that the

---

1. Olen Leonard and C. P. Loomis, Culture of a Contemporary
   Rural Community, El Cerrito, New Mexico, pp. 3-4.
2. Loc. cit.
3. Gov. Lionel A. Sheldon, Report to Secretary of Interior,
   1881, as quoted by W. A. Keleher, Maxwell Land Grant, pp.
   8-9.

economic development of New Mexico was served by the exploita-
tion of its land by new owners. Assessment of guilt is not the
purpose of this paper, however. Rather, it is to point out
factors which make for political differences between the two
dominant groups in New Mexico. In this connection it is sufficient to indicate that the Hispano has lost control of hundreds
of thousands of acres which he once owned.

The Treaty of Guadalupe Hidalgo guaranteed Spanish and
Mexican titles; statutory law extended further protection in this
unmistakable fashion:

> Rights of persons in possession under Spanish
> and Mexican grants: Every person or persons being of the
> class or condition that have held or hold, in lawful
> possession under a legitimate title, derived from the
> authorities of Spain or Mexico, which, according to the
> laws at that time, had legitimate authority to grant such
> title to property, upon whatever lands belonging to said
> governments, prior to the treaty of peace by the latter
> with the United States, who actually find themselves in
> legal possession upon said lands, in quiet and peaceful
> possession, and without being interrupted, from the time
> that the government of the United States comprised within
> its limits this state; the said persons are entitled to a
> lawful claim of property and legal ownership under the
> limits thereof, to the lands mentioned, in the same man-
> ner as those who had acquired by purchase, inheritance
> or legal conveyance, be the same whatever it may be,
> according to law, exclusively and against any other per-
> son whatsoever, who lay claim subsequent to that date.
> (Laws 1863-4, p. 54.)[1]

Yet powerful social and economic forces set in motion
by the American conquest changed the system of land tenure. Of
5,000,000 acres of private grant lands confirmed by Congress and
the Court of Private Land Claims, less than 3,000,000 remained
in 1930. Of the 2,000,000 acres of community grants only

-----

1. New Mexico Statutes, Annotated 1941, V. 5, p. 961.

300,000 were left in 1930.[1] It was these community grants which
for centuries had provided Hispano villages with their principal
grazing lands.

The ill feeling engendered by the transfer of ownership from Hispano to Anglo has been widely noted in case studies
of Hispanic-American villages. The following quotations from
a study made by A. B. Chavez are typical enough to serve as
examples:

> The Americanos who are buying these lands from
> the state, the county and the conservancy (district) must
> have no soul, for why should the rich Americanos covet
> the meagerness of the poor.. . .These "gringos" who buy
> these lands don't intend to settle and work them. They
> don't love the soil nor the plants, nor the animals. All
> they intend to do is to hold on to these lands and then
> sell out to the agricultural corporations for profit. All
> they are capable of loving is money and tractors.[2]

> The conservancy taxes got heavier and heavier
> on my land. We never made enough from the land to cover
> the taxes. Finally I had to sell it for what I could get
> or lose it completely. Truly things were in a bad way.
> But about ten years ago that rich cattleman from ----
> bought many of these lands that were tax delinquent. How
> he managed to do it, I don't know, but these days men with
> money find the doors open to them anywhere.[3]

Common Law vs. Civil Law

No discussion of the conflicting conception of ownership and its effect on Anglo-Hispano relations would be complete
without mention of mineral and water rights. When the common law
followed American arms into the vast Mexican cession, it came
into conflict with Spanish civil law. Riparian rights in water

1. Allan G. Harper and others, Man and Resources in the Middle
   Rio Grande Valley, pp. 61-2.
2. The Use of the Personal Interview to Study the Subjective
   Impact of Culture Contacts, p. 104.
3. Ibid., p. 115.

was the rule in English common law; water rights by appropriation was the rule under the Spanish civil law. An immense body of law dealing with community irrigation ditches (acequias) had developed in New Mexico between 1540 and 1847. Where water was so precious, where human organization was so utterly dependent upon a complex irrigation system, it was natural that water rights should seem almost sacrosanct.

Among Americans there was no appreciation of this attitude, for until the acquisition of Texas and the Mexican Cession there had been no irrigated deserts in the United States. In the end, English water law gave way to, or was greatly modified by Spanish water law, as an examination of the statutes of New Mexico will reveal.[1] But the accommodation of English to Spanish concepts was marked by endless litigation and hostility between Anglo and Hispano. All too frequently blood was shed.

Mineral rights also proved vexatious. In colonial times, the wealth of the New Mexican sub-soil had been an exclusive possession of the Crown. The right to exploit it was granted by temporary concession with payment of royalties. When Mexico declared its independence, sub-soil rights passed into the hands of the nation.[2]

English law, on the contrary, vested sub-soil rights in the owner of the surface. Here again was cause for prolonged conflict between Anglo and Hispano. In some instances, both the Spanish Crown and the Mexican government had granted land with

---

1. Edward D. Tittman, "The First Irrigation Lawsuit," p. 363.
2. Alfonso Teja Zabre, Guide to the History of Mexico, p. 348.

no reference to sub-soil mineral rights. As noted above, the
Treaty of Guadalupe Hidalgo guaranteed the title of Mexican
nationals in such rights as they had at the time of the annexation of New Mexico.

> The nationals of Mexico in (another) type of
> grant not having acquired a right in the minerals under
> their grants, such rights became vested in the United
> States. The United States owning these rights, appar-
> ently, have no right to issue a permit for mineral ex-
> ploration to a stranger to the title, because the fed-
> eral government has no right to the land itself.[1]

This curious situation also gave rise to litigation.

Aristocracy vs. Democracy

Conflicting concepts of land, water, and mineral rights
ranged Anglo against Hispano almost from the moment New Mexico
became part of the United States. Also influential in determining relationships were several less obvious socio-economic
differences.

New Mexico was sheep country before the arrival of the
Anglo, and single Hispano families owned as many as 2,000,000
head.[2] But vast herds of cattle were introduced by Texans
shortly after New Mexico became an American territory The cattle
population rose from 90,000 in 1860 to 1,000,000 in 1910.[3] As
the competition for the range became more intense, the proverbial
antipathy of cattlemen for sheep men became translated into
antipathy of Anglo for Hispano.

In New Mexico the distrust of the villager for the out-

---

1. W. A. Keleher, "Law of the New Mexico Land Grant," p. 369.
2. Thomas C. Donnelly, Rocky Mountain Politics, p. 223.
3. Charles F. Coan, A History of New Mexico, V. I., p. 475.

lander also was exhibited. Before its annexation by the United
States, the province of New Mexico was largely made up of com-
munal settlements, each dominated by a village. In this respect,
the territory was distinctly feudal in organization. But the
Anglo-American

> . . .introduced a radically different method of settlement.
> The homesteader was primarily a dry-farmer, not an irriga-
> tionist; he was a seeker after a cash crop, not mere sub-
> sistence. He tended to disperse over the area; to him the
> highway, rather than the village, was the link between his
> home and school, church, postoffice and trader's store. If
> he were a rancher, he made his headquarters out on the range
> at some desirable water-hole, remote from the villages.[1]

The Hispanic resident of New Mexico not only found it
difficult to accept the Anglo system of ownership, taxation,
animal husbandry, and settlement; far more important, he found
it hard to comprehend the Anglo-American conception of government.
For in 1848 New Mexico was feudal; its government was aristocratic; its people were completely unprepared for self-rule.
The idea of democracy was as alien as the idea of a money economy
or of a religion other than Catholicism.

As one authority on the government of New Mexico com-
mented, "Democracy was as unknown to the New Mexican of 1848 as
it was to the German of 1919. The Hispanic-American's concept
of church and state was completely foreign to the Anglo-American;
moreover, the patron-peon relationship which characterized the
entire political and social structure of New Mexico was frowned
upon by the fiercely democratic Anglo settler.[2]

---

1. Allan G. Harper and others, Man and Resources in the Middle
   Rio Grande Valley, p. 21.
2. Interview, Dorothy Cline, Department of Government, University
   of New Mexico, Albuquerque, July 15, 1949.

Reason for the almost complete ignorance of democratic government at the time of the American conquest is not hard to find. Throughout the Spanish colonial period, New Mexico was ruled by appointive governors who enjoyed virtually dictatorial power. And throughout the entire period of Mexican rule "the province was corruptly and despotically 'bossed' by one man, Manuel Armijo."[1] The authority of the governor was buttressed by the Church and by a tightknit, feudal aristocracy--the patrones. The bulk of the population was formed of a serflike class, the peones.

The absence of a middle class in New Mexico prevented the incoming Anglo-American from making contact with the native New Mexican. Both the privileged land-owning aristocracy and the lowly serfs were repugnant to the democratic concepts of the newcomer.

The Anglo-American's belief that the "native" people could not operate any form of self-government was brought out in the prolonged debate on the subject of statehood. Vigorous opposition to the admission of New Mexico developed among segments of the Anglo-American population; the spokesmen of such groups feared that the state government would fall into the hands of a few Hispano families who still regarded themselves as feudal lords.

> Each of these families has from five hundred to two thousand dependents, some of whom were their peons before that system was abolished, and continue to yield obedience by nature and habit. If a state, this would be a most complete "rotten borough"--the worst "carpet-bag"

1. Carey McWilliams, North from Mexico, p. 69.

state in the Union. Fifteen families with ease would
rule the state.[1]

> They (the Hispanic-Americans) know not the
> independence of thought and action common to the American
> voter. They are led by a few old and wealthy families,
> and any movement these leaders may agree upon will be
> sure of securing a majority of the votes cast.[2]

Particular attention has been directed to this phase
of the history of New Mexico because it is a commonly held belief of contemporary social scientists that the patron-peon
relationship still exists among Hispanic-Americans, and that
its political consequences are of major importance.

> Both political and economic life in New Mexico still
> suffer from (the Hispano's) instinctive love of a feudal
> relationship to some leader. Shrewd politicians have
> built up some of the most perfectly working and perfectly
> corrupt political machines that ever existed by taking
> proper care of their henchmen.[3]

> An economic atus as thoroughly ingrained in a people
> as peonage in the Spanish-American people cannot be
> wiped out i_ generation or two. As a result, political
> and economic life in New Mexico still suffer to a great
> extent from the subservient attitude of the Spanish-
> Americans toward some leader.[4]

Summary

A glance at the history of New Mexico reveals that Anglo-
Americans and Spanish-Americans were brought into conflict with
the occupation of the territory by the United States. Divergent
views on land ownership led to ill feeling, particularly on the
part of the Hispanic-American. Conflicting philosophies of law

---

1. J. H. Beadle, The Undeveloped West, p. 454, (Quoted, Archie
    M. McDowell, Opposition to Statehood Within the Territory of
    New Mexico, 1888-1903, p. 13.)
2. Ibid., pp. 21-2.
3. Harvey Fergusson, Rio Grande, p. 116.
4. John C. Russell, "State Regionalism in New Mexico," p. 36.

likewise led to prolonged litigation and recrimination. Moreover, the feudal and aristocratic principles which long had
characterized New Mexican society made for misunderstanding
between the "native people" and the aggressively democratic newcomers. Even today, many Anglo-Americans insist that Spanish-
American political concepts are dominated by the patron-peon
relationship, a holdover from the period of Spanish-Mexican
domination.

CHAPTER IV

THE SOCIO-ECONOMIC BASE OF POLITICS

From a financial point of view, New Mexico is a poor
state. The per capita income for the period 1944-1946 was
$762.00, which gave New Mexico the rank of forty-second among
the 48 states. In comparison, the per capita income for the
United States as a whole during the period was $1,141.00, and
for the wealthiest state, $1,579.00.[1]

Within the state of New Mexico itself there are notable disparities. The difference in per capita income in the
richest county and the poorest county is as marked as the difference between the poorest state in the Union and the richest.
Since the counties of New Mexico may be classified as Hispanic-
American or Anglo-American, a comparison of their respective per
capita incomes gives some indication of the economic status of
the two major groups.

In comparing the seven counties having an Anglo-American
population in excess of 75 per cent of the total with a similar
number of counties having a comparable Hispanic-American population, some pertinent facts emerge. Figures released by the New
Mexico Department of Public Health in September, 1947, show that
the average per capita income in the seven most Hispanic counties

1. Department of Public Health, New Mexico Health Officer,
   (Sept., 1947), p. 12.

ranged from $291.32 in Rio Arriba county to $732.63 in Guadalupe
county, with an average of $452.26. On the other hand, the av-
erage per capita income in the seven most Anglo counties ranged
from $536.84 in De Baca county to $1282.11 in Curry county, with
an average of $870.04.

In other words, the average per capita income in seven
counties having the highest percentage of Anglo residents was
almost double the average per capita income in seven corresponding
Hispano counties.

Data and sources of information for all counties under
study are shown in Diagram 1.

Differences in the economic status of the two groups
also may be sought in comparing assessed valuation of property
in Anglo and in Hispano counties on a per capita basis. Again,
only those counties with a respective Anglo or Hispano population in excess of 75 per cent of the total are used.

Here the contrast between Anglo and Hispano counties
is more striking than in the preceding comparison. The per
capita assessed valuation of property in the seven most Hispanic
counties in 1949 ranged from $200.64 in Rio Arriba county to
$993.65 in Guadalupe county, with an average of $516.88. The
per capita assessed valuation of property in the seven most
Anglo counties in the same year ranged from $566.63 in Curry
county to $2,865.18 in Lea county, with an average of $1,244.97.

Thus, the average per capita assessed valuation of
property in seven counties having an Anglo population in excess
of 75 per cent of the total was more than double the per capita
assessed valuation of property in seven corresponding Hispanic

DIAGRAM 1

ESTIMATED PER CAPITA INCOME BY COUNTY

A. Counties having highest percent of Hispanic-Americans

Guadalupe	$ 732.63
San Miguel	531.05
Socorro	495.79
Taos	395.26
Mora	380.00
Sandoval	339.74
Rio Arriba	291.32

B. Counties having highest percent of Anglo-Americans

Curry	$1282.11
Lea	1153.68
Quay	871.32
Union	848.42
Chaves	796.05
Roosevelt	601.84
De Baca	536.84

C. Average per capita income:

Anglo counties	$ 870.04
Hispanic counties	452.26

Key: 1/16" = $20

Source of data: New Mexico Department of Public Health,
New Mexico Health Officer, Sept., 1947, p. 60.

counties.

Data for all counties under study are shown in Diagram 2.

While neither the federal nor the state government
classifies income tax returns according to county, tax data are
available in another form. The New Mexico Taxpayers Association
compiles total state, county, municipal, and school taxes annually collected in each county.

Comparison of the total property taxes collected in
Hispanic and in Anglo counties in 1947 sheds further light on
economic differences which may influence politics. In the
seven most Hispanic counties of New Mexico, total state, county,
municipal, and school taxes on a per capita basis ranged from
$4.91 in Sandoval county to $18.53 in Guadalupe county, with an
average of $10.25. In the seven most Anglo counties of New Mex-
ico, total state, county, municipal, and school property taxes
on a per capita basis ranged from $12.25 in Curry county to
$35.41 in Lea county, with an average of $21.84.

In other words, Anglo counties had a per capita property tax receipts double those of corresponding Hispano counties.

Complete data and sources are shown in Diagram 3.

A comparison of the average number of persons annually
receiving public assistance per capita by county likewise assists
in comparing the economic status of the two groups under study.
Again by comparing seven counties having respective Anglo and
Hispano populations exceeding 75 per cent of the total, the
following facts emerge.

In seven Hispano counties, the estimated average number

DIAGRAM 2

PER CAPITA ASSESSED VALUATION OF PROPERTY

A. Counties having highest percent of Hispanic-Americans

Guadalupe	$$$$$$$$$$$$$	$ 993.65
Socorro	$$$$$$$$$$$$$	906.81
San Miguel	$$$$$$$	536.17
Mora	$$$$$$	480.22
Sandoval	$$$	256.05
Taos	$$$	244.60
Rio Arriba	$$$	200.64

B. Counties having highest percent of Anglo-Americans

Lea	$$$$$$$$$$$$$$$$$$$$$$$$$$$$$$$$$$$$$$$	$2865.18
De Baca	$$$$$$$$$$$$$$$$$$$$$$$$	1730.55
Union	$$$$$$$$$$$$$$$$	1139.31
Quay	$$$$$$$$$$$$$	922.36
Roosevelt	$$$$$$$$$$	755.87
Chaves	$$$$$$$$$$	734.89
Curry	$$$$$$$$	566.63

C. Average per capita valuation:

Anglo counties	$$$$$$$$$$$$$$$$$	$1244.97
Hispanic counties	$$$$$$$	516.88

Key: $ = $75

Source of data: Taxpayers Association of New Mexico, New Mexico
Tax Bulletin, July 1949, p. 702.

Bureau of Business Research, University of New
Mexico, Population of New Mexico Counties, 1948
(Processed)

DIAGRAM 3

STATE, COUNTY, MUNICIPAL AND SCHOOL PROPERTY TAXES

PER CAPITA BY COUNTY

A. Counties having highest percent of Hispanic-Americans

County	Per Capita Tax
Guadalupe	$18.53
Socorro	18.26
San Miguel	12.13
Mora	9.27
Sandoval	4.91
Taos	4.79
Rio Arriba	3.83

B. Counties having highest percent of Anglo-Americans

County	Per Capita Tax
Lea	$35.41
De Baca	32.64
Union	21.87
Quay	18.76
Roosevelt	16.01
Chaves	15.93
Curry	12.25

C. Average per capita property tax:

	Per Capita Tax
Anglo counties	$21.84
Hispanic counties	10.25

Key: 1/8" = $1

Source of data: Taxpayers Association of New Mexico, New Mexico
Tax Bulletin, June 1948, p. 485.

Bureau of Business Research, University of New
Mexico, Population of New Mexico Counties, 1948,
(Processed)

of persons receiving public assistance on a per capita basis
ranged from .0333 in Sandoval county to .1118 in Mora county,
with an average of .0741. In seven Anglo counties, the estimated
average number of persons receiving public assistance on a per
capita basis ranged from .0062 in Lea county to .0433 in Union
county, with an average of .0237. In other words, the average
for Hispano counties was more than three times the average in
Anglo counties.

Complete data are shown in Chart 1.

A fifth clue to differences in the economic status of
the Anglo-American and the Hispanic-American population of New
Mexico may be found in an evaluation of the population of the
Civilian Conservation Corps for the year 1940-1941. Since admission to the corps was on the basis of family need, the procedure throws some light on economic status. Again the comparison
is on a per capita basis, using the same Anglo and Hispano
counties for purposes of evaluation.

In seven counties having an Hispanic population in excess of 75 per cent of the total, the average number of enrollees
per capita by county ranged from .0061 in Sandoval to .0147 in
San Miguel, with an average of .01025.

In seven corresponding Anglo counties, the average number of enrollees per capita by county ranged from .00089 in Lea
county to .00510 in De Baca county, with an average of .00255.

To put it another way, on a per capita basis, the CCC
enrollment from Hispano counties was almost five times that of
Anglo counties.

Data and sources are shown in Chart 2.

CHART 1

ESTIMATED AVERAGE NUMBER OF PERSONS RECEIVING PUBLIC ASSISTANCE
PER CAPITA BY COUNTY

A. Counties having highest percent of Hispanic-Americans

County	Total Persons	Total Population	Per Capita
Rio Arriba	1,991	27,300	.0729
Taos	1,027	21,300	.0482
Mora	1,096	9,800	.1118
Guadalupe	582	8,500	.0684
Sandoval	634	19,000	.0333
San Miguel	3,187	28,600	.1114
Socorro	618	8,500	.0727

B. Counties having highest percent of Anglo-Americans

County	Total Persons	Total Population	Per Capita
Lea	182	29,200	.0062
Union	360	8,300	.0433
Chaves	487	30,500	.0159
Curry	382	29,100	.0131
Quay	393	14,600	.0269
Roosevelt	310	17,700	.0175
De Baca	172	4,000	.0430

C. Average per capita receiving public assistance:

Hispanic counties .0741

Anglo counties .0237

Source of data: New Mexico Department of Public Welfare, Annual
Report, 1948, p. 38.

Bureau of Business Research, University of New Mexico,
Population of New Mexico Counties, 1948, (processed)

CIVILIAN CONSERVATION CORPS: AVERAGE NUMBER OF ENROLLEES
PER CAPITA BY COUNTY

A. Counties having highest percent of Hispanic-Americans

County	No. Enrollees	Population	Per Capita
Rio Arriba	314	25,352	.0123
Taos	149	18,528	.0080
Mora	106	10,981	.0096
Guadalupe	82	8,646	.0094
Sandoval	86	13,898	.0061
San Miguel	413	27,910	.0147
Socorro	133	11,422	.0117

B. Counties having highest percent of Anglo-Americans

County	No. Enrollees	Population	Per Capita
Lea	19	21,154	.00089
Union	28	9,095	.00307
Chaves	80	23,980	.00333
Curry	31	18,159	.00170
Quay	33	12,111	.00272
Roosevelt	16	14,549	.00109
De Baca	19	3,725	.00510

C. Average number of enrollees in Civilian Conservation Corps

Per Capita

		Per Capita
Hispanic counties	🧍🧍🧍🧍🧍🧍🧍🧍🧍	.01025
Anglo counties	🧍🧍	.00255

Source of data: New Mexico Department Public Welfare, Annual
Report (1940-41), p. 27.

United States Census, 1940.

Health Records as Keys to Status

When compared with the United States as a whole, the over-all health record of New Mexico is very poor. There were in 1946 a total of 1,866 persons for each physician in the state, while the ratio for the nation was one physician per 1,091 persons.[1] The infant mortality rate is consistently the highest in the country. Thus, in 1946 the infant mortality rate for the nation was 33.8, while the New Mexico rate was 86, which was more than twice as high as that of any other state.[2]

New Mexico has a death rate from contagious and infectious diseases three times the national average; its death rate places it forty-seventh among the states; it is thirty-eighth in matters of sanitation and forty-fifth in hospitalization insurance.[3] According to a sampling of housing conditions reported in the Housing Census of the United States (1940), 32 per cent of New Mexico homes were overcrowded, as compared to 9.0 per cent for all states.[4]

Examination of county health records reveals great extremes within the state itself. Thus, certain sections of New Mexico show a higher incidence of disease and a higher death rate than other areas. Such disparities not only indicate extremes in health care, but they also indicate economic differences, for there is "a definite trend toward correlation of per capita income, children under medical care per day per 1,000 children, and

1. New Mexico Health Officer, (Sept., 1947), p. 26.
2. Ibid., p. 12.
3. Division of Surveys and Field Services, George Peabody College, Public Education in New Mexico, pp. 9-10.
4. Helen H. Ellis, Public Welfare Problems in New Mexico, p. 6.

the infant mortality rate."[1]

Thus, comparisons of counties having a high concentration of Hispanic-Americans with counties which have an
overwhelming majority of Anglo-Americans throws some light on
the relative socio-economic position of the two groups.

It is commonly held that the number of doctors and
dentists per 1,000 population is an index of the socio-economic
status of a specific locality. If this yardstick is used in
assessing differences between Anglo and Hispano counties, these
facts are revealed in Table I.

Public health authorities generally agree that a high
correlation exists between socio-economic status and infant
mortality. If this is a correct assumption, comparison of
infant mortality rates in Anglo-American districts and Hispanic-
American sections contributes to an understanding of the socio-
economic basis of politics in New Mexico.

Writing in El Palacio in 1942, Reginald Fisher reported
that in the Hispanic villages of the Rio Grande the infant mortality rate was approximately 150 per 1,000, or 24 per 1,000 higher
than for New Mexico as a whole.[2]

Statistics of the United Public Health Service are more
extensive, more recent, and more exact. They indicate that in
1946 the Hispanic-American and the Anglo-American counties ranked
according to the data in Table II.

In 1949, the Santa Fe New Mexican reported that "Figures

1. New Mexico Health Officer, op. cit., p. 18.
2. "Hispanic People of the Rio Grande," El Palacio, (August, 1942),
   p. 158.

TABLE I

Number of Physicians and Dentists per 1,000
Children by County

A. Hispanic Counties

County	Number of Physicians per 1,000 Children	Number of Dentists per 1,000 Children
Guadalupe	.64	.00
Mora	.00	.00
Rio Arriba	.62	.10
Sandoval	.18	.00
San Miguel	.49	.39
Socorro	1.04	.26
Taos	1.40	.13

B. Anglo Counties

County	Number of Physicians per 1,000 Children	Number of Dentists per 1,000 Children
Chaves	1.72	.86
Curry	2.02	1.09
De Baca	.00	.00
Lea	1.11	.48
Quay	1.72	.49
Roosevelt	.60	.20
Union	1.67	.83

C. Anglo-Hispano Ratio

	Number of Physicians per 1,000 Children	Number of Dentists per 1,000 Children
Average, Hispano Counties	.48	.13
Average, Anglo Counties	1.28	.56

Source of Data: Department of Public Health, New Mexico Health Officer, (Sept., 1947), Table III.

TABLE II

Number of Deaths under One Year per 1,000

Live Births by County

A. Hispanic-American Counties

County	Deaths under One Year per 1,000 Live Births
Mora	143.8
Rio Arriba	127.1
Sandoval	101.0
San Miguel	99.8
Taos	80.9
Socorro	73.3
Guadalupe	52.4

B. Anglo-American Counties

County	Deaths under One Year per 1,000 Live Births
Chaves	60.9
Quay	56.9
Union	48.1
Curry	42.1
Roosevelt	35.6
Lea	33.8
De Baca	17.7

C. Anglo-Hispano Ratio

	Deaths under One Year per 1,000 Live Births
Average, Hispanic-American Counties	96.9
Average, Anglo-American Counties	42.1

Source of Data: Vital Statistics of the United States, Part II, (1946), pp. 72-3.

released by the state health department show that the infant
mortality rate is highest in counties of northern New Mexico.

"One out of 10 babies die during the first year of life
in Mora, San Miguel, De Baca, Rio Arriba, McKinley, Sandoval,
Valencia, and San Juan counties.

"The death rate for infants in other counties averages
about six out of 100 births."[1] The significance of this report
lies in the fact that only one of the named counties is predominantly Anglo-American in population.

Another index often related to low economic and social
status is the incidence of tuberculosis in a given area. If this
yardstick is used in comparing the Anglo and the Hispano communities of New Mexico, the latter appear at a great disadvantage.
Hammond and Donnelly report that twice as many Spanish-American
children are infected with tuberculosis as Anglo-American
children.[2]

The New Mexico Department of Public Health also provides information on this score. For administrative purposes,
the state is divided into 10 health districts, three of which
have a predominantly Hispanic-American population and three a
predominantly Anglo-American population. The three Hispano districts (1, 3, 5) have respective tuberculosis mortality indices
of 28.3, 62.1, and 65.5 per 100,000 population. The three Anglo
districts (6, 9, 10) in the same year, had indices of 19.1, 19.8,
and 18.3 respectively.[3]

---

1. March 6, 1949.
2. George P. Hammond and T. C. Donnelly, Story of New Mexico, p.
   209.
3. State of New Mexico, Dept. Public Health, "Tuberculosis
   Mortality by Health Districts," June 24, 1949.

The average index of tuberculosis mortality in the
three predominantly Hispanic-American districts was 51.9 per
100,000 population; in the three predominantly Anglo-American
districts the index was 19.1, a difference of 32.8.

The Spanish-American in Social Groupings

Further indication that socio-economic differences divide the Anglo-Americans and the Hispanic-Americans of New Mexico may be found by examining the membership of social and oc-
cupational groups. Thus, the predominance of Anglo-Americans in
business affairs and in the professions is brought out in the
city directory of Albuquerque and in the state business directory compiled by the Bureau of Business Research of the University
of New Mexico. The former volume reveals that the overwhelming
majority of all business concerns are owned or managed by Anglos.
The same statement applies to the professions. In May, 1949,
there were 114 physicians in Albuquerque, of whom three were
Hispanic-American; of 126 lawyers, 11 were Hispanos; of 50 dentists, two were Hispano; of the 27 osteopathic physicians and
surgeons, none were Hispanic-American; of 11 certified public
accountants, none were Hispano; likewise all of the 12 architects
and 13 engineers were Anglo-American.[1]

The New Mexico State Business Directory and Economic
Handbook (1946-47)[2] shows that of the 143 dentists in the state,
eight are Hispanos; of 402 physicians and surgeons, 10 are Hispanos;

---

1. New Mexico Bell Telephone Company, Albuquerque Directory,
    May, 1949.
2. Bureau of Business Research, University of New Mexico, 1947.

of 272 lawyers, 24 are Hispano; and of 19 certified public
accountants, none are Hispanic-American. Examination of this
state directory indicates that members of the professional
classes are highly concentrated in counties commonly regarded
as Anglo-American.

Study of the New Mexico Educational Directory (1948-49)[1]
provides similar results. Of 31 county superintendents, eight
were Hispano. The total number of public school teachers was
4,654, of whom 1,062 were Hispanic-American. Another check on
the character of New Mexico business and professional leadership
may be found in Who's Who in New Mexico.[2] Of 1,093 listings, 57
persons are Hispanic-American.

The foregoing would indicate that the business and professional life of New Mexico is dominated by Anglo-Americans.
The relationship of Anglo and Hispano within the ranks of organized labor is more difficult to define. Writing in 1936,
Swayne observed that the nature and organization of New Mexican
labor is profoundly affected by the "racial" factor.

> Relative to the racial question, there is a big
> problem in obtaining an adequate representation of the
> Spanish-American group in organized labor. The Spanish-
> speaking people of New Mexico have supported organized
> labor, and practically every local union in the state has
> both Spanish and "Anglo" members. However, due to the
> economic status of a great portion of the Spanish-speaking
> population, membership in the various craft unions is
> impossible. Furthermore, the only union within the state
> which can admit common labor is the Hod Carrier's Union,
> and the expense of belonging to this union is prohibitive
> to most of the above-mentioned group[3]

1. State Department of Education, 1949.
2. Michel D. Abousleman, 1937.
3. James B. Swayne, A Survey of the Economic, Political and Legal
   Aspects of the Labor Problem in New Mexico, p. 32.

After careful investigation, Swayne reported that he found no evidence that state and local unions discriminate against Hispanic-Americans. It was evident that the economic and social status of the group made it impossible for Hispanos "to avail themselves of the opportunities of advancement afforded by the various trade and labor unions."[1]

In the thirteen-year period, 1936-49, Hispanic-Americans showed increasing interest in labor unions. The official yearbook of the State Federation of Labor[2] indicates, however, that Anglo-Americans still provide most of union leadership. The yearbook lists some 117 local officers, of whom 18 are Hispano.

According to the secretary of the Central Labor Union in Albuquerque (perhaps the largest and most powerful local organization in the state) such facts do not present the true position of the Hispano. This official states that Hispanic-Americans are interested and well organized; that the percentage of Hispanos in labor organizations is increasing; and that in some unions, Hispanos outnumber Anglos. (In the Hod-Carrier's Union, for example, 1,800 of 2,000 members are Hispanos.) More significant, young Hispanos are entering the craft unions, where they now constitute about 50 per cent of all apprentices.[3]

Since all but two unions in New Mexico are affiliated with the American Federation of Labor,[4] the Anglo-Hispano ratio within the state federation is of some interest. Earl J.

1. Ibid., p. 33.
2. New Mexico State Federation of Labor, Official Yearbook, 1947.
3. Interview, Frank McCoy, Albuquerque, August 1, 1949.
4. Loc. cit.

McDonald, state secretary-treasurer, estimated in October, 1949, that 35 per cent of all union members are Hispanic-American.[1]

The position of the Hispanic-American within the ranks of organized labor is only one small facet of the total economic problem. Actually, union membership indicates desire to improve economic status. And this is difficult for the Hispanic-American to achieve, for there is considerable evidence to support the charge that highly discriminatory wage differentials have been established in New Mexico. To state it bluntly, Anglo and Hispano workmen frequently are paid different wages for doing identical labor. Or, Hispanic-Americans are barred from certain types of work.

For example, in the two largest grocery stores in Santa Fe, there is one wage scale for Hispano and another for Anglo employees. In a Taos garage, G. I. apprentices of Anglo ancestry were paid $25.00 per week while their Hispano counterparts received $15.00.[2]

In Albuquerque, no Hispano bus drivers are employed by the comprehensive transportation system.[3]

In Grant county copper mines and in the Carlsbad potash mines jobs as mechanics, pumpmen, timekeepers, and hoistmen are reserved for Anglos, while low-bracket jobs are allocated to Hispanic-Americans. Some mines refuse to hire Hispanos altogether.[4]

---

1. Letter to writer, Oct. 26, 1949.
2. Interview, R. L. Chambers, Chief, United Press, Santa Fe, Dec. 29, 1949.
3. Interview, David B. Keleher, confidential secretary, United States Senator Dennis Chavez, Albuquerque, Dec. 28, 1949.
4. Interview, Alfredo Montoya, National President, Asociacion Nacional Mexicana-Americana, Albuquerque, Dec. 28, 1949.

A committee of the Social Action Department of the
National Catholic Welfare Conference reported that,

> A prior incidental task in the case of Latin
> Americans is to remove the notion that these people are
> inferior workers to be paid accordingly. We call for
> careful research to show that Latin Americans can
> accomplish as much as other workers; so that, on the
> basis of substantial evidence, wage differentials may
> be eliminated and obstacles to upgrading removed.[1]

Reports of Region Ten of the Fair Employment Practices
Commission, in which New Mexico was considered, showed that 37
per cent of all complaints received involved discrimination
against "Mexicans."[2]

At hearings on the proposed New Mexico Fair Employment
Practices Act, conclusive evidence was offered that discrimination against Hispanic-Americans exists in the state, particularly
in the eastern section.[3]

Since voting on the FEP bill was according to language,
rather than party lines, there is some reason to believe that
the Hispanic-Americans of New Mexico feel that they are discriminated against as a group.

Social Differentiation

If the Hispanic-American of New Mexico is sure that he
is the object of economic discrimination, he is equally convinced
that he is the victim of social discrimination. Again there is
evidence to support such charges.

---

1. National Catholic Welfare Conference, Proceedings, Second
   Seminar on Spanish-Speaking of Southwest and West, Denver,
   1944, p. 44.
2. Carey McWilliams, North from Mexico, p. 198.
3. Interview, Monsignor William Bradley, Superintendent of Schools,
   Archdiocese of Santa Fe, Santa Fe, July 21, 1949.

For instance, on a recent tour of New Mexico, the
national president of the Federation of Women's Republican Clubs
was "shocked to sense any consciousness at all of race when it
is within a race entirely of Caucasian ancestry."[1] The speaker,
Mrs. Joseph Farrington, wife of Hawaii's representative in Congress, then compared New Mexico and the island unfavorably as
far as inter-group relations are concerned. The speaker perhaps
had in mind such items as the following:

In many towns in eastern New Mexico, Hispanos are
barred from the "better" barber shops, restaurants, hotels, and
places of amusement. Hispano children in that section of the
state frequently attend schools which in practice, though not in
theory, are segregated. Anglo and Hispano attend separate churches,
engage in different forms of recreation, very rarely meet socially.[2]

A young Hispano living in Santa Fe was drafted into the
army and was stationed in Roswell--an Anglo town. When he
attempted to rent a bathing suit at a local pool, he was told
that none were available. A friend lent him a suit, and at that
point the young Hispano soldier was bluntly told that no member
of his "race" could use the pool. When reports of the episode
reached Santa Fe, feeling among the Hispanic community ran high.[3]

R. L. Chambers cites other examples in a recent article
in Common Ground:

> In almost all Little Texas (eastern New Mexico)
> communities, a Hispano veteran is never permitted to join
> the American Legion, for instance, unless there is a post

---

1. Santa Fe New Mexican, Nov. 10, 1949.
2. This statement is based upon direct observation in many eastern
    towns over a period of many years.
3. Interview, Manuel Lujan, Republican gubernatorial candidate,
    1948, Santa Fe, Dec. 29, 1949.

set up exclusively for Hispanos. But discrimination
doesn't stop there. Last year, when the Carlsbad
Legion donated its hall for a public dance, Hispanos
were stopped at the door. They were told that by the
order of some post official no "Mexicans" were to be
admitted.[1]

At the University of New Mexico, social discrimination

is practiced, despite the opposition of the administration. This

statement is based upon numerous conversations with Anglo and

Hispano university students and upon a sociological study of

the University, made by Carolyn Zeleny and reported by Carey

McWilliams.[2] Anglo girls will not date Hispano men; Hispanos

are barred from Greek-letter fraternities and sororities (al-

though "token" pledges sometimes are made from the ranks of the

Spanish-speaking aristocracy to combat charges of discrimination).

Discriminatory practices meet with strong opposition from the

faculty and administrative officers of the University, as well

as from "liberal" student groups. In athletics and in scholastic

activities discrimination is not in evidence, but otherwise

Hispanic students move in a social orbit of their own.

A state senator--well educated, prominent lawyer,

financially successful--applied for membership in the Albuquerque

Country Club. He was "blackballed" on the ground that he was

an Hispano.[3]

It goes without saying that social discrimination has

---

1. "The New Mexican Pattern," Summer, 1949, p. 22.
2. McWilliams, op. cit., p. 79.
3. Interview, David B. Keleher, confidential secretary,
   United States Senator Dennis Chavez, Albuquerque, Dec. 28,
   1949.

political repercussions. These will be discussed in succeeding
sections of this study, particularly in connection with the
legislative battle which resulted in the passage of Fair Employment Practices legislation.

It should be noted here that while certain Anglo-
Americans discriminate against Spanish-Americans, others stren-
uously oppose such practices. A vigorous campaign against discrimination has been waged for many years, both by individuals
and by organized groups. New Mexico is the home of many nationally known writers, and almost without exception they have
denounced discrimination and have sought to promote understanding
between the two major groups. Immediately there come to mind
Mary Austin, Erna and Harvey Fergusson, Oliver La Farge, and
Kyle Crichton. The Anti-Defamation League, the Council on Human
Relations, the C. I. O., and other organizations have fought
social and economic discrimination, while newspapers, notably the
Albuquerque Journal and the Santa Fe New Mexican, have decried
malpractices of this type. Nor must one overlook the notable
work of the church, particularly the Roman Catholic Church, in
this connection.

Summary

Comparisons of the socio-economic status of counties
predominantly Hispanic-American in population with counties predominantly Anglo-American in composition reveal considerable disparity. The per capita income and the per capita assessed valuation of property in Anglo counties are considerably higher than
in Hispano counties. A comparison of total property taxes

collected, and the number of persons receiving public assistance
per capita likewise indicates the economic superiority of Anglo
counties. In matters of health, Anglo counties have a distinctly
higher rating.

Further indications that socio-economic differences
divide the Anglo-Americans and the Hispanic-Americans of New
Mexico may be found by examining the membership of social and oc-
cupational groups. This reveals the marked predominance of the
Anglo in business affairs and in the professions. Although
organized labor is dominated by Anglo-Americans, there is some
indication that Spanish-Americans are becoming increasingly
numerous in unions. There is some evidence that Spanish-Americans
are subject to economic discrimination in the form of wage differentials and are subject to social discrimination in the form
of restrictive practices.

CHAPTER V

EDUCATION AND POLITICS

In calling attention to aspects of the educational system of New Mexico which have political significance, it is well to bear in mind that the state has financial problems which provide at least partial explanation for the charges of parsimony, indifference, and discrimination sometimes brought by Hispanic-American critics. The gravity of the public school problem in New Mexico is underlined in a report, The Forty-Eight State School Systems, released by the Council of State Governments in 1949.

According to this study, New Mexico has the heaviest educational load of any state in the Union, in that it has the highest ratio of children-to-be-educated to the adult population. There are 283 school-age children per 1,000 population in New Mexico, while New Jersey has 166, and the national average is 205.[1] Yet New Mexico ranks thirty-eighth in its ability to support an educational system, for its income per pupil in daily attendance is $5,316.00, whereas New York has an income of $15,739.00 per student in attendance, and the national average is $8,981.00.[2]

That New Mexico makes an heroic effort to support education is indicated by the fact that it has first rank among the

---

1. New Mexico Education Association, State Governors Look at Schools, (July, 1949), p. 2.
2. Loc. cit.

48 states in the per cent of total income appropriated for
public education.[1]

Prior to 1934, the public school system was financed
almost entirely by property taxes. The crisis produced by the
depression of 1929-39 caused the legislature to provide both an
income and a sales tax to replace the property tax as the chief
source of school support. Revenue from the sales tax, income
tax, and mineral lands leases supports the state public school
equalization fund. Money distributed to the schools from this
fund accounts for about 70 per cent of all public school revenue
in New Mexico, exclusive of the proceeds of bond issues for
capital outlay.[2] Distribution is based upon the ratio which the
average daily attendance of each county bears to the total average
daily attendance of the state. Before the fund is distributed,
however, deductions are made to cover the cost of pupil transportation and administrative expenses.

The public schools of New Mexico also receive moneys
from the current school fund, which was established by the constitution. Revenue for this fund accrues from income from state
lands, from the permanent school fund, fines, forfeits and escheats,
and from a one-half mill state property tax. The fund is distributed to local districts on the basis of the total number of
school-age children in the district.

County schools also receive funds from motor vehicle
licenses, merchandise leases, and from any federal forest lands

1. Loc. cit.
2. Taxpayers Association of New Mexico, This Is How Public Schools
   Are Financed in New Mexico, (July, 1949), p. 7.

which may be situated in the county. In addition to these
sources of revenue, each county generally levies a tax of five
mills for school maintenance.

The amount of revenue produced by the five-mill
school maintenance levy varies considerably from county
to county, depending upon the wealth of the county, which
sets up a basic inequality to start with, and the distribution of state aid, rather than tending to equalize this inequality, merely piles inequality on top of inequality.
Evidence of the inequality is seen in the cash balances
which have accumulated in some counties; about 57 per
cent of the cash balances held by the schools is seen in
seven counties.[1]

Since distribution of state aid works to the disadvantage of poorer counties, the Hispanic-American population of
New Mexico is adversely affected. For as indicated in the preceding chapter, Hispano counties tend to have lower property
valuations than Anglo counties.

Charge and Counter-Charge

From the time the public school system was established
in 1890 until the present, Hispanic-American leaders have been
critical of the educational opportunities afforded members of
their group. George I. Sanchez, himself an educator of note,
gave succinct expression to this attitude when he wrote,

. . .careful analysis reveals that as the percentage of
Spanish-speaking population increases, educational opportunity decreases.[2]

The record is easy to read. During the period of
phenomenal educational expansion elsewhere in the nation
and in the world, New Mexico was abandoned to the doubtful ministrations of church and private endeavor. Public
education, the keystone of democratic nationality, was
not recognized as of serious import to the policy followed

1. Ibid., p. 23.
2. Forgotten People, p. 31.

by the United States with respect to New Mexicans. And this cannot be attributed to lack of interest on the part of native leaders.[1]

Charges of discrimination are frequently made by Hispanic-American interest groups. Thus, the president of the Asociacion Nacional Mexicana-Americana reports that "we have begun to line up cases of violations of the FEP law. There are examples of this in McKinley County, where not one Mexican-American teacher is hired, despite the 50 per cent of the population which is Mexican-American; in Grant County, there are several segregated schools.. . ."[2]

And such statements as the following are not unusual in publications slanted for an Hispanic-American audience: "We all know by heart just what those rights are that we should enjoy as residents and citizens of this great country of ours. . .but many of our unfortunate brothers who have been denied the privilege of an education in some counties, and, as a result, have been deprived of competing in the economic struggle must accept whatever is given them for their toil and labor."[3]

In contending that the Hispanic-Americans of New Mexico are educationally disadvantaged, Hispano leaders find support among Anglo-American educators. For instance, Loyd S. Tireman of the University of New Mexico calls attention to the fact that Spanish-speaking children present a special problem, since the course of study now followed in New Mexico was originally designed for English-speaking children of the Atlantic seacoast.

---

1. "New Mexico Acculturation," New Mexico Quarterly, (Feb., 1941), p. 65.
2. Letter to writer, Alfredo Montoya, Sept. 29, 1949.
3. Philip J. Montalbo, "Our Rights," Lulac News, (Feb., 1938), p. 3.

The curriculum was based on the accepted
principle that all children should go to high school
and college.. . .But the Spanish-speaking people of
New Mexico had no such body of accepted principles.[1]

. . .The Spanish-speaking people were expected to adjust themselves to the American pattern..
. .When soberly viewed from an historical perspective,
it is rather remarkable that New Mexico has accomplished
so much. Yet the appalling fact is that the common
school has helped very little.[2]

Such charges meet flat denial on the part of many Anglo-
Americans; others contend that inequality of educational opportunity has nothing to do with language patterns, or that if inequities exist, they are the fault of the Hispanic-Americans
themselves. Since this debate on educational status has political
connotations, it becomes necessary to examine the basis of charges
and counter-charges.

Measurement of Educational Opportunity

In order to determine whether or not the Hispanic-
Americans and the Anglo-Americans of New Mexico enjoy equal educational opportunities, a number of comparisons will be made. While
no one study will provide a satisfactory answer, each will con-
tribute to an understanding of the issue.

Total expenditure per pupil in average daily attendance
is one criterion for determining educational opportunity. By
comparing seven counties having an Hispanic-American population
in excess of 75 per cent with seven counties having a comparable

1. Loyd S. Tireman and Mary Watson, A Community School in a
   Spanish-Speaking Village, pp. 15-16.
2. Ibid., p. 17.

concentration of Anglo-Americans, some light is thrown on the educational advantages offered to members of the respective groups. Figures released by the Taxpayers Association of New Mexico in July, 1949, as indicated in Table III, are used for this purpose.

Analysis of the figures revealed in Table III indicates that a considerable disparity exists between Anglo-American and Hispanic-American counties. For example, the average expenditure per pupil in Anglo counties is $74.26 higher than in Hispano counties. In other words, an increase of more than one third in Hispanic county budgets would be required to bring the average to the level of Anglo counties. Attention also should be directed to the fact that the expenditure per pupil in all but two of the seven Anglo counties exceeds the expenditure per pupil in the highest Hispano county.

The method of distributing state aid to counties has been a matter of concern for some years, and criticism from both Hispanic-American and Anglo-American quarters has been severe. An education board appointed by the governor (1947) recommended legislation which put the distribution of state aid on a classroom basis, taking into consideration the wealth of counties, qualifications of teachers, and other sources of revenue. The object of the proposed legislation "was to guarantee each classroom unit a minimum amount for operation and to encourage school units to employ better qualified teachers by a system of rewards for teacher qualifications."[1] Had the bill passed, money would

---

1. Taxpayers Association of New Mexico, This Is How Public Schools Are Financed in New Mexico, (July, 1949), p. 23.

TABLE III

Total Expenditure per Pupil in Average

Daily Attendance by County

A. Hispanic Counties

County	Total Expenditure per Pupil in Average Daily Attendance
Guadalupe	$247.87
Mora	214.02
Rio Arriba	193.50
Sandoval	189.62
San Miguel	199.74
Socorro	213.96
Taos	192.42

B. Anglo Counties

County	Total Expenditure per Pupil in Average Daily Attendance
Chaves	$220.18
Curry	225.67
De Baca	274.46
Lea	360.17
Quay	261.89
Roosevelt	258.42
Union	370.14

C. Anglo-Hispanic Ratio

	Total Expenditure per Pupil in Average Daily Attendance
Hispanic-American Counties	$207.30
Anglo-American Counties	281.56

Source of Data: Taxpayers Association of New Mexico, This Is How Public Schools Are Financed in New Mexico, (July, 1949), p. 19.

have been taken from seven or eight of the wealthier counties
and redistributed to poorer ones.

Opponents of the proposed change in the status quo
prevented either the senate or the house from considering legislation which would have corrected some of the inequities brought
out in Table III. It would be easy to assume that the wealthier
Anglo counties thus prevented improvement of the educational status
of the Hispanic counties. It is worthy of note, however, that several of the counties having large cash surpluses also contained
large Spanish-speaking minorities.[1]

Comparison of enrollment and average daily attendance is
another device employed in assessing educational status. On this
basis, seven Hispanic-American counties and seven Anglo-American
counties make the showing which is revealed in Table IV. Figures
on rural schools released by the Taxpayers Association of New
Mexico in June, 1948, are used for this purpose as indicated in
Table IV.

Teachers salaries also are used as an index of educational opportunity, on the theory that better instruction is
offered in those schools which are able to attract more highly
qualified teachers. In comparing seven representative Hispanic-
American counties with seven corresponding Anglo-American counties
the facts presented in Table V emerge.

Yet another check on educational opportunity may be had
by comparing the percentage of teachers holding college degrees.
Using figures released by the Taxpayers Association of New Mexico

---

1. *Ibid.*, Table 10.

TABLE IV

Comparison between Enrollment and Average Daily

Attendance in Rural Schools by County

A. Hispanic Counties

County	Average Daily Attendance
Guadalupe	81 per cent
Mora	83 " "
Rio Arriba	82 " "
Sandoval	83 " "
San Miguel	85 " "
Socorro	79 " "
Taos	73 " "

B. Anglo Counties

County	Average Daily Attendance
Chaves	50 per cent
Curry	82 " "
De Baca	83 " "
Lea	81 " "
Quay	83 " "
Roosevelt	80 " "
Union	88 " "

C. Anglo-Hispanic Ratio

	Average Daily Attendance
Hispanic-American Counties	81 per cent
Anglo-American Counties	78.1 " "

Source of Data: Taxpayers Association of New Mexico, New Mexico
Tax Bulletin, (June, 1948), p. 492.

TABLE V

Average Salary per Teacher

by County

A. **Hispanic Counties**

County	Average Salary
Guadalupe	$2373
Mora	2475
Rio Arriba	2091
Sandoval	2568
San Miguel	2447
Socorro	2486
Taos	2323

B. **Anglo Counties**

County	Average Salary
Chaves	$2831
Curry	2776
De Baca	2631
Lea	2828
Quay	2617
Roosevelt	2822
Union	2362

C. **Anglo-Hispanic Ratio**

	Average Salary
Hispanic-American Counties	$2395
Anglo-American Counties	2695

Source of Data: New Mexico Tax Bulletin, (June, 1948), p. 489.

in February, 1949, the Hispanic and the Anglo counties may be ranked according to the data presented in Table VI.

Yet another appraisal of educational opportunity may be had by comparing the length of school terms in Anglo and in Hispano counties. Until recent years, the length of the school year varied from 120 days to 180 days. There was a notable tendency for school terms to be shorter in Hispanic-American neighborhoods than in Anglo-American districts. This disparity has, in large part, been corrected as a result of the equalization law which requires a minimum of 176 school days for participation.[1]

Since the 1940 census does not list illiteracy rates by county, reliance must be placed upon earlier statistics. Figures published by George I. Sanchez and presented in Table VII are used in comparing the seven most Anglo and the seven most Hispanic counties on the basis of illiteracy rates. (Here "illiteracy" is defined as inability to read and write Spanish or English.)

The Language Issue

Comparison of illiteracy rates provides introduction to one of the most difficult socio-political problems of New Mexico: the language issue. For as one authority points out, "In the bundle of issues that is called the 'Mexican problem,' none has occasioned more discussion and controversy than the language issue in the schools."[2] This issue was precipitated by the conquest, aggravated by the establishment of a public school system, and

---

1. Interview, Rupert Asplund, Secretary, New Mexico Taxpayers Association, Santa Fe, July 29, 1949.
2. Carey McWilliams, North from Mexico, p. 298.

TABLE VI

Per Cent of Public School Teachers Holding

College Degrees by County

A. **Hispanic Counties**

County	Per Cent of Public School Teachers Holding Degrees
Guadalupe	48.1
Mora	25.3
Rio Arriba	42.1
Sandoval	47.3
San Miguel	54.1
Socorro	54.1
Taos	36.9

B. **Anglo Counties**

County	Per Cent of Public School Teachers Holding Degrees
Chaves	89.5
Curry	84.4
De Baca	79.4
Lea	94.5
Quay	80.3
Roosevelt	88.4
Union	63.3

C. **Anglo-Hispanic Ratio**

	Per Cent of Public School Teachers Holding Degrees
Hispanic-American Counties	46.6
Anglo-American Counties	82.2

Source of Data: Taxpayers Association of New Mexico, _New Mexico Tax Bulletin_, (Feb., 1949), pp. 611-13.

TABLE VII

Per Cent of Illiteracy

by County

A. Hispanic Counties

County	Per Cent of Illiteracy
Guadalupe	11.5
Mora	13.9
Rio Arriba	18.9
Sandoval	22.6
San Miguel	17.3
Socorro	16.3
Taos	15.5

B. Anglo Counties

County	Per Cent of Illiteracy
Chaves	4.6
Curry	1.1
De Baca	8.1
Lea	.6
Quay	3.3
Roosevelt	.9
Union	2.9

C. Anglo-Hispanic Ratio

	Per Cent of Illiteracy
Hispanic-American Counties	16.6
Anglo-American Counties	3.1

Source of Data: George I. Sanchez, Education of Bilinguals in a State School System, p. 45.

given a political cast by the constitution.

Prior to 1846, New Mexico was without schools, and illiteracy was almost complete. Spanish was the universal language. Schools were established by Catholic, Protestant, and non-sectarian organizations shortly after the conquest, and English was introduced as a competing language. That few Hispanic-Americans mastered the new tongue in the first half-century of American tutelage is indicated by the fact that as late as 1917, it was estimated that not one Hispanic-American family out of 100 in New Mexico had entirely abandoned Spanish as the language of the home.[1]

But steady expansion of the Anglo-American population and the organization of a public school system in 1890 made New Mexico increasingly bilingual. The state constitution furthered the use of English in unmistakable fashion: "Provision shall be made for the establishment and maintenance of a system of public schools which shall be open to all the children of the state and free from sectarian control, and said schools shall always be conducted in English."[2]

A number of grave educational problems immediately presented themselves, and they still complicate the social and political life of New Mexico. An Anglo-American philosophy of education was introduced to a people who had no comprehension of its principles, and only a smattering knowledge of the language which was to be the official vehicle.

---

1. Ibid., pp. 297-98.
2. State Department of Education, New Mexico Public School Code, 1941 Supplement, 1938 Compilation, p. 78.

The problem of securing teachers capable of dealing
with the complex educational problem thus presented would have
been difficult under the most perfect conditions. Since New
Mexico was a sparsely populated and economically poor state, the
obstacles were well-nigh insuperable. This should be borne in
mind as one reads charges that the educational system of New Mexico has produced illiteracy in two languages.

Yet even more difficult than securing teachers was the
determination of policy. Perhaps the most important question was
whether or not an attempt should be made to preserve the Spanish
language and culture. An effort in that direction might tend to
fix the Spanish-Americans as a marginal group, completely isolated
from the community as a whole.

> The attractiveness of the Anglo culture pattern
> especially in its material aspects, for an isolated people
> is so great that it constantly tends to assimilate them,
> willingly or unwillingly. The new generations clearly
> show the confusion brought about by the two forces acting
> upon them, one centripetal which prompts them for self
> preservation to take refuge in their own culture in the
> face of the unkindness of the dominant culture, and another
> centrifugal which prompts them to imitate the Anglos.[1]

In the earlier years of public education, the tendency
was to force the English language and the Anglo-Saxon culture on
the Spanish-Americans. Thus, the educational policy introduced
in New Mexico offers a striking parallel to the policy later
adopted by the United States in Puerto Rico and the Philippines.

Recent years have witnessed a change. Now there is a
studied attempt on the part of many educational leaders to preserve
the Spanish language and to acquaint Anglo-Americans with the

---

1. School of Inter-American Affairs, University of New Mexico,
   "Conference on the Problems of Education among Spanish-Speaking
   Populations of Our Southwest," pp. 5-6.

Hispanic culture. Not all this effort may be written off as
an attempt to preserve the quaint character of the native people.

Official recognition of this attitude came with the
adoption (1941) of legislation which required that Spanish be
taught in public schools.

> In all public grade schools of this state, rural
> or municipal, having at least three teachers or an average
> daily attendance of ninety (90) pupils, the Spanish lan-
> guage shall be taught in the fifth to the eighth grades in-
> clusive of such schools; except and unless the governing
> boards of education of the county wherein such school is
> located, shall, by resolution spread of record upon its
> minutes, specifically naming the school or schools to
> which the order applies, may dispense, as to such school,
> with the teaching of Spanish during any scholastic year.
> Provided however, that no pupil attending any public school
> in the state shall be required to take the course in Spanish
> in any school in this state, where the parent or guardian of
> such pupil specifically objects in writing to the super-
> intendent or principal in charge of such school, to the pu-
> pil taking such Spanish course.[1]

It will be noted that the law provides loopholes which
make it possible for administrators to secure release from its
provisions. However, in the last five years, no public school
superintendent has requested a waiver.[2] This does not imply that
all elementary and junior high schools include Spanish in their
curricula. Scarcity of trained teachers, and curriculum restrictions imposed by the small size of most New Mexico public
schools preclude a successful campaign to make all public school
children bilingual. Yet the goal remains as an official objective.

The legislature in the same connection also established
a research fund to "Determine the extent to which the Spanish lan-

1. *New Mexico Statutes, Annotated*, Laws 1941, Ch. 143, p. 250.
2. Interview, Gail Barber, State Supervisor of Elementary Education, Santa Fe, July 29, 1949.

guage should be taught in the schools of this state to the profit
and benefit of its citizens, and to determine the most practical
manner and methods of teaching such language."[1] In this manner
an attempt was made to remove the language question from politics.

Since Spanish is still the home language of most Hispanic-
Americans, youngsters entering public schools are at a great disadvantage, for by law instruction must be in English. Young Hispanos are taught a basic English vocabulary in pre-first grade
classes and then enter the first grade. This establishes a line
of cleavage between Anglo and Hispano at the outset. That cleavage persists, for Spanish-speaking children tend to remain retarded throughout their school career.[2]

Pupil Mortality

A survey conducted by George Peabody College (1948)
emphasizes the fact that retardation is a peculiarly serious problem in New Mexico. On the basis of data submitted by five representative counties, the Peabody survey reported that 28 per
cent of all pupils in grades 1 - 7 are overage. The proportion
of retarded children is 50 per cent larger in rural schools
(where Hispanic-Americans are concentrated) than in urban schools.[3]
Retardation is higher in Hispano than in Anglo counties. "One
of the principal causes of overageness in the Spanish-speaking
areas is the linguistic handicap of the children and the in-

1. T. F. Conway, "Bilingual Problem in the Schools of New Mexico,"
   Alianza, (Feb., 1943), p. 13.
2. Thomas C. Donnelly, The State Educational System, p. 29.
3. Division of Surveys and Field Services, George Peabody College
   for Teachers, Public Education in New Mexico, p. 133.

adequacy of the means used to develop good language habits."[1]

Closely related to the problem of retardation is that
of pupil mortality. Here the Hispanic-American again appears at
a disadvantage. This is indicated by a study conducted by R. J.
Mullins, executive secretary of the New Mexico Education Association in the period 1935-1948. The Mullins report was based upon
a comparison of all public schools in five counties (Mora, Rio
Arriba, Sandoval, San Miguel, and Taos) having an overwhelming
Hispanic-American population and all public schools in five
counties (Curry, De Baca, Luna, McKinley, and Roosevelt) having
a predominantly Anglo-American population.

Of each 100 pupils enrolled in grade two in Hispano
counties in 1937-38, 70 reached grade four; 35 reached grade eight;
23 enrolled in grade nine; 12 reached the twelfth grade, and 11
graduated in May, 1948.

Of each 100 pupils enrolled in grade two in Anglo
counties in 1937-38, 100 reached grade four; 86 reached grade eight;
78 enrolled in grade nine; 47 reached grade 12; and 42 graduated
in May, 1948.[2]

In other words, the ratio of pupils in Anglo counties
who reached grades eight, nine, and twelve and graduated from high
school to those in Hispanic counties was about four to one.

Explanation for the high pupil mortality among Hispanic-
Americans has been variously attributed. George I. Sanchez has
stressed the socio-economic factor and has called attention to

1. Ibid., p. 134.
2. R. J. Mullins, (Reprint), "Where Did They Go? And Why?",
   New Mexico School Review, (May, 1949).

the unsuitability of the curriculum. He concludes that, "It
seems evident that there is a tendency in the schools of New
Mexico to provide diminishing degrees or educational opportunity,
as measured in this study, as the proportion of Spanish-speaking
children enrolled in the schools increases."[1]

After noting that the curriculum was completely un-
suited to the needs of the children in question, the famous study
of the Spanish-American village, El Cerrito, pointed up parental
apathy as a major reason for pupil mortality.

> Parents are neither consulted nor are they
> willing to offer anything in the way of criticism or
> support.. . .Although few parents expect their children
> to complete more than eight grades of school, this mini-
> mum is considered essential. Any less would not give
> the pupil the necessary working knowledge of English.[2]

Mullins, author of the comprehensive study of pupil
mortality cited above, offers a completely different explanation.
The disparity between Anglo and Hispano schools is not one of
money he states. For, "Long have we placed our best efforts,
with a degree of success, into a plan for better financing of
schools in the neglected areas."[3] He then remarks that,

> Currently 88 per cent of the operating costs
> of the schools in all these counties are being financed
> from state sources. To this extent the amount available
> for each child in school is approximately the same in
> each county, and the differential in production of local
> tax levy is not more than ten per cent of the total avail-
> able per pupil, hence lack of money is not the cause of
> poor school attendance.[4]

1. The Education of Bilinguals in a State School System, p. 96.
2. Olen Leonard and C. P. Loomis, Culture of a Contemporary
   Rural Community, El Cerrito, New Mexico, p. 52.
3. Mullins, op. cit.
4. Loc. cit.

Having ruled out the economic factor and parental
background as chief factors in pupil mortality, Mullins bluntly
states that political domination of schools in Hispanic counties
is the principal reason for high pupil "mortality."

> In our capacity as representative of teachers
> in tenure and contractual problems, we have been called
> on repeatedly in each of these counties in cases involving
> dismissal for political reprisals, transfers to less desir-
> able positions, late employment and assignment. On the
> other hand we have never been called on, nor have we heard
> of a teacher employment problem in Group Two (Anglo).
> Neither the people nor the teachers would tolerate polit-
> ical interference with schools in that area.[1]

Segregation in New Mexico

The constitution of New Mexico specifically forbids
the segregation of Spanish-speaking children in the public schools
of the state.[2] Nevertheless, Hispanic-American leaders have long
contended that such discriminatory practices prevail in many
counties.

Sanchez states that "Side by side with indifference to
the educational needs of the Spanish-speaking children is the
vexing and questionable practice of segregation."[3] He then adds
that segregation sometimes is admitted, sometimes disguised, but
that always it is carried on under one guise or another.

Alfredo Montoya charged that segregation is practiced
in Grant county, as reported earlier in this chapter,[4] and R. L.
Chambers reports that "A school board meeting was recently called

---

1. Loc. cit.
2. Article 12, Section 10.
3. George I. Sanchez, The Education of Bilinguals in a State
School System, p. 33.
4. Supra, p. 54.

in an eastern New Mexico community for the express purpose of setting up a 'Spanish school' in an abandoned church."[1]

Observation in the larger communities of eastern and southern New Mexico led the writer to conclude that segregation is widely practiced. In one case, his attention was called to the fact that the legislature in 1923 authorized separate rooms for students of "African descent," and that "Negroes and Mexicans are the same as far as we are concerned."

However, conversations with a number of superintendents during a state meeting of public school administrators[2] provided the other side of the picture. Socio-economic differences, rather than racial discrimination, account for segregated schools in certain communities, so the schoolmen said. In such localities, Hispanic-Americans gravitate into specific areas because of low financial resources. Inevitably Hispano children congregate in certain schools, for the same reason that Negro children congregate in certain schools in Harlem, south side Chicago, and other urban centers. Economic status, rather than linguistic or cultural patterns, determines the school a child attends.

Officials of the state department of education have opposed efforts to establish segregated schools. Since attention has been called to the attempt at segregation in eastern New Mexico as reported by Chambers,[3] it should be pointed out that the proposed "Spanish" school was not established because of

---

1. "The New Mexico Pattern," Common Ground, (Summer, 1949), p. 23.
2. Santa Fe, July 28, 1949. In particular, Patrick Murphy, Carlsbad; F. Robert Wegner, Los Alamos.
3. R. L. Chambers, Supra, p. 67.

state intervention. while successful attempts to segregate Hispanic-American children do occur, they are violations of the spirit and not the letter of the law.

Further evidence could be offered that Hispanic-American pupils are segregated in certain counties of New Mexico. And further evidence could be offered to indicate that such practices meet the strenuous opposition of state officials and private organizations. But it is sufficient for the purposes of this study to indicate that segregation is an issue which affects relations between Anglo-Americans and Hispanic-Americans.

Summary

The educational problem of New Mexico is complicated by the fact that the state not only is financially poor but it also has the heaviest educational load of any state in the Union. Despite noteworthy and generally successful efforts to improve public instruction, Hispanic-Americans frequently charge that their group is poorly served.

A comparison of expenditures per pupil in average daily attendance and average salary per teacher in representative Anglo and Hispano counties provides some evidence that the quality of education in "native" counties is somewhat inferior t. that in Anglo counties. The disparity is more apparent when the percentage of teachers holding college degrees and the rate of illiteracy are considered. Thanks to vigorous state financial support, the gap has been narrowed to a marked degree.

Bilingualism is a problem which vexes the relationship between Anglo and Hispano. While instruction is in English, in

recent years an official effort has been made to introduce the
study of Spanish in elementary schools to encourage Anglo children
to become bilingual. Pupil mortality is considerably higher in
Hispanic counties than in Anglo counties; a comprehensive study
indicates that the cause is political, rather than socio-economic.
While segregation exists in some schools, it meets with the full
opposition of state education authorities.

CHAPTER VI

CHURCH AND STATE

Since religious differences have been known to make for political differences, it becomes necessary to examine the religious affiliations of the Hispanic-Americans and the Anglo-Americans of New Mexico.

The very landscape of New Mexico is a reminder that the territory was conquered in the name of a Catholic monarch, Christianized by Catholic missionaries, and peopled by Catholic settlers. There was but one church, the Roman Catholic, until the American conquest. Today it dominates the religious scene, as its structures dominate the man-made portion of the landscape.

Any religious census of New Mexico reveals how complete that domination is. The 1930 federal census shows that approximately one half of the total non-Indian population belonged to some church. Roman Catholics constituted 82 per cent of the total, while Protestant sects accounted for 16 per cent.[1] A directory of churches and religious organizations compiled by the Works Progress Administration in 1940 gave the total Catholic population of the state as 200,000, while non-Catholic religious groups had a membership of approximately 82,300.[2]

---

1. Thomas C. Donnelly, Rocky Mountain Politics, p. 235.
2. New Mexico Historical Records Survey, Directory of Churches and Religious Organizations, pp. 1-385.

While the boundaries of the state of New Mexico and the archdiocese of Santa Fe do not coincide, the Catholic population of the state is concentrated within that archdiocese. For that reason, recent statistics from the chancery office are of some interest. The Official Catholic Directory (1949) reveals that the total population of the archdiocese of Santa Fe is 430,000 of whom 205,000 are Roman Catholic.[1]

Map 3 indicates that the Roman Catholic population of New Mexico is highly concentrated in Hispano counties. It merely illustrates what has long been accepted as established fact: that the average Hispanic-American is at least nominally a Catholic, and that the average Anglo-American is at least nominally a Protestant. This commonly held belief also is borne out by statements of the clergy of the respective faiths. For instance, a representative of the New Mexico Baptist Convention in 1949 stated that no more than 25,000--or 10 per cent of the Hispanic population--can be classified as Protestant, while between 80 and 90 per cent of the Anglo population calls itself Protestant.[2]

Moreover, one astute commentator on religion in New Mexico points out that Anglo-Americans of Catholic persuasion are somewhat alienated from their Hispanic-American co-religionists because of the peculiar character of the Hispano's faith:

> Particularly in religion the Mexican is a Spaniard--that is a Catholic with the ascetic, self-torturing instinct.

> But even with the restraining guidance of the clergy, the Mexicano tends toward a bizarre note in his

1. P. J. Kenedy & Sons, New York, pp. 208-11.
2. Letter to writer, Rev. C. W. Stumph, Oct. 13, 1949, (Albuquerque)

MAP 3
ROMAN CATHOLIC MISSIONS BY COUNTY

1940

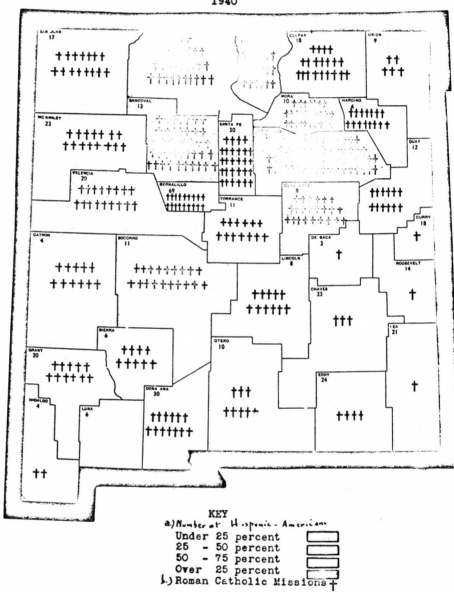

KEY
a.) Number of Hispanic-Americans
Under 25 percent
25 - 50 percent
50 - 75 percent
Over 25 percent
b.) Roman Catholic Missions +

Source of data: <u>Directory of Churches and Religious Organizations in New Mexico</u>, Works Progress Administration, p. 220.

religion, of which his American Catholic neighbor has neither understanding nor approval.[1]

Certainly the cult of the Penitentes still flourishes in sections of Hispanic New Mexico as a reminder that wide deviations exist within the Catholic church itself. And certainly the cult of flagellants finds no acceptance among Anglo-American Catholics who are heirs of northern European concepts and traditions. Yet it must be observed that extremists such as the brotherhood of Penitentes also find no support among the more discerning Hispanos, and that in recent years the hierarchy has discouraged the Penitentes' fanatical manifestation of faith.

Areas of Conflict

The latent hostility between Protestant and Catholic sometimes expresses itself openly in New Mexico, particularly in regard to church-state relationships. Protestants, particularly clergymen, express concern at what they consider the political influence of the Roman Catholic church in New Mexico. Donnelly furnishes partial explanation of this concern: "Religiously and otherwise, the padre has a hold on his communicants that the Protestant minister cannot approach. Politicians pay their respect to this detail . . .by the gingerly manner in which they treat issues in which the papal hierarchy manifests an interest."[2]

One of the most spectacular legislative battles in recent history was that which marked the passage of the Fair Employment Practices Act in 1949. As indicated earlier in this

---

1. Ross Calvin, Sky Determines, p. 216.
2. Donnelly, Rocky Mountain Politics, op. cit., p. 235.

study, the stormy debate often assumed the complexion of an
Anglo-Hispano controversy. The Roman Catholic church, in the
person of a very able monsignor, openly lobbied for the measure,
sometimes on the floor of the legislature, and thus invoked the
wrath of a number of Anglo-Americans. The archbishop's public
letter in support of the measure likewise aroused the ire of
some Protestant leaders, as well as Anglo-American members of
the legislature.[1]

The peculiar organization of public schools in several
Hispano counties also precipitated a Catholic-Protestant controversy on the issue of church and state. Again there were
political repercussions.

The crisis developed as the result of an arrangement
whereby the school boards and superintendents of ten counties
established a number of tax-supported public schools which were
taught by priests or nuns in church-owned buildings. The arrangement was not challenged for a number of years, but eventually
28 persons from seven of the 10 affected counties brought suit
in an effort to terminate church-state cooperation. In March,
1949, the famous Dixon ruling was handed down.

This sweeping decision had far-reaching effect, not
only on the educational system, but also upon Catholic-Protestant
relations. E. Turner Hensley, the district judge who made the
ruling, declared that 12 schools on the list were "in fact, Roman
Catholic parochial schools and are being subsidized in part by

---

1. Interview, John F. Simms, Jr., Speaker of House of Represent-
    atives, Albuquerque, August 1, 1949.

funds raised through taxation by the State of New Mexico."[1]

His decision permanently barred 143 Catholic nuns, priests, and brothers then employed in 10 counties from teaching in tax-supported schools, and required the replacement of Catholic-owned buildings with structures owned by the respective public school districts. The ruling also decreed that students of parochial and private schools cannot be provided with free transportation in public school buses or with free textbooks owned by the state.[2]

The Dixon ruling was bitterly denounced by Catholic leaders, some of whom interpreted it as the result of a Protestant effort to cripple the Roman Catholic church. The superintendent of parochial schools for the archdiocese of Santa Fe told the writer that prohibitions against the use of buildings owned by the church or the employment of priests and nuns in public schools were at least understandable to Catholic officials. But the ban on state-financed textbooks and bus transportation was not comprehensible, since it injured children, rather than the Catholic church.[3] Pending clarification and enforcement of the decree by the state board of education, the church expressed willingness to comply with its provisions.

Two other recent events reveal non-Catholic opposition to any move which would strengthen the church in affairs of state. On November 7, 1949, the daily newspapers of New Mexico

---

1. Santa Fe New Mexican, March 13, 1949.
2. "The Dixon Ruling," New Mexico School Review (May, 1949), p. 14.
3. Interview, Monsignor William T. Bradley, Superintendent of Schools, Archdiocese of Santa Fe, July 21, 1949.

carried a front-page account of the Pope's decree that Roman
Catholic judges must not grant civil divorces for marriages
recognized by the church. Ranged alongside the story was a
statement from one of the most prominent Hispanic-American
jurists in New Mexico, District Judge Luis E. Armijo. The judge
announced that he would refuse to be bound by the order from
Pope Pius XII. "Armijo announced emphatically that his oath of
office as a judge would come first in his attitude toward any
matters of jurisprudence. . .(and that) he would stick by his
decision despite the consequences as far as the church was concerned."[1]

The official organ of the archdiocese of Santa Fe
was prompt in its response: a stinging rebuke was administered
the judge in the editorial column. Shortly thereafter the judge
issued a lengthy statement which again was featured in the
leading newspapers of the state. It was regarded by non-Catholics
as a public retraction, since it contained these submissive words:
"I wish to make it clear that I will uphold the divine law and,
in my official duties as judge will adhere to the principles
which have been set down by His Holiness as an expression of the
law of God."[2]

Public criticism of the apparent change in Judge
Armijo's attitude was not forthcoming. In private, however, the
writer found a hostile attitude among those non-Catholics who
were familiar with the episode. The incident was cited as clear

---

1. Santa Fe New Mexican, Nov. 7, 1949.
2. Santa Fe New Mexican, Dec. 8, 1949.

proof that the Roman Catholic church openly interferes in the civil affairs of New Mexico.

Plans to enlarge St. Vincent's hospital, a Santa Fe institution operated by Catholic sisters, also precipitated a Protestant-Catholic conflict. The ambitious project called for the use of public funds, and this fact caused the Protestant ministers of Santa Fe to express their opposition in an organized manner.[1] Instead of a Catholic hospital, the Protestant leaders proposed a second hospital which would be non-sectarian. When plans for the Catholic project were approved by local, state, and federal authorities, certain non-Catholic leaders spoke of "another victory for Romanism."

More recently, the church became subject to attack as a result of the suspension of the Santa Fe chief of police. A Catholic parochial church proposed to conduct a lottery with an automobile as the prize. The city council approved the project, but the chief of police refused to give his sanction on the ground that the lottery constituted a form of gambling. "Several secret meetings were held on the subject (of the chief's ouster for his anti-gambling activities), but definite action was undertaken only after an issue had arisen that seemed to involve the powerful Catholic church."[2]

When the city council suspended the chief of police, there was a loud outcry that the church had intervened in politics. However, a front-page editorial in the leading news

---

1. Editorial, Santa Fe New Mexican, Dec. 8, 1949.
2. Santa Fe New Mexican, June 4, 1950.

organ offered contrary evidence:

> The council bloc that voted to suspend the
> chief appeared to side with the church, an appearance
> which was about as far wrong as possible. There is no
> greater advocate of morality in public office than
> Catholic Archbishop Edwin V. Byrne. His statements
> Friday to the St. Michael graduates and his consistent
> record of years past demand honest, unswerving ob-
> servance of the law.[1]

Observation over a period of years leads the writer
to conclude that the average Anglo-American, like the average
Hispanic-American, is scarcely aware of, and therefore scarcely
concerned with Catholic-Protestant rivalries. But the foregoing paragraphs indicate that sharp differences between the two
religious groups exist, and that the leadership in each body is
highly sensitive to the political aspect of organized religion.
When differences are brought into the open, there frequently is
cleavage along Anglo-Hispano lines.

Summary

New Mexico may be considered the most Catholic state
in the Union if the Catholic-non-Catholic ratio is used as
criterion. The Catholic population is highly concentrated in
the Hispanic sections of the state. Latent antagonism between
Catholic and Protestant occasionally becomes open; this sometimes assumes the complexion of an Anglo-Hispano conflict because of the divergent religious affiliations of the two groups.

---

1. Loc. cit.

CHAPTER VII
ACTION GROUPS

In examining the roots of political behavior, attention
must be focused on organizations which represent linguistic or
cultural groups. For where minorities exist, and where such
minorities consider themselves disadvantaged, they frequently
intervene in politics on an organized basis. The Hispanic-
Americans of New Mexico are no exception, for through the years
they have formed associations which are politically influential.

The Alianza Hispana-Americana was founded in Tucson,
Arizona, in 1895.[1] It is primarily a fraternal organization,
comparable to the Knights of Pythias or the Benevolent and Protective Order of Elks. It has more than 300 lodges in the southwestern states, and maintains numerous clubhouses. In New Mexico, the strength of Alianza is centered in Albuquerque, where
the association maintains an active program which has its head-
quarters in a large clubhouse in the northern part of the city.
According to its executive secretary, Alianza has "several
thousand" members in New Mexico.[2]

Alianza Hispana-Americana is based upon three principles: Protection, Morality, and Instruction. The organization
had its inception in a desire to protect the Hispanic-American

---

1. _Alianza_ (December, 1948), p. 8
2. Interview, Paul Sanchez, Albuquerque, Dec. 27, 1949.

population from the rising tide of Anglos. Later, "protection"
came to include economic as well as socio-political matters.
This led to the establishment of a comprehensive insurance program. Today, members of Alianza take out life insurance policies,
the maximum being $2,500.

While the chief emphasis has come to be protection
through insurance, Alianza Hispana-Americana has not neglected
the educational phase of its program. The association promotes
the showing of educational films, brings speakers into Hispanic-
American communities, and encourages young Hispanic-American
artists by sponsoring concerts.

Alianza Hispana-Americana is perhaps the least political
of the major ethnic organizations under consideration. It rarely
lobbies; however, if measures introduced into the legislature are
regarded as adverse to the interests of the Hispanic people of
New Mexico, Alianza will bring pressure. Recently, the organization secured the defeat of a bill which would have made physical
examination a prerequisite to the issuance of life insurance
policies. Alianza regarded the measure as detrimental to the
welfare of the Hispanos, many of whom have no access to medical
service. For that reason, the organization successfully fought
the proposed legislation.[1]

Perusal of the monthly magazine, Alianza, reveals only
occasional preoccupation with Anglo-Hispano relations. The bulk
of the reading matter is made up of accounts of lodge activities,
social notes, "canned" essays on tolerance, inter-racial co-

---

1. Interview, Paul Sanchez, loc. cit.

operation and the like.

The League of United Latin American Citizens (LULAC) was organized in Harlingen, Texas, in 1927, and shortly thereafter chapters were established in New Mexico, Arizona, Colorado, and California. Today the League has approximately 2,000 members in New Mexico.[1] Active chapters are found in most of the larger communities, and in several places Junior Lulac societies have been formed to attract younger Hispanic-Americans.

In membership, Lulac represents a somewhat privileged group, for it is distinctly middle-class in composition, and admittedly is made up of "men of prominence in diverse professions and. . .persons truly cosmopolitan and capable not only of bringing honor to their race but to all humanity."[2] Although Lulac represents the Hispanic-American middle class in New Mexico, it is not homogeneous. It has its liberal and its conservative elements; anti-Negro, anti-Semitic, and anti-peon feeling exists on the part of some, while others display complete tolerance.[3] This diversity in the ranks of the League of United Latin American Citizens sometimes has made it difficult to secure a united front on matters affecting the entire Spanish-speaking community.

The aims and purposes of the League, as set forth in the official publication, Lulac News, fall into several categories. Few of the stated aims have purely ethnic appeal, but the following

1. Interview, Daniel T. Valdes, State Governor, Lulac, Santa Fe, Dec. 30, 1949.
2. Antonio Rebolledo, "Lo Que Nos Toca Hacer," Lulac News (Sept., 1940), p. 19.
3. Interview, Valdes, op. cit.

citations indicate an acute awareness of minority status.

> We solemnly declare once and for all to main-
> tain a sincere and respectful reverence for our racial
> origin, for which we are proud.. . .To eradicate from
> our body politic all intents and tendencies to estab-
> lish discriminations among our fellow citizens on
> account of race, religion or social position.. . .We
> shall destroy any attempt to create racial prejudices
> against our people, and any infamous stigma, which may
> be cast upon them. We shall demand for them the re-
> spect and prerogatives which the Constitution grants
> to us all.. . .Secretly and openly, by all lawful means
> at our command, we shall assist the education and
> guidance of Latin Americans.. . .We shall oppose any
> tendency to separate our children in the schools of
> this country.[1]

Concern for the socio-economic status of Hispanic-

Americans is manifested in a number of objectives listed in the

official aims and purposes.

> The acquisition of the English language, which
> is the official language of our country, being necessary
> for the enjoyment of our rights and privileges, we de-
> clare it to be the official language of this Organiza-
> tion, and we pledge ourselves to learn, and speak and
> teach same to our children.. . .We shall encourage the
> creation of educational institutions for Latin Americans
> and we shall lend our support to those already in exist-
> ence.[2]

The official aims and purposes of the League states

that "This organization is not a political club," but the re-

mainder of this particular statement reads:

> . . .but as citizens we shall participate in all local,
> state and national political contests. However, in
> doing so, we shall ever bear in mind the general welfare
> of our people, and we disregard and abjure once for all
> any personal obligation which is not in harmony with
> these principles. With our vote and influence we shall
> endeavor to place in public office men who show by their
> deeds, respect and consideration for our people.. . .In
> order that we may enjoy our rights more fully, we, as
> well as the members of our families, shall comply with

---

1. Lulac News (October, 1940), p. 27.
2. Loc. cit.

the laws of the state in which we reside governing the
right of franchise.. . .We shall endeavor to secure
equal representation for our people on juries and in
the administration of Governmental affairs.. . .We
shall resist and attack energetically all machinations
tending to prevent our social and political unification.[1]

The New Mexico Chapter of the League of United Latin
American Citizens has had able, and sometimes, aggressive leadership. Its most recent governor, Daniel T. Valdes, a young university graduate, spearheaded the drive for a state Fair Employment
Practices law. Although the bitter legislative battle which
that campaign precipitated is discussed in a succeeding chapter,
it should be pointed in this connection that the League was the
single most important factor in the passage of that controversial
legislation.

The campaign for a Fair Employment Practices act was
the culmination of a long campaign waged against alleged discrimination. The pages of Lulac News have been filled with such
statements as these:

> I saw them (Hispanos) working in the fields,
> in the factories, digging ditches, serving the tables,
> and everywhere with brawn and muscle they toiled, they
> were the underdogs of the new conquistadores. Ignored
> and forgotten, the glory that was theirs faded into
> oblivion. Mostly fate was unkind to them. Hate and
> racial discrimination was their lot, accepted spoils
> of victory of the conquerors.[2]
>
> . . .and to bear out the truth of my statement, as to
> the bitterness and resentment and contempt that the
> American public has for us, I have only to remind you
> that many American ecomomists and historians when
> speaking of us in their writings on the economic,
> social and historical picture of the United States,
> classify us. . .as non-white or colored. . .let each

1. Loc. cit.
2. F. Valencia, "March Onward Lulac Soldiers," Lulac News,
   (Feb., 1938), p. 7.

of you ask yourself, "Am I going to sit by and meekly allow this indignity, this insult to my blood, to my ancestors, to my very soul go unchallenged?"[1]

Not only did Lulac attempt to bring an end to discrimination in the socio-economic field, but it also insisted upon equality of political opportunity. In particular, the organization sought the inclusion of Hispanic-Americans on grand and petty juries. The Hispano's case was succinctly stated by Philip J. Montalbo:

> We should make a concerted effort to have every qualified member of our race serve on a Grand Jury in each of the respective localities.. . .Only a handful of men of our extraction rotate on our grand juries. A Grand Jury is supposed to represent every member of a community.. . . . . .The sad part about the jury system is that in the great majority of cases, when a petty jury is being selected, not one person of our extraction is called or selected to serve on a jury.[2]

But the League of United Latin American Citizens has been active in fields other than social and political. As Senator Dennis Chavez has pointed out on a number of occasions, one reason "why some of our people do not enjoy all the rights and privileges of the Constitution has been the lack of education in the language of this country."[3] For that reason, leaders of this Hispanic-American organization constantly have reminded members of their responsibility to master the English language, to teach it to their children, and to assist other Hispanos to learn the language as a step toward economic equality.

---

1. Edward A. Guiterrez, "Darkness Lifts to the Dawn," Lulac News (April, 1939), p. 12.
2. "Our Rights," Lulac News (Feb., 1938), pp. 3-4.
3. Speech to National Lulac Convention, Lulac News (July,1938), p. 35.

To develop pride and _esprit de corps_ in the Hispanic-American community, the League promotes varied social activities. Motion pictures, dances, benefits, and similar affairs not only bring Hispanos together, but they also may be used to raise funds for the educational and political projects of the organization. In larger communities, an auxiliary branch for children, Junior Lulacs, exists and acts as a feeder for the parent organization.

New Offensive

A possible indication that the Hispanic-Americans of New Mexico are increasingly conscious of minority status may be seen in the recent organization of two aggressive and potentially powerful organizations--the Asociacion Nacional Mexicana-Americana and the Association for the Advancement of Spanish-Americans.

Founded in May, 1949, in Grant county, New Mexico, the Asociacion Nacional Mexicana-Americana (ANMA) now has 1,500 members, and aims at a state membership of 5,000 when the first national convention is held in the spring of 1950.[1]

The organization of ANMA was the direct outgrowth of a clash between Hispano miners and Anglo law enforcement officers in the village of Fierro in May, 1949. The fracas led to the Hispano charge that "The police force, on the whole, looks down upon the Mexican-Americans as an 'inferior' people. Instead of safeguarding the rights of the people, it uses intimidation and

---

1. Letter to writer, Alfredo Montoya, National President, Asociacion Nacional Mexicana-Americana, December 8, 1949.

force to cow them."[1] With strong backing from the C. I. O., a
local chapter of ANMA was launched in Grant county at a time
when public opinion was inflamed. On August 14, 1949, the
national organization of Asociacion Nacional Mexicana-Americana
was set in motion in Albuquerque.[2]

According to its national president, the young, highly
educated, politically astute Alfredo Montoya, ANMA is a grass
roots movement. It is interested in reaching all segments of
the Hispanic community and in wielding them into a unified force.
Unlike the older organizations, it seeks out the disadvantaged
Hispano and offers him positions of leadership which will give
him a feeling of "belonging." The purpose of the Asociacion
is not to organize Hispanos into a hyper-sensitive minority group,
but to make the Mexican-American as proud of his origin as is the
Irish-American or the German-American.

ANMA has a close connection with the labor movement,
particularly with the C. I. O. It urges its members to join
unions, and having joined to seek positions of leadership within
the organization. For that reason, ANMA has been opposed by
certain Anglo officers of the AF of L who seemingly are jealous
of their leadership. Asociacion Nacional Mexicana-Americana
likewise has encountered the disapproval of a number of the
Roman Catholic clergy because of its refusal to issue a blanket
condemnation of communists and other subversive elements. By
pinning the label "communist" to ANMA, its opponents have hindered its membership campaign in New Mexico. In California,

1. Abusos e Injusticia Contra los de Origen Mexicano, Asociacion
   Nacional Mexicana-Americana, June, 1949.
2. Albuquerque Journal, August 15, 1949.

Colorado, and Arizona the organization has made far greater headway.[1]

Unlike Alianza and Lulac, the Asociacion aims for a national, rather than a regional, organization of Hispanic-Americans. Membership drives in the "Mexican" communities in Chicago, Detroit, and other industrial centers are under way, and a link with the large Puerto Rican colony in New York city is contemplated. Likewise, ANMA makes a strong bid for the support of liberal Anglo-Americans. It proposes a coalition of all progressive forces to enact a comprehensive New Deal-Fair Deal program, including comprehensive civil rights legislation.

In the meantime, Asociacion Nacional Mexicana-Americana extends its protection to disadvantaged Hispanos. In particular, it offers to intervene in cases where aged persons and dependent children are denied social security benefits, where veterans run into difficulty with the Veterans Administration, or where householders are threatened with eviction. ANMA also has interested itself in cases of alleged police brutality. Besides its civil rights program, The Asociacion is engaged in an educational program, where stress is laid upon health, and in a drive for low-rent housing projects in the Spanish-speaking sections of larger cities.

To conclude: the very name chosen by the founders of ANMA is indicative of the character and purpose of the organization. The idea that the Hispanos of New Mexico are of pure

---

1. Interview, Alfredo Montoya, op. cit., Albuquerque, Dec.. 28, 1949.

Spanish stock is repudiated. Instead, their New World, Mexican background is recognized. By calling attention to the cultural contributions of the American of Mexican descent, ANMA seeks to inculcate self-respect in the Hispano of today, to provide him with a goal and the instrument for achieving that goal.[1]

Full Dress Politics

On February 1, 1950 the most political of all Hispanic-American organizations was announced. The Association for the Advancement of Spanish-Americans had as its head Daniel T. Valdes, former governor of the League of United Latin American Citizens and former chairman of the New Mexico Council on Human Relations.

The new organization is a non-profit corporation established for the purpose of promoting political activity. To this end it proposes to set up non-partisan political action committees in every precinct in the state. According to Valdes, the action groups are "for the purpose of working for good government and governmental programs necessary to improve the economic, cultural, and social status of the Americans of Spanish ancestry in New Mexico."[2]

That the Association for the Advancement of Spanish-Americans is non-partisan is indicated by the fact that the first chapter (Santa Fe county) has an executive board composed of 24 Republicans and 24 Democrats. That it will engage actively in politics is indicated by the fact that it has two full-time, paid organizers in Santa Fe county, with similar officials promised for

1. Loc. cit.
2. Santa Fe New Mexican, February 1, 1950.

other sections of the state.

Like Asociacion Nacional Mexicana-Americana, the
Association for the Advancement of Spanish-Americans makes a
bid for support from labor and from "liberal" Anglo-Americans.
It advocates expansion of state and federal social security programs, health and educational facilities and public housing. The
conservation and development of natural resources is one of its
objectives, along with comprehensive civil rights and labor
legislation.[1]

Formation of the Association was a reminder that the
Hispanic-Americans of New Mexico now were organized on a purely
political basis.

Summary

The Spanish-Americans of New Mexico have formed several
organizations designed to forward their interests. These associations vary from the Alianza-Hispana-Americana, primarily a
fraternal organization, to the Association for the Advancement
of Spanish-Americans, a political action group. Between the
two extremes are the League of United Latin American citizens,
an organization catering to the somewhat privileged middle class,
and the Asociacion Nacional Mexicana-Americana, an organization
which champions the less advantaged segment of the Spanish-
American population and stresses cooperation with organized labor
and "liberal" Anglo groups.

---

1. Interview, Daniel T. Valdes, Chairman, AASA, Santa Fe,
    December 30, 1949.

CHAPTER VIII

PARTY AFFILIATION IN NEW MEXICO

Statistics, historical data, and other information
presented in preceding chapters indicate that visible differences exist between the Anglo-Americans and the Spanish-
Americans of New Mexico. Some of these differences represent
the residue of past conflicts over land, water and mineral
rights; divergent concepts of law and politics; and differing
patterns of land settlement, economic goals and social organization. Attention has been called to other factors which represent differences in the economic and social advantages now
enjoyed by Anglos as a group as compared with Hispanos as a
group. These differences are magnified by the manner in which
the population of New Mexico is distributed. There is a marked
tendency for the state to be divided into Anglo-American and
Hispanic-American areas. This has encouraged members of each
group to regard themselves as part of a bloc operating in opposition to a similar bloc.

At this point, the purpose of the study is to discover whether or not the differences outlined above bring the
Anglo-American and the Hispanic-American populations of New
Mexico into political opposition. Also a matter of concern is
the manner in which possible opposition exhibits itself.

It would be natural to assume that where two groups

find themselves in opposition in a democratic society, rival
political parties would develop as the official vehicles of
the respective groups. Certainly it would have simplified this
particular political study if such a situation existed in New
Mexico. Such is not the case, however. The record of party
affiliation is highly complex, as the following recital will
indicate. The ethnic factor is but one of many complications.

Rise and Fall of Party Power

Roughly, the political history of New Mexico may be
divided into three periods: 1850-1911, Republican domination;
1911-1930, Republican-Democratic balance of power; 1930-1950,
Democratic ascendancy.

In the period when New Mexico was a territory of the
United States, Republicanism was a national trend. With the exception of Cleveland, all Presidents were Republicans; that party
generally was in control of both houses of Congress; its members
had almost exclusive possession of the Supreme Court. It was a
period of national expansion, shared alike by the humble work-
man, the independent farmer, and the mighty financier.

It was in that period that the mines, the forests, and
other resources of New Mexico were exploited; the railroads built;
and large-scale irrigation begun. It was logical for the Republican party to be in charge of the territory at this time. Government became an instrument in the hands of those who controlled
the economic resources of the area.

Control of the national administration also gave the
Republican party a firm hold on the administration of New Mexico.

The President not only appointed the territorial governor and federal judge, but he also named a host of lesser officers. The power of patronage quite naturally drew many of the hesitant into the Republican fold.

As far as the Hispanic-American population was concerned, there were added reasons for the hold of Republicanism. As Charles B. Judah has pointed out, the great Spanish landowners of New Mexico readily accepted the tenets of the Republican party:

> For longer than the English had been in America, a handful of Spanish masters had exploited the land and its people. The Americans had put an end to the "master-servant" law, a euphuism for peonage, but that done, patron and capitalist found little over which to quarrel. They could be and were good Republicans together.[1]

The importance of the hidalgo's conversion to Republicanism becomes apparent when one remembers that each great landowner was the patron of numerous peones, landless workmen. The political ramifications of this relationship will be considered at some length in a subsequent chapter (X), but it should be noted that almost without exception historians emphasize the fact that the patron voted his peones as he saw fit:

> Each of these (Spanish) families has from five hundred to two thousand dependents, some of whom were their peons before that system was abolished, and continue to yield obedience by nature and habit.[2]

> Both political and economic life in New Mexico still suffer from (the Hispano's) instinctive love of a feudal relationship to some leader. . . .Of one of

---

1. The Republican Party in New Mexico, p. 4.
2. J. H. Beadle, The Undeveloped West, as quoted by Archie M. McDowell, Opposition to Statehood Within the Territory of New Mexico, p. 13.

them it was said that when an election was in doubt he could always win it by voting the sheep.[1]

Politics among one of the groups in New Mexico, the Spanish-Americans, is characterized by their proneness to follow some leader with a blind, solemn devotion. The behavior is found and is a recognized phenomenon among all peoples and groups, but among the Spanish-Americans it appears to a startling degree.[2]

In short, as one reads the standard histories of New Mexico which are cited in the appended bibliography, he comes to the conclusion that in this period the strength of the Republican party was derived from an alliance of the privileged Anglo and the privileged Hispano. But it was the peon vote provided by the latter group which enabled the party to remain in power.

In territorial days, the Spanish-Americans of New Mexico were overwhelmingly Republican in sentiment. It was freely acknowledged that the real strength of the party was based in the "native" counties. This is borne out by an analysis of election returns. It also finds demonstration in the composition of the famous constitutional convention of 1910, that event which signalized the end of territorial status. Of the 100 delegates, 71 were Republican, and 29 were Democratic. The Republican group was almost evenly divided between Anglo and Hispano: 38 Anglo-Americans and 33 Hispanic-Americans. But not one Democrat was an Hispano.[3]

The Rise of the Democratic Party

The period of 1850-1911 was one of almost complete

---

1. Harvey Fergusson, Rio Grande, p. 116.
2. John C. Russell, State Regionalism in New Mexico, p. 30.
3. Ibid., p. 73.

Republican domination. The period of 1911-1930 was characterized by the rise of the Democratic party and the emergence of New Mexico as a two-party state.

The composition of the state legislature, as revealed in the Blue Books of New Mexico, indicates that Republicans had surrendered many seats to the rival party. The two parties likewise fought on somewhat equal terms as far as the governorship was concerned. Democrats captured that important office in 1911, 1916, 1922, 1924, and 1930. Republicans occupied the governor's chair in 1918, 1920, 1926, and 1928. In other words, the score was 5-4 in favor of the Democrats. The even balance of power was illustrated in the fact that "with two exceptions the victorious party's margin of victory was narrow, ranging from approximately two hundred to thirty-seven hundred votes."[1]

If the period 1850-1911 may be termed the golden age of the Republican party in New Mexico, the same appellation may be used in describing the sway of the Democratic party in the years 1930-1950. For during this period the Republican party almost disappeared as a major force in New Mexico. Certainly it never was successful in capturing the state administration. It was declared officially dead by several of its leaders, and political commentators referred to New Mexico as part of the Solid South. Since the transfer of power from Republican to Democrat involved a shift in the party loyalty of many Hispanic-Americans, it may be well to consider the reasons for this major change in the politics of New Mexico.

----

1. Charles B. Judah, op. cit., p. 7.

The most obvious explanation is the fact that the national trend was toward the Democratic party. The Democrats captured Congress in 1930, and with one exception controlled succeeding ones in the period under discussion. The Presidency fell into the hands of the Democrats in 1932, and they managed to keep that office thereafter. Even the Supreme Court assumed a Democratic complexion.

Control of the national administration gave the Democratic party control in New Mexico to an unparalleled degree. The explanation is simple: a large portion of the state of New Mexico is owned outright by the federal government. Federal expenditures completely overshadow any other source of revenue. The United States government is by far the most important employer. The patronage power is enormous. The inference is obvious: the Democratic party can count on the support of thousands of officeholders, both civil service and appointive. According to the chairman of the state Democratic committee, the Republican party never will stage a comeback in New Mexico until there is a Republican President who can dispense patronage.[1]

When compared with the federal Democratic machine, the state organization appears somewhat minor. Yet it is a force to reckon with: approximately 5,000 state jobs are at its disposal, and it is estimated that these individuals and their families represent a tight-knit bloc of 25,000 votes which can be delivered to the Democratic party at each election.[2]

---

1. Interview, Bryan Johnson, Albuquerque, December 27, 1949.
2. Interview, Manuel Lujan, onetime mayor of Santa Fe, Dec. 29, 1949.

The control of the Democratic party has been expressed in terms of patronage because patronage is of peculiar
importance to the Spanish-American of New Mexico. As a group,
the "native" people are economically disadvantaged; as a group,
they find many avenues closed to them; state, county, and federal jobs provide an avenue of escape. For this reason, government jobs of all types are of immense importance to the Hispanos
of New Mexico.

Senator Dennis Chavez, acknowledged leader of the
Spanish-Americans of New Mexico, frequently has deplored their
dependence upon politics for jobs.[1] Dorothy Cline of the Department of Government of the University of New Mexico characterized
public offices as employment bureaus and indicated that this
would be true until more economic opportunities developed for the
Hispanic-Americans.[2] The famed study of El Cerrito contains this
observation: "(A candidate's) attitude toward national or state
issues concerning such factors as business or labor are passed
over lightly. Instead, he is measured in terms of the number of
jobs and the amount of grants and relief he has obtained for his
constituents. These are what matter."[3]

Among political leaders interviewed during the course
of this investigation there was general agreement that the relief
policy of the Democratic administration during the Great Depression
was the single most important factor in changing New Mexico from

1. Interview, David B. Keleher, confidential secretary, United
   States Senator Dennis Chavez, Albuquerque, December 28, 1949.
2. Interview, Albuquerque, July 20, 1949.
3. Olen Leonard and C. P. Loomis, Culture of a Contemporary Rural
   Community, El Cerrito, New Mexico, p. 57.

a Republican to a Democratic state. This was acknowledged
by Democrats, as well as by discouraged Republicans. Such statements find corroboration in the writings of Thomas C. Donnelly,
perhaps the foremost authority on the government of New Mexico.
After stating that the capture of the Spanish-American vote was
the chief reason for Democratic success, Donnelly stresses the
effect of the relief policies of the Roosevelt administration.

> In January, 1935 more than 135,000 people or
> almost one third of the total population of the state,
> was on relief. Democratic politicians were quick to
> take political advantage of the opportunity to claim the
> loyalty of the relief group, and a change in the voting
> habits of a number of counties was effected. Control of
> relief administration became a powerful political in-
> fluence in both state and local elections.[1]

This is not to say that the Spanish-Americans of New
Mexico were the exclusive recipients of relief. On the contrary,
for in some of the Dust Bowl counties of New Mexico, largely
peopled by Anglo-Americans, those on relief sometimes outnumbered
those who were not. It is obvious, however, that a group as
economically disadvantaged as the Hispanos would be unusually
sensitive to relief policies. It is perfectly logical to expect
"Candidates running for office during the heyday of the New Deal
(to make) capital of the administrative gifts lavished upon the
poorer classes."[2]

The population study found in Chapter II of this study
reveals another factor affecting the rise of the Democratic party
--the phenomenal growth of Little Texas or eastern New Mexico.

---

1. Thomas C. Donnelly, Rocky Mountain Politics, pp. 243-44.
2. Walter L. McNutt, An Inquiry into the Operation of the
   Primary System of New Mexico, p. 2.

As indicated in the cited chapter, the majority of the newcomers were from Texas and Oklahoma. They brought with them a belief in racism and a devotion to the Democratic party. The importance of this influx becomes apparent when one studies election returns. "Between the first state election in 1911 and the election of 1948 the vote cast for governor from the six counties forming what is generally considered the Democratic eastside increased from fifteen per cent of the total to twenty-one per cent."[1] To put it another way: an influx of southerners spelled the doom of Republicanism in New Mexico.

As already noted, this incursion of people from Texas and Oklahoma also widened the rift between Anglo-American and Spanish-American and made the ethnic factor of major importance in politics. It is somewhat ironical that an uneasy alliance between "Little Texans" and "natives" should have contributed so heavily to the success of the Democratic party.

In concluding this explanation for the shift from the Republican party to the Democratic party, mention must be made of the role played by one of the most colorful figures in New Mexican politics, Bronson Cutting. A full-length study of this leader will be made in another connection. (Chapter X) Here it is sufficient to say that this wealthy Anglo was the stormy petrel of the Republican party in New Mexico for two decades. His importance at this point lies in the fact that he exercised rigid control over the Spanish-American vote. And to the admiration of his supporters and the despair of his foes, Bronson Cutting

1.   Charles B. Judah, op. cit., p. 15.

frequently led the Hispano voter outside of the Republican fold. Thus Cutting broke the Hispano's habit of voting straight Republican and facilitated a transfer of allegiance to the Democratic party.

Party Allegiance Today

It has been noted that the switch of large numbers of Hispanic-Americans from the Republican to the Democratic ranks accounted in part for the rise of the latter party. It now should be observed that despite this defection, the strength of the Republican party in New Mexico still lies in the "native" counties. Figures from the Blue Book of New Mexico (1947-48) showing total registration by county demonstrate this fact as indicated in Table VIII. For the purpose of this study, the seven counties having the highest concentration of Anglo-Americans will be compared with seven corresponding Hispanic-American counties.

"Because of the great predominance of Spanish-Americans in the small list of those registered Republican,"[1] Democratic politicians, especially Spanish-American Democrats, have shown considerable interest in Republican affairs. This manifests itself in several ways. On a number of occasions, Spanish-American Democrats have given open support to members of their own group who were running on the Republican ticket. Thus J. O. Gallegos, once co-chairman of Anglo Governor Mabry's campaign as Democratic nominee, swung his support behind Manuel Lujan, Republican nominee.[2]

---

1. Will Harrison, "At the Capitol," Santa Fe New Mexican, May 9, 1950.
2. Clovis News Journal, Sept. 19, 1948.

TABLE VIII

Total Party Registration

by County

A. **Hispanic-American** Counties

County	Democrats	Republicans
Guadalupe	2830	1765
Mora	2685	2651
Rio Arriba	7442	4375
Sandoval	2785	2400
San Miguel	9510	4212
Socorro	3830	1947
Taos	4934	3527
Total	34016	20877

B. **Anglo-American** Counties

County	Democrats	Republicans
Chaves	9236	2075
Curry	9963	1622
De Baca	1592	324
Lea	7570	894
Quay	5197	780
Roosevelt	7578	662
Union	2592	1095
Total	43728	7452

C. **Democratic-Republican** Ratio

	Democrats	Republicans
Hispanic-American Counties	1.6	1.
Anglo-American Counties	5.7	1.

Source of Data: Blue Book of New Mexico (1947-48), p. 152.

On other occasions, the support has been undercover. For example, in 1948 several New Mexico newspapers accused United States Senator Dennis Chavez of giving secret aid to the Republican gubernatorial nominee, Lujan, despite the fact that Chavez was a key figure in the Democratic party. Chavez denied the charges, but it is interesting to note that the chairman of the state democratic committee termed such statements true. "Dennis Chavez gave strong but undercover support to Lujan in the 1948 campaign."[1]

The fact that Republican strength centers in the "native" counties permits Democratic leaders to destroy their Republican opposition, if they choose. Democratic politicians see to it that a weak or completely unknown Spanish-American candidate enters the Republican primary. Frequently his very name assures him the nomination. Then in the general election the Democratic nominee has only token opposition. This device has been described by one of the most powerful figures in the Democratic party, the "second-floor governor" and dispenser of patronage in the Mabry administration (1946-50), Victor Salazar, state commissioner of revenue.

> Here's what we can do in the open primary. I can go to Galisteo and get some sheepherder to sign his name to a GOP nominating petition for governor. Since so many natives are Republican, I can get him to be on the ticket with 500 signatures and he can win the primary. Then in the open general election all we have to do is to say: "Look at this guy, a poor imbecile who's never made more than $30.00 a month working for Jose Ortiz y Pino." I can do that to their (Republican) whole ticket.[2]

The Future of Party Affiliation

---

1. Interview, Bryan Johnson, Chairman State Democratic Committee, Albuquerque, December 27, 1949.
2. Interview, Victor Salazar, Santa Fe, December 29, 1949 (Through Melvin Mencher).

Views on the future party affiliation of the Hispanic-Americans of New Mexico vary. One thought dominates: the inevitable capture of the Democratic party by the Anglo eastern and southern sections of New Mexico. Incomplete 1950 census returns underline the fact that Little Texas is destined to overshadow northern New Mexico, stronghold of the Hispanic element.

Shift in control of the Democratic party will be hastened if the primary election revision recently passed by the legislature finally becomes law. Candidates who run in primary elections are to be chosen by conventions. Representation at the convention is based upon the number of votes cast in the previous gubernatorial election. After noting that southern and eastern New Mexico (Anglo) would have a total of 298 votes out of 1,040 delegates at the Democratic convention, R. L. Chambers, writing in the Taos Star, observes that this would be the largest bloc of votes. "The northern (Hispano) counties can muster 227 at the very most."[1]

In view of the fact that the Republican party, which the Hispano once made strong, no longer is a potent force in New Mexican politics; in view of the fact that the Democratic party, which the Hispano aided in coming to power, apparently is to be dominated by a group somewhat hostile to the Hispano; in view of these two developments, what is to be the role of the Hispanic-American voter from 1950 on?

Almost without exception, the Anglo politicians who were interviewed in connection with this study indicated that

---

1. March 23, 1949.

they had given this question little thought or that they considered it of little consequence. Ordinarily they minimized the
role of "race" in politics or referred to it as a passing stage
in political development.

On the other hand, Hispano political leaders showed
much interest in future party affiliation and activity. There
was no unanimity of opinion, however. Manuel Lujan, once mayor
of Santa Fe and recently a gubernatorial candidate, believes that
the future of the Hispanic people lies with the Republican party,
the party of their fathers.[1] On the other hand, Victor Salazar,
key figure in the state Democratic machine, believes that Anglo-
Hispano differences can be composed within the dominant party.
"I don't want to cram race equality down anyone's throat. It's
a matter of education and getting people to be intelligent."[2]

A third view was expressed by Sam Sosa, Democratic city
chairman in Santa Fe. He believes that eventually the Hispanic-
Americans of New Mexico will be forced to organize a party of
their own. This will wield a balance of power between conflicting
Anglo groups.[3] This view was strongly expressed by one of the
most astute observers of the New Mexican scene, Joaquin Ortega,
formerly director of the School of Inter-American Affairs of the
University of New Mexico.[4] A fourth point of view was offered
by Daniel T. Valdes, chairman of the Association for the Advancement of Spanish-Americans and lieutenant of the Chavez forces.

---

1. Interview, Santa Fe, December 29, 1949.
2. Interview, Santa Fe, December 29, 1949.
3. Interview, Santa Fe, July 19, 1949.
4. Interview, Albuquerque, July 18, 1949.

Valdes believes that the Hispanic-Americans of New Mexico will
ally themselves with organized labor and the liberal element
within the two major parties. Only by enlisting the support of
Anglo allies can the grave economic and social problems of the
Hispanic people be alleviated through political activity.[1]
Support for this position came from Alfredo Montoya, president of
the Asociacion Nacional Mexicana-Americana,[2] and in general from
those younger Hispanos described by Dorothy Cline of the University
of New Mexico as the future leaders who know that education and
economic status are powerful political weapons.[3]

The question posed at the beginning of this section
cannot be answered conclusively. The party affiliation of the
majority of the Hispanic-Americans of New Mexico will be governed
by future events. Observation would lead one to believe, however,
that the majority of Spanish-Americans will continue to register
as Democrats. Whether they become a submerged minority within
that party or effect a coalition with progressive Democrats and
thus consolidate power is a question which younger Hispanic
politicians will answer.

Summary

The political history of New Mexico may be divided into
three periods. Between 1850 and 1911, the Republican party was
in power; between 1911 and 1930 the Republicans and Democrats
divided power; after 1930 the Democrats were in full control. In

---

1. Interview, Santa Fe, December 30, 1949.
2. Interview, Albuquerque, December 29, 1949.
3. Interview, Albuquerque, July 20, 1949.

days when New Mexico was a territory, the Hispanic population
was staunchly Republican. The patron-peon relationship which
characterized Hispanic society contributed to this situation.
Large numbers of Hispanic-Americans switched to the Democratic
party after 1930. In part, this was due to a national trend.
The peculiar dependence of the Spanish-American on politically
derived jobs also has been offered in explanation. Relief
policies of the Roosevelt administration won the loyalty of
many Spanish-Americans. A rising tide of Democrats from Texas
and Oklahoma, and the divisive tactics of Bronson Cutting also
strengthened the Democratic party. In each case, the Spanish-
American population was affected.

Despite the fact that a switch in party allegiance on
the part of Spanish-Americans enabled the Democrats to achieve
power, the "native" counties still are strongholds of Republicanism. This fact has caused Democratic politicians, especially
those of Hispanic descent, to assume great interest in Republican
affairs. Interference has been both open and secret.

Hispanic-Americans see their future party affiliation
from various points of view. Return to the Republican party and
the formation of a new party, based on ethnic origin, are men-
tioned. It is probable that Spanish-Americans will continue to
register as Democrats. Possibly a coalition will be effected
among Hispano, organized labor, and liberal Anglo.

CHAPTER IX

INTER-GROUP ASPECTS OF POLITICAL INTEREST

From a purely legal point of view, no state in the
Union has fewer restrictions on the franchise than New Mexico.
Provisos which so drastically restrict the suffrage in Mis-
sissippi and Alabama are entirely lacking in the constitution
and statutes of this western state. Even the strictures on
illiteracy, which are incorporated in most state election laws,
are missing in regulations governing the franchise.

As far as voting goes, the citizens of New Mexico,
regardless of race, religion, financial position or educational
attainment, are placed on an equal footing. The constitution
explicitly states that inability to speak, read or write the
English or Spanish languages shall not be the basis for with-
holding the franchise. In fact, provision is made for encouraging
the illiterate citizen to vote:

> If any person seeking to register shall be unable to
> read or write either the English or Spanish language,
> . . .the application of such person shall be filled
> out by one of the registration officers and the name
> of such person so registering shall be signed by the
> mark of such person and sworn to by him and witnessed
> by two (2) qualified electors of the county.[1]

When the convention system of naming candidates was
discarded in favor of the open primary, legislation was adopted
which reiterated the principle laid down in the constitution:

---

1. New Mexico Statutes, Annotated 1941, V. 4, p. 1138.

At any and all primary elections held in the state of
New Mexico. . .no such qualified registered elector of
the state shall be denied the right to freely vote or
in any manner hindered in freely voting at such primary election by reason of lack of education or possession of property, or by reason of race, descent or religion or by reason of the lack of ability to read, write
or speak any language.[1]

That "the right of any citizen of the state to vote,
hold office, or sit upon juries, shall never be restricted,
abridged or impaired on account of religion, race, language or
color, or inability to speak, read or write the English or Spanish
languages"[2] became a fundamental of New Mexico politics was due
to pressure which Hispanic-American delegates exerted at the
constitutional convention. The cited clause was made almost impossible to amend, and attempts to modify it have met with concerted
opposition on the part of Hispanic leaders, particularly those
changes which have been regarded as efforts to restrict the
franchise.[3]

The right to vote, shared alike by Anglo New Mexican
and Hispano New Mexican, has not been equally regarded, as the
above comment would indicate. Moreover, the Hispanic-American not
only has been more concerned with the franchise, but he also has
been more concerned than his Anglo neighbor with politics itself.
Thus since the earliest days of statehood, commentators have declared the Hispano citizen to be more politically minded than the
Anglo citizen. The jealousy with which he has regarded his vote
has been but one indication of this intense preoccupation with
political affairs.

1. Ibid., p. 1251.
2. Constitution of the State of New Mexico, Art. 7, Sec. 3.
3. Cf. Chapter XI.

But there are other reasons for believing that of the two major groups, the Hispanic-Americans have shown more interest in politics. These include a virtual unanimity of opinion among social scientists, participation in political campaigns and other party activities, and the record of registration and voting.

This active interest in politics has been demonstrated in the studies of Tewa Basin[1] and El Cerrito,[2] conducted under government auspices, as well as in the case studies of Spanish-American villages made by Chavez,[3] Kluckhohn,[4] Walter[5] and other private investigators. Maurice G. Fulton and Paul Horgan, for example, describe Spanish-Americans as excellent politicians, a view popular with both the Anglo and the Hispano citizen of New Mexico. Hispano politicos "throw a personal passion into the performance of their functions; they shame their American colleagues, for there is nothing perfunctory, nothing cold-blooded"[6] about their politics. This point of view is supported by Donnelly, who writes that "The Spanish-American takes readily and with enthusiasm to political activity and seems to derive intense enjoyment from the drama of political campaigns."[7]

This preoccupation with politics is described by Walter and an explanation is offered:

1. Division of Economic Surveys, Soil Conservation Service, Tewa Basin Study, V. II, The Spanish-American.
2. Olen Leonard and C. P. Loomis, Culture of a Contemporary Rural Community, El Cerrito, New Mexico.
3. A. B. Chavez, Use of the Personal Interview to Study the Subjective Impact of Culture Contacts.
4. Florence Kluckhohn, Los Atarquenos, (2 V.).
5. Paul A. F. Walter, Jr., A Study of Isolation and Social Change in Three Spanish Speaking Villages of New Mexico.
6. New Mexico's Own Chronicle, pp. 347-48.
7. Thomas C. Donnelly, Rocky Mountain Politics, p. 233.

The interest of the Spanish-speaking people in the world at large is limited mainly to partisan politics. Unable to adapt themselves readily to the American economic system, lagging behind in educational attainment, they must achieve their recognition in a realm where their numerical preponderance, until recently, gave them an easy avenue to actual and vicarious distinction. This realm is controlled by the ballot box.. . .

Needing the majority of the vote, which for so long resided in the Spanish-speaking people, it became the common practice among successful politicians in New Mexico to use flattery of every kind to win them. Such reciprocity and recognition have not been possible in other fields of activity.[1]

Walter concludes that it is because of their preoccupation with politics that most Spanish-speaking men are accomplished orators, even when they are not able to read or write.

According to the highly publicized case study, El Cerrito, the interest and participation of the Spanish-American people in politics has increased as the functions of government have become more important to their very existence. "Although Government may be the source of relief and public works, politics governs the machinery by which these are made available to them."[2] This has led to a belief that a person's benefit from a government program will be in direct proportion to his participation in politics.

Basic Pattern of Political Interest

The Spanish-Americans of New Mexico exert their influence and express their needs through countless small clubs, at least one of which may be found in every northern village. Observation of a number of these groups in action leads one to believe that the

---

1. Paul A. F. Walter, Jr., op. cit., pp. 72-73.
2. Olen Leonard and C. P. Loomis, op. cit., p. 57.

basic pattern is the same. A group of the younger people organize
a social-political club, giving it a very high-sounding name. The
prime mover may be an aspiring officeholder, or a rising young
politico who wishes to unseat the local boss (jefe politico).
The club arouses interest and generates good will by sponsoring
dances and fiestas. More important, it offers an informal, highly
articulate forum where local people can discuss politics in their
own way.

S. Omar Barker has given a colorful description of a
club meeting, typical of the "native" counties. Arriving politicians are profusely greeted by the owner of the house where the
meeting takes place, as well as by the club officials. Men,
women and children are packed into the only large room in the
adobe house. They sit Quaker style, men on one side, women on
the other. Introductions are lengthy, and oratory is flowery,
in true Latin style. The acknowledged best speaker of the village
winds up the serious part of the evening with a stirring panegyric
of the party in power. Then follows the inevitable baile or
dance in which both young and old participate.[1]

As pointed out in the study of El Cerrito, most Spanish-
American villages are divided into warring factions.[2] This fact
further stimulates interest in politics, for it is by capturing
public office that one faction achieves the power to thwart its
rival. "Because of the resulting friction, local political issues
are on a par with or of more importance than county or state issues.

---

1. "La Politica," New Mexico Quarterly, Feb., 1934, pp. 3-13.
2. Olen Leonard and C. P. Loomis, op. cit., p. 57.

The broader issue may be forgotten in a desire to thwart the purpose or objective of a rival local group."[1] This negative aspect of political interest is nowhere more evident than in school affairs. Struggle for control of the school board, acrimonious discussion over educational policy, and fistic encounters over the location of a school are somewhat commonplace in the "native" counties, if newspaper accounts may be believed. Recently the executive secretary of the New Mexico Education Association wrote a bitter indictment of this manifestation of political interest in "native" counties.

> We are convinced, however that political domina-
> tion of schools is the principal cause of lack of holding
> power of schools in Group One (Spanish-American counties.)
> In our capacity as representative of teachers in tenure
> and contractual problems, we have been called on repeatedly
> in each of these counties in cases involving dismissal for
> political reprisals (etc.).. . .On the other hand, we have
> never been called on, nor have we heard of a teacher employ-
> ment problem in Group Two (Anglo-American counties.)[2]

If great interest in politics has caused the Spanish-Americans of New Mexico to become involved in petty bickering and to mix politics and education, it also has caused the Hispano to accept certain of his civic responsibilities more readily than in the case of his Anglo neighbor. This is particularly apparent in the exercise of the franchise.

Differences between the voting records of the Hispanic-Americans and the Anglo-Americans of New Mexico are not revealed by comparing the ratio between total population and total registered voters in Anglo counties with the equivalent ratio in Hispano

1. Loc. cit.
2. R. J. Mullins, "Where Did They Go? and Why?," New Mexico School
   Review, May, 1949 (reprint).

counties. For as the statistics presented in Table IX   indicate, the population: registered voters ratio in the seven most Anglo counties is closely comparable to that of the seven most Hispano counties. If the mere act of registration is an indication of interest in the franchise, then the Anglo New Mexican and the Hispano New Mexican are on equal footing.

The significant difference between the Anglo voter and the Hispano voter is displayed, not at time of registration, but at time of election. For it is proverbial in New Mexico politics that the Anglo vote is "hard to get out" while the Hispanos freely exercise the right of franchise. Thus in discussing the operation of the primary system, McNutt writes that, "The drama of the political campaign has long been an integral part of the lives of a large portion of the population. The temperament of the Spanish-American people lends itself to the pageantry of campaign politics. This interest results in a large percentage of voters participating in campaigns and elections."[1] And in commenting on the exceedingly light vote in the first primary election, the same author notes that "As usual, there was greater voting participation by the Spanish-American population."[2]

Recent statistics bear out the assertions made by political scientists. At a time when the governor complained that only about one-third of New Mexico's potential voters go to the polls,[3] those counties which were predominantly Hispanic in population made a far better showing. In the 1948 election, for example, 56

1. Walter L. McNutt, An Inquiry into the Operation of the Primary System of New Mexico, pp. 1-2.
2. Ibid., p. 42.
3. Santa Fe New Mexican, Dec. 6, 1949.

TABLE IX

Population: Registered Voters Ratio, 1940

A. Seven Most Hispano Counties

County	Population	Registered Voters	Per Cent
Guadalupe	8,646	3,822	44
Mora	10,981	4,204	40
Rio Arriba	25,352	8,767	35
Sandoval	13,898	4,012	29
San Miguel	27,910	10,672	39
Socorro	11,422	4,841	42
Taos	18,528	5,859	32
Average			37.3

B. Seven Most Anglo Counties

County	Population	Registered Voters	Per Cent
Chaves	23,980	8,996	33
Curry	18,159	7,705	42
De Baca	3,725	1,307	35
Lea	21,154	8,805	42
Quay	12,111	5,119	42
Roosevelt	14,549	5,653	39
Union	9,095	4,013	44
Average			39.6

Sources of Data: New Mexico Blue Book, 1939-40, p. 58.
New Mexico Blue Book, 1945-46, p. 55.

per cent of the registered voters of Rio Arriba went to the
polls, 54.5 per cent in Sandoval, 52 in Mora and the same per
cent in Taos county. In contrast to the voting record in the
Hispano counties was that in the most Anglo counties of New
Mexico. Less than 21 per cent of the qualified electors of
Roosevelt county voted, less than 26 per cent in Lea, less than
33 in Dona Ana and less than 34 per cent in Eddy county.[1]

The figures have a twofold significance. In the first
place they underline the fact that the Hispanic-American voter
exercises the franchise far more readily than his Anglo neighbor
does. In the second place, the voting habits of the Spanish-
speaking citizens of New Mexico have given them political importance disproportionate to their numerical strength. While the
population of many Hispanic counties is small when compared with
some of the eastern Anglo counties, the Hispano counties tally
more votes. It is for this reason that politicians place such
stress upon the "native" counties.

Anglo-Hispano Balance in Party Leadership

The fact that the Hispanic-Americans of New Mexico display marked interest in partisan politics, coupled with the fact
that the Hispano voting record is superior to that of the Anglo
element, would lead one to suspect that a disproportionate number
of party officials have been Spanish-speaking. The validity of
this assumption has been examined by considering the ethnic
composition of the state central committees of the two major
parties during the period of statehood.

1. Joe Clark, "Capitol Slant," Albuquerque Journal, Aug. 29, 1949.

TABLE X

Ethnic Composition of State Central Committees, 1916-1948

A. Democratic Party

Year	Total Committeemen	Hispanic	Per Cent of Total
1916	52	13	25
1918	52	12	23
1920	56	13	23
1922	118	18	15
1924	123	23	19
1926	121	27	22
1928	121	26	21
1930	124	29	23
1932	134	30	22
1934	134	32	24
1936	151	36	23
1938	154	38	24
1940	154	45	30
1942	155	38	25
1944	155	45	30
1946	154	44	29
1948	154	53	35

B. Republican Party

Year	Total Committeemen	Hispanic	Per Cent of Total
1916	52	23	44
1918	52	20	39
1920	86	31	36
1922	154	54	35
1924	86	24	29
1926	84	29	34
1928	95	29	31
1930	147	53	36
1932	153	49	32
1934	153	44	29
1936	190	82	43
1938	166	62	37
1940	165	52	32
1942	174	53	30
1944	138	42	30
1946	164	46	29
1948	173	48	28

Source of Data: Blue Books of New Mexico, 1915-16 to 1947-48.

The data presented in Table   X   indicate that the
number of Hispanic Democratic committeemen has increased slightly
over a period of years. This reflects the shift in party allegiance on the part of Hispanic-Americans as outlined in the previous chapter of thi. study. At no time, however, has the number
of Hispanic-Americans on the Democratic state committee reflected
the Anglo-Hispano balance in the general population of the state.
And, considering the magnitude of the Hispanic shift to the Democratic party after 1930, the Spanish-speaking representation on
the state committee probably has not been proportionate. In
1948, as in 1916, Spanish-speaking members of the highest party
council have been in a distinct minority. Examination of committee membership throughout the period of statehood also shows that
it is rare for an Hispanic-American committeeman to represent
any but a district which is distinctly Hispano in population.
Even where the Anglo population only slightly exceeds the Hispano
population, Anglo-Americans tend to monopolize the Democratic high
command.

As noted in the preceding chapter, the stronghold of
the Republican party always has been the "native" counties. This
is reflected in the composition of the Republican state committee.
In the early days of statehood, a higher percentage of Spanish-
speaking members sat on the Republican central committee than
was true in the case of the Democratic party. However, comparison
of the data presented in Table   X   also will show that Hispanic
representation on the Republican state committee has declined in
recent years. This reflects the Hispanic swing to the opposing
party. In the period under study, Hispanic-American representation

on the Republican state committee rarely was proportionate to
the total Hispanic-American population. As was true in the case
of the Democratic party, Spanish-speaking committeemen always
have been in the minority, even when the Hispanic population
was a majority of the total.

It is apparent, then, that the high command of each
major party has been dominated by Anglos, despite the fact that
the Hispanic-Americans of New Mexico have shown extraordinary
interest in politics, and despite the fact that their constancy
in voting has contrasted with the less regular voting of the
Anglo population. To the extent that political influence is
expressed in terms of party leadership, the Spanish-speaking
population has had a subordinate role.

<u>Summary</u>

From a purely legal point of view, the franchise in New
Mexico is perhaps the least restricted of any state in the Union.
Illiteracy is no bar to voting; there are no racial restrictions;
strict provisions in the constitution otherwise guarantee the
franchise.

Social scientists long have pointed out that the Hispanic-
Americans of New Mexico are more politically minded than their
Anglo-American neighbors. The major case studies which have
been made of Hispano communities underline this extraordinary
preoccupation with politics, oftentimes at a very petty level.
Political scientists have explained this interest in various ways.
It may be ascribed to a realization that government is the source
of jobs, relief and other aids, and that politics is the vehicle

through which government is influenced. On the other hand it
is attributable to the fact that in politics the "native" element
competes on equal terms with the Anglo populace, whereas in
education, business and other activities, the Spanish-speaking
population is at a disadvantage.

Comparison of the ratio between total population and
total registered voters in seven Anglo counties and seven Hispano
counties does not reveal major differences. Thus if the mere act
of registration is an indication of interest in the franchise,
then the Anglo New Mexican and the Hispano New Mexican are on
equal footing.

The significant difference between the Anglo voter and
the Hispano voter is displayed at time of election. In the 1948
election, for instance, the percentage of registered voters who
actually went to the polls in Hispanic counties was far in excess
of the registered voters who cast ballots in Anglo counties. In
some instances the ratio was more than 2:1.

The voting habits of the Spanish-speaking citizens of
New Mexico have given them political importance disproportionate
to their numerical strength. However, this political strength is
not reflected in the composition of party leadership at the state
level. Even when the Hispanic-American population exceeded the
Anglo-American population, Spanish-speaking committeemen were in
a distinct minority on both Republican and Democratic state central
committees. As the allegiance of the Hispanic voter has gravitated
in the direction of the Democratic party, there has been an increase in the percentage of Democratic committeemen; a corresponding decrease is notable in the Republican central committee. The

Hispanic percentage has remained a fairly constant minority,
when the entire period of statehood is considered. Thus when
political influence is expressed in terms of party leadership,
the Spanish-speaking population has had a subordinate role.

CHAPTER X

THE PATRON IN NEW MEXICO POLITICS

Historically, the Spanish-American culture group of New Mexico is a product of the medieval feudal system of Europe. Its forebears came to the Southwest long before the Industrial Revolution completely altered the fabric of western European social and political organization. The feudal system introduced into New Mexico in the sixteenth century survived almost without alteration until the American occupation in the nineteenth century, thanks to the geographical isolation of the upper Rio Grande.

At a time when the English colonists along the Atlantic were in constant communication with Europe, the Spanish settlers of New Mexico virtually had no contact with that continent; at a time when the English colonists had elective legislatures and other evidences of self government, the Spanish colonists were ruled in a completely autocratic manner by a governor appointed by a viceroy who in turn owed his own office to a king; and at a time when a well developed middle class was usurping the power of the aristocracy in the English colonies in America, Spanish colonists remained divided into a small, highly privileged upper class and a large, unprivileged lower class. Political, social, economic--even religious--control was retained by a handful of patrones; the role of the numerous peones was that of submissive vassals to the overlords.

A way of life which persisted for almost a thousand years in Europe and almost a third that long in New Mexico was not to be altered overnight. At first thought it would seem that the impact of the dynamic, democratic, capitalistic American culture on the static, aristocratic, feudalistic Spanish culture would have produced a new pattern within a generation. But as one reads the history of New Mexico for the period 1850-1900, he finds that many Americans accommodated themselves to the Spanish system, in fact, did much to perpetuate it. For it was in alliance with the patrones that the great American entrepreneurs exploited the mines and forests of New Mexico.

On the whole, the patron principle suited the purposes of the American magnates and they adopted it. The sharing of economic power by American patron and Spanish patron also dictated the sharing of social and political power. Certainly the chronicle of political events as outlined by Twitchell,[1] Coan,[2] Vaughn[3] and other historians indicates that a small group of men ruled American New Mexico in the same manner that the patrones had ruled Spanish New Mexico. Otero, Fall, Luna and Springer--the new rulers were both Anglo and Hispano. The great mass of those who were ruled still were the Hispanic-Americans who voted as they were told.

The statutory abolition of peonage and the extension of the franchise to master and servant alike did not bring an end to the patron system. The incursion of small Anglo landholders into

---

1. Ralph E. Twitchell, Leading Facts in New Mexican History.
2. Charles F. Coan, A History of New Mexico.
3. John H. Vaughn, History and Government of New Mexico.

eastern New Mexico, the unionization of mines and the expansion
of educational facilities--each of these developments tended to
weaken the institution. But the patron system, relic of feudal
New Mexico, remains a characteristic of the state today. It is
nowhere more evident than in the realm of politics, where a few
leaders still maintain extraordinary control over the mass of
voters.

That the patron system is particularly characteristic
of the Spanish-American culture group has been emphasized by
social scientists for many years. "An economic status as thoroughly ingrained in a people as peonage was in the Spanish-
American people cannot be wiped out in a generation or two. As
a result, political and economic life in New Mexico still suffer
to a great extent from the subservient attitude of the Spanish-
Americans toward some leader."[1] In his study of Spanish-American
villages, Walter calls attention to the important position occupied by the local patron. Where he does not hold office, he
constitutes the power behind the throne. Even "the court and
other officials are the creatures of the jefe politico and do his
bidding in matters touching upon the community welfare."[2] If the
leader changes his political allegiance, "his entire constituency
is expected to change with him. Political insubordination is
promptly disciplined by all the pressure which the jefe can bring
to bear."[3] Control extends to school affairs and to irrigation
rights, as well as to more political matters.

---

1. John C. Russell, State Regionalism in New Mexico, p. 36.
2. Paul A. F. Walter, A Study of Isolation and Social Change in
    Three Spanish Speaking Villages of New Mexico, pp. 70-71.
3. Loc. cit.

After commenting that "Both political and economic life in New Mexico still suffer from the (Spanish-American's) instinctive love of a feudal relationship to some leader,"[1] Harvey Fergusson observes that the patron system has enabled shrewd politicians to build perfectly working machines.

At their best, these machines operated to the mutual advantage of the patron and his political retainers. In every Spanish-American village there was a local strong man, who sometimes was likened to patriarch, sometimes to feudal lord. He was shrewd, he was politically well informed, he was respected. His advice was sought on every occasion, and in time of death, illness or other emergency he readily extended aid. He sponsored dances, directed the local fiesta, took a leading role in religious activities. More important, he dispensed jobs. In return for the almost feudal protection which he extended, the patron exacted one payment: the complete support of his political vassals, especially on election day.

At their worst, the political machines operated by the patrones corrupted government. For when the newly enfranchised peon discovered that his vote was desired by Anglo and Hispano politician alike, he often placed a price on his ballot. The political history of New Mexico is replete with accounts of wholesale vote-buying. The economic disadvantage of the Hispanic-Americans as a group has made them particularly susceptible to this practice; the patron system has facilitated its operation; Anglo politicians frequently have provided the incentive and

_____

1. Rio Grande, p. 116.

supplied the money, as succeeding biographical detail will
indicate.

A few examples will suffice to illustrate the manner in
which the patron delivered the vote of his political vassals.
Owen P. White, onetime editor of Collier's, describes the campaign
tour which he made with the Republican gubernatorial candidate in
1924. Spanish-American patrones approached the governor's en-
tourage "with information about vote buying. On one occasion a
boss had quoted three dollars as the standard price of votes in
his county but stated that the Democrats had given him only two
dollars. If, he bargained, the Republicans would give him three
dollars, he would vote the community for them."[1]

In his study of an Hispanic-American village, A. B.
Chavez quotes the somewhat philosophical patron as saying that
"The people elect the officers who administer the law and if in
the process of getting elected a candidate buys votes it is only
because those who sell their votes are not duly appreciative of
those rights which the constitution gives them." The patron then
observes that the rule applies to Anglos and Hispanos alike "because I have bought them both."[2] Chavez concludes that the
patron's failure to admit the irresponsibility of his behavior in
vote-buying was "traceable to the strong influence of semi-
autocratic, patriarchal authority, which is not questioned to any
great degree by those under it."[3]

In 1926, the United States district attorney filed a

---

1. Quoted, Jonathan R. Cunningham, Bronson Cutting, pp. 111-12.
2. Use of the Personal Interview to Study the Subjective Impact
   of Culture Contacts, p. 88.
3. Ibid., p. 44.

complaint against three Spanish-American politicians from San
Miguel county, charging them with bribery and conspiracy to
bribe in connection with the election.[1] A far more serious
charge was made by the editor of the Roy Record when he wrote
that "In the last election, as in elections gone by, the natives
sold and delivered votes by the hundred."[2] The editorial raised
an outcry in the state legislature, and the publisher was charged
with anti-Hispano bias. But the matter was promptly dropped when
the editor offered to appear before the legislature to show pos-
itive evidence in support of his statement.

That the vote-buying aspect of the patron system still
is a factor in New Mexico politics finds ready proof. The head
of the United Press in Santa Fe reported that Hispano votes were
bought on a large scale in many counties in the 1948 election.
At times, the price went as high as eight dollars a vote. Hispano
voters were herded to the polls by the local jefe politico.[3] In
1949, extension of the Albuquerque bus franchise became subject
to popular referendum. When Anglo sections of the city voted
against renewal of the franchise and Hispano sections voted for
confirmation, it was commonly reported that the Hispano vote had
been bought by the bus company.[4] In 1950, the Archbishop of Santa
Fe, in a widely publicized address, condemned the "vote buying
and ballot stealing" reported prevalent in the state. "I wish to
point out that it is a serious dereliction of civic duty to buy

1. Jonathan R. Cunningham, op. cit., p. 142.
2. Ibid., p. 181.
3. Interview, Melvin Mencher, Santa Fe, Dec. 30, 1949.
4. Interview, Dorothy Cline, Department of Government, University
   of New Mexico, Albuquerque, July 15, 1949.

or to sell votes for candidates."[1] While the archbishop did not
exclude Anglos from his condemnation, the fact that he addressed
his remarks to a Spanish-American audience was significant.

The practice of buying votes is not limited to the state
of New Mexico, as even one with a scant knowledge of American
politics would admit. Nor would anyone claim that the practice
is restricted to the Spanish-Americans of New Mexico. It is rather
clear, however, that many Hispanos are apt to regard the franchise
as a marketable item because of their economic disadvantage, their
lack of educational opportunity and their domination by the patron
system.

The Patron in State Politics

Carlyle once remarked that history is but a compendium
of the biographies of the great men of the earth. Considerable
support for this thesis may be found in the political record of
New Mexico. From the establishment of the first permanent settlement in 1598 until the present day, a series of powerful leaders
have occupied the center of the stage. Always these leaders have
assumed the role of patron; generally they have sought and received the unswerving support of the Hispanic-Americans; often
they have led a crusade in behalf of the "native" people.

The continued operation of the patron principle becomes
clear when one reflects that throughout the period of statehood,
the Hispanic-Americans of New Mexico have recognized the para-
mount leadership of one particular individual. There always has
been a single major figure who owed his power to an ability to

---

1. Santa Fe New Mexican, June 2, 1950.

deliver the Hispanic vote. The operation of the _patron_ system
can best be described in terms of the individual careers of the
four men who successively have led the Spanish-American people.

Solomon Luna was one of the leading citizens of New
Mexico at the time the constitutional convention met in 1910.
Not only was he reputed to own more sheep than any other person
in the territory, but he also had the largest number of employees.
That   itself gave him political power. The fact that he desired
no office for himself and that he had the friendship of many
wealthy Anglo railroad builders, mine operators and lumbermen
gave him added stature. He was acknowledged as one of the great
patrones of New Mexico.[1]

In his dual role as leader of the Hispanic-Americans and
as "perhaps the most powerful figure in the Republican party,"[2]
Luna took a prominent part in the constitutional convention. The
extraordinary protection offered the Spanish-speaking people by
the constitution was attributed to Luna and his Anglo friend,
Bursum.[3]

Luna's leadership of the Hispanic people did not end
with the drafting of the constitution, for his ability to influence the "native" vote was recognized in the first state elections. His power as _patron_ of Valencia county was illustrated
in the fact that he delivered better than 75 per cent of the vote
to the Republican candidate in 1911 and in 1914 improved the

1. Interview, Thomas J. Mabry, Governor of New Mexico and member
   of the constitutional convention of 1910, Santa Fe, December
   30, 1949.
2. Charles B. Judah, The Republican Party in New Mexico, p. 1.
3. Dorothy Thomas, The Final Years of New Mexico's Struggle for
   Statehood, pp. 96-7.

count by delivering 88 per cent of the Valencia vote.[1]

Solomon Luna was succeeded as leader of the "native" people by a far more aggressive and politically more ambitious patron, O. A. Larrazolo. Unlike Luna, who was content to be the power behind the throne, Larrazolo made numerous bids for state office. And where Luna minimized inter-group differences, Larrazolo magnified them; in fact Anglo-Hispano hostility became his central theme and formed the basis of his appeals for the support of the Spanish-speaking people. "Whether for good or for evil, it is because of the impress he gave his day that the cleavage between the descendants of the Spanish conquerors and colonists and those who came from other states continues to be accentuated in political life and is felt even in business, in the professions and in social activities."[2]

It is somewhat ironical that two of the four patrones who have achieved power through the support of the "native" people, were themselves not natives of New Mexico. Larrazolo, for instance, was born in Mexico and grew up there during the French intervention. He came to the United States as the protege of the Bishop of Tucson and followed that prelate to New Mexico when the latter became Archbishop of Santa Fe. After his admission to the bar in 1888, he held several judicial positions in Texas, then returned to New Mexico and entered politics.[3]

Larrazolo had many qualities which inspired the unswerving loyalty of the Hispanos. He was "tall, of vigorous frame and hand-

---

1. Charles B. Judah, op. cit.
2. Paul A. F. Walter, "Octaviano Ambrosio Larrazolo," p. 97.
3. Who's Who in America (1928-29), p. 1259.

some, with the proud, courtly and punctilious bearing of a
Spanish gentleman."[1] Moreover, he was recognized as a brilliant
lawyer, and was an eloquent speaker, whether he addressed his
audience in English or in Spanish. It was not long before he
was recognized as the new _patron_, the "champion of the native
population."[2]

Larrazolo was Democratic candidate for delegate to Congress in 1900, 1906 and 1908. Despite the fact that Spanish-
Americans traditionally were Republican, Larrazolo carried the
northern counties, where Hispanos predominate. However, he was
defeated in each of the three elections, a humiliation which he
blamed upon the refusal of the Anglo Democrats of eastern New
Mexico to vote for a Spanish-speaking candidate.[3] Although not a
member of the constitutional convention, he worked behind the
scenes to have protections for the Hispanic people incorporated
into the final document. Alleged Democratic opposition to these
safeguards caused Larrazolo to repudiate the party and to join
the Republicans. Thereafter he was the stormy petrel of that
party.

His brilliance as a speaker made him an effective cam-
paigner, and his hold on the Spanish-speaking voters of New Mexico
gave him a position of leadership in the party, even though many
Republican politicians feared the consequences of "the Larrazolo
native-son propaganda which had been most industriously dis-

---

1. Lansing B. Bloom, "O. A. Larrazolo," _Dictionary_ _American_
   Biography, V. XI, pp. 7-8.
2. _Loc. cit._
3. Lansing B. Bloom, _op. cit._, p. 8.

seminated for more than a year in certain northern counties."[1]

Despite his switch to the Republican party, Larrazolo campaigned for a Democratic gubernatorial candidate of Spanish extraction in 1916. As patron, Larrazolo delivered enough Hispanic votes to the Democratic nominee to guarantee his election. Two years later Larrazolo himself became governor of New Mexico, the second and the last Spanish-speaking governor of the state. Although his position as undisputed leader of the Hispanic-Americans had enabled him to achieve the coveted post, it also was responsible for his failure to secure re-nomination. In the eyes of certain GOP chieftains, the inter-group antagonism which Larrazolo had generated threatened to disrupt the party, and they determined to oust the governor. Ironically enough, the patron who long had won the support of many Hispanos by alleging that they were discriminated against, himself was accused of favoring Spanish-speaking citizens in his appointments.[2]

The opposition of Old Guard Republicans not only was based upon Larrazolo's "racism," but also because he was considered too progressive. But party lieutenants, however opposed they may have been to the Hispanic firebrand, were forced to nominate him for office. His control of the Spanish-speaking voters was in the best tradition of the patron. In part, this was attributable to the fact that "his eloquence in speaking could not be matched by anyone in New Mexico,"[3] thus making him the symbol of Hispanic accomplishment; in part, his control was based upon the distribution of political patronage.

---

1. Paul A. F. Walter, op. cit., p. 98.
2. Jonathan R. Cunningham, Bronson Cutting, pp. 88-9.
3. Vorley M. Rexroad, The Two Administrations of Governor Richard C. Dillon, p. 99.

Larrazolo was nominated for the supreme court in 1924, and he made a strenuous attempt to win that post in order to break the Anglo monopoly of that tribunal. The election returns again underlined his position with the Spanish-speaking voters, and again aroused his antagonism toward Anglo-Americans. For he carried each of the "native" counties by a substantial majority, but was overwhelmed by the Anglo vote of eastern New Mexico.[1]

Although "both friend and foe apparently questioned his sincerity in any position he took on policies of government and statesmanship outside of his fervent racial propaganda,"[2] he was not to be denied political power. In 1928 he was nominated for United States Senator; he gained the seat, but his triumph was short lived, for he died shortly after taking office.

The Good Don of Santa Fe

Long before Larrazolo's death, his position as patron was disputed by one of the most controversial and one of the most complex figures in American political history, Bronson Cutting. This Anglo-American, non-Catholic New Yorker exerted more complete control over his Hispanic-American followers than either of the Spanish-speaking patrons who preceded him or the one who succeeded him. Fifteen years after his death, he still was venerated by thousands of humble villagers in the northern counties. And fifteen years after his death, his shadow still loomed over the politics of New Mexico.

Bronson Murray Cutting, scion of a distinguished and very

---

1. Blue Book of New Mexico (1925-26).
2. Paul A. F. Walter, op. cit., p. 99.

wealthy New York family, was a graduate of Groton and was elected to Phi Beta Kappa before he was forced to leave Harvard for reasons of health. He toured the Southwest for some time, eventually settling in Santa Fe in 1910, when New Mexico was yet a territory. He was then twenty-two.[1]

Cutting began an intense study of his new environment. With characteristic energy he mastered the Spanish language, studied the cultures of the American Indian and the Spanish-American, and traced the development of social and political institutions. It soon became apparent that the young easterner had decided upon a political career. He was a delegate to the first Republican state convention in 1911, and in the same year helped to found the New Mexico Progressive Republican League. Cutting joined the Progressive party in 1912 and took a leading part in its activities thereafter.[2] He acquired a mouthpiece when he bought the controlling share of the New Mexico Printing company in 1912. This gave him the editorial columns of one of the most influential English-language newspapers, as well as those of the chief Spanish-language publication in the state. From that time until his death almost a quarter century later, "The story of the political career of Bronson Murray Cutting and the story of New Mexico's political life since statehood are so inextricably interwoven that one cannot be told without the other."[3]

At first the politicians of New Mexico did not regard Bronson Cutting very seriously. He was young, he was liberal, and

1. Dictionary of American Biography, V. XXI, pp. 215-16.
2. Who's Who in America (1934-35), p. 658.
   Dictionary of American Biography, loc. cit.
3. Jonathan R. Cunningham, op. cit., p. 1.

he was an outsider--all of which damned him in the eyes of party
lieutenants. Furthermore, they distrusted his intellectualism
and found him difficult to approach because of his excessive shy-
ness. For such reasons they tended to brush aside his suggestions
and offers of support.

Within a short time, however, they found that Cutting
had acquired tremendous political influence. It was not so much
the aggressive quality of his newspapers. It was the tremendous
hold which he secured on the "native" people. A patron far more
powerful than Larrazolo had emerged.

> (Cutting) bided his time. While he waited he
> learned the approach he must make to the Mexican people,
> and word got about that a Mexican major domo could bor-
> row from him a few dollars to tide him over until he
> sold his sheep or cattle or harvested his crops. Mr.
> Cutting became interested in the younger generation of
> Mexicans and helped them to advance to positions of power
> in the state.[1]

News spread quickly among the Hispanic-Americans that in case of
death or other emergency, the good don of Santa Fe would see the
family through. He also supplied money for the education of prom-
ising young Hispanos, and took Spanish-speaking leaders as his
close associates. Frequently this aristocratic young millionaire
who shrank from the social activities of Santa Fe's upper stratum,
journeyed over back-mountain roads to attend a dance in an Hispanic
village or to launch a fiesta.

Whether or not Cutting's cultivation of the Hispanic-
Americans was sincere or not has long been debated. Many of his
contemporaries, including the present governor and the senior
United States Senator, are convinced that Cutting was a remarkably

---

1. Jan Speiss, "Feudalism and Senator Cutting," p. 373.

astute politician who "played" the Hispano vote in a cynical
manner.[1] On the other hand, his biographer answers such accusations by pointing out that the notoriously sensitive Hispanos
were thoroughly convinced of his genuine interest, and that his
will provided handsomely for his Spanish-speaking friends, among
his bequests being the newspaper enterprise itself.[2]

 An intermediate position, and perhaps a more judicious
one, has been suggested by a state government specialist at the
University of New Mexico: "Cutting always managed to be on the
side of God, even when he arrived there by purely Machiavellian
means."[3] Support for this position is found in Judah's statement
that "Cutting was opposed to the vested interests and the machine
politicians who, in his opinion, served them. He was in favor of
government which represented and served all the people equally,
and he seems to have believed that such government could be
achieved through perfecting the machinery of politics."[4]

 Cutting's attitude toward the Spanish-speaking people
fitted into this frame of reference. He quickly learned that the
government of New Mexico did not serve all the people equally.
Most disadvantaged were the Hispanic-Americans, whose educational
and economic status as a group relegated them to a position of
inferiority. Moreover, he foresaw that the Hispanic element, then
a majority, was destined to be a minority within a short time be-

---

1. Interviews, Thomas J. Mabry, Governor of New Mexico, Santa Fe,
   December 30, 1949, and David B. Keleher, confidential secretary,
   United States Senator Dennis Chavez, Albuquerque, December 28,
   1949.
2. Jonathan R. Cunningham, op. cit., pp. 114-15.
3. Interview, Jack E. Holmes, professor state and local government,
   University of New Mexico, August 1, 1949.
4. Charles B. Judah, Governor Richard C. Dillon, p. 11.

cause of the influx of Anglo-Americans from other states. He
believed that it was necessary to use political authority to
guarantee the welfare of the Hispanos. Only through the facilities of government could the educational status of the Spanish-
speaking be improved; only through government intervention could
their economic betterment be assured.[1]

The end which Cutting sought was democratic, in that he
aspired to have Anglo-American and Hispanic-American living in
harmony on a basis of equality. The means he employed sometimes
were anti-democratic in that he made full use of the feudalistic
patron system. For centuries the great landowners had taken a
paternal interest in all who worked for them. The average Hispano
had become so accustomed to this form of patronage that it was
impossible to rid him of the idea that he not only tilled the
great man's land and guarded his sheep, but that he also voted as
he was told. As for the don himself, "he went to political
meetings where the speeches of the Americans were interpreted, and
he learned that if fifty of his peons voted as he insisted his
prestige with the Americans was greatly enhanced. That could be
arranged by personal persuasion. That is today the understanding
of politics which the Mexican in New Mexico brings to the polls."[2]

By making himself patron of all Spanish-speaking New
Mexico, Bronson Cutting achieved the political power he sought.

It is doubtful if any Spanish patron or Anglo boss in
territorial or state history has ever personally controlled more votes than Bronson Cutting.[3]

---

1. Jonathan R. Cunningham, op. cit., pp. 220-221.
2. Jan Speiss, op. cit., p. 373.
3. Charles B. Judah, op. cit., p. 12.

Cutting was now firmly building his political machine
which was made up to a very large extent of the native
people.. . .(He) had gained the support and confidence
of the Spanish-American people as no other individual
had done. Because of his personal and political influence, he could easily lead his followers from one
party to another and could successfully oppose native
leaders.[1]

Although the Spanish-American vote was the most impor-

tant cog in the Cutting machine, another important part of the

mechanism was the support of the American Legion. Health reasons

prevented Cutting from active participation in World War I, but

he did serve as assistant military attache in London. When he

returned to New Mexico, he helped to found the American Legion,

and as long as he lived he remained very active in its affairs.[2]

He became the champion of the war veterans of New Mexico, thereby

winning their political support.

In Legion affairs, as in politics, Cutting showed

marked interest in the "native." He bitterly opposed the dis-

crimination against Spanish-speaking Legionnaires which was

practiced by some predominantly Anglo posts, encouraged young

Hispanos to take an active role, and gave financial support to

posts in the northern counties.

Having achieved political influence as patron of the

Spanish-American people, Cutting pushed their interests. He

freely dug into his personal fortune to support the Spanish-

American normal school and the training school at San Juan; sub-

sidized and encouraged young Hispano politicians; demanded

legislation fostering the economic and social welfare of the

1. Jonathan R. Cunningham, op. cit., p. 111.
2. Dictionary of American Biography, op. cit., pp. 215-216.

"native" people; and secured jobs for the Spanish-speaking. He was so successful in this respect that he invoked Anglo criticism. Thus an otherwise friendly commentator wrote that Cutting held "his power in New Mexico as the don who loans money in time of need, or gives a job to the young Mexican in preference to the young American" and that "Mr. Cutting has somehow ignored the young Americans who are aspiring to power; he turns the force of CWA and PWA to the good of the native worker."[1]

As champion of the Hispanic-Americans, Cutting sometimes took a position which his Anglo supporters considered extreme. Thus in 1924 a Democratic governor set up a bi-partisan board to recommend needed reform in New Mexico's election laws. The proposed code forbade the practice of permitting persons to accompany the voter into the election booth. Spanish-American leaders claimed that this proviso would disfranchise thousands of illiterate "natives" and they attacked the proposal bitterly. Cutting entered the fray, conducting a vigorous editorial and speaking campaign against the measure. He succeeded in defeating the Democratic governor who sponsored the legislation. Four years later, a Republican judge who had served on the bi-partisan committee which had drafted the code was nominated by the Republicans-- Cutting's own party. This time Cutting swung his Spanish-Americans into the Democratic camp in order to defeat a gubernatorial candidate accused of being anti-Hispano. This split the Republican party into two factions.[2] Cutting's action divided the Republican party into two warring factions; to this day there remain Cutting

---

1. Jan Speiss, op. cit., p. 374.
2. John C. Russell, State Regionalism in New Mexico, pp. 186-87.

and anti-Cutting factions, with the latter blaming the subsequent collapse of the party to the tactics of the great patron.

Although Cutting was a power in New Mexico politics
for almost a generation, he held only one elective office, that
of United States Senator. He first came to that office by appointment in December, 1927, upon the death of Senator Jones, and sub-
sequently was elected. His elevation to that post provoked a
storm of criticism. His practice of leading his loyal supporters
from party to party had exasperated the Old Guard Republicans who
could not cope with his financial and political power. And
conservative Democratic opinion was summarized by a former
governor who said that "Cutting as a United States Senator is and
will be a joke, but unfortunately the joke will be upon the people
of New Mexico."[1] Such opinion was based upon Cutting's alleged
inexperience in public affairs, particularly as regarded office-
holding.

However critical the conservative element in each of the
major parties may have been, the appointment pleased thousands of
New Mexicans, particularly those who regarded Cutting as their
patron.

> He also saw his influence with the Spanish-Americans in-
> crease.. . .Not only was Cutting a rich man who could
> always be counted on for a loan of a few dollars to a few
> thousand dollars, but he was now a United States Senator
> to whom they might look for a possible political job.
> Thus the native political leaders, always shrewd bar-
> gainers, could see very definite results from their
> support of Cutting.[2]

With the career of Bronson Murray Cutting, national

---

1. Albuquerque Journal, December 30, 1927.
2. Jonathan R. Cunningham, op. cit., p. 151.

figure, this study has no part. It is sufficient to point out
that the New Mexico Senator joined Norris and LaFollette as
among the most distinguished legislators to sit in Congress, and
that his aggressive liberalism attracted wide publicity and served
to facilitate the introduction of the New Deal. Actually Cutting
attempted to transport to the national stage those goals which
he had long sought in New Mexico. Perhaps foremost among them
was a fierce determination to bring a measure of equality, even
if that involved the use of undemocratic methods. This helps to
explain why, although now dead more than 15 years, Cutting is a
vivid memory in the lives of many New Mexicans.

Patron, Modern Style

The mantle of the great patron, Bronson Murray Cutting,
fell upon one who in almost every respect was his antithesis.
True, the two leaders were born in the same year, 1888, but a
common birth date was one of the few points they had in common.
Cutting, a Protestant and an aristocrat, was the scion of a
wealthy New York family which had produced many public figures.
Dennis Chavez, Catholic and New Mexico-born, was the son of
poverty-stricken parents. Cutting graduated from a swank prepar-
atory school and was a Harvard man; Chavez left school early, was
largely self-educated, and did not earn a degree until he was
thirty-two. Cutting, however great his political talent, bought
his way into New Mexico politics with the purchase of three leading newspapers. Chavez had no resources other than tremendous
drive and uncommon sagacity. To paraphrase John Gunther's description of Franklin Delano Roosevelt, the disadvantaged Hispanos
chose Cutting, a prince, to lead them, and he did things for them,

as a good prince should. What was Cutting's career but a vast
exercise of noblesse oblige? Chavez, on the contrary, was a
"commoner" who rose from the ranks and retained power, not because he dispensed gifts as a generous prince but as a fortunate
brother who understands the needs of his family and is solicitous
of its welfare.

Dennis Chavez, the only Spanish-descended senator in
recent times, has been called the chief spokesman of the Hispanic-
Americans of the United States and its territories, as well as the
last of the great patrones of New Mexico. His career reads like
a page from the Great American Success Story--a fact which helps
to explain his hold on many people in his native state. They derive vicarious satisfaction from regarding the rise of an un-
tutored boy from their midst to a position of great power and
prestige.

Born Dionisio Chavez, the future United States Senator
became "Dennis" when he entered school. His formal education
soon ended, however, for he found it necessary to go to work. He
became involved in politics before he could vote, but his first
great opportunity came when he served as United States Senator A.
A. Jones' interpreter in the 1916 campaign. A Senate clerkship
was his reward--a reward which made possible his completion of
law school at Georgetown University.[1]

Although Dennis Chavez had served as member of the
United States House of Representatives, he did not become a prominent figure until 1934, when he challenged Bronson Cutting. Two

1. Interview, David B. Keleher, confidential secretary, United
    States Senator Dennis Chavez, Albuquerque, December 28, 1949.
    Current Biography, 1946, p. 110.

Senate posts fell vacant that year, and Chavez was advised to run
for the short term, where his victory was almost assured. However, he displayed the political boldness for which he was to become famous by attempting to unseat the great don of Santa Fe.
Cutting's biographer gives two reasons for the fateful decision.
In the first place, Chavez realized the strength of Cutting's
position as the Republican candidate and felt that he alone had
a chance to win for the Democratic party. But there was a more
important reason for Chavez' decision to challenge the great
Cutting. It was his ambition, in case he secured the senatorship,
to supplant Cutting as leader of the "native" people. "Chavez,
himself a Spanish-American, had frequently accused Cutting of
catering to the Spanish-American people merely for their votes."[1]
In political vernacular, this simply meant that Chavez proposed
to replace Bronson Cutting as the great patron of New Mexico.

Because of the able support he had given to many New
Deal measures during his term in the Senate, Cutting expected to
receive backing from the national Democratic organization, even
though theoretically he was a Republican. To his great chagrin,
however, administration support was thrown to Chavez. It was
then that a hotly contested senatorial race became inevitable.
An Hispano candidate, assured of a large vote from the almost
fanatically Democratic eastern half of New Mexico was attempting
to capture the Spanish-speaking vote controlled by a powerful
Anglo patron. The race which ensued was hard-fought, and when
the ballots were counted the margin between the two candidates

1. Jonathan R. Cunningham, Bronson Cutting, A Political Biography,
    p. 192.

proved even narrower than had been anticipated. For the state
canvassing board announced the returns as Cutting--75,759, Chavez
--74,498, a difference of only 1,261.[1]

Chavez and his supporters immediately leveled charges
of fraud and corruption at Cutting, alleging that the election
had been stolen from the Democratic nominee. The Chavez group
went further: redress was sought through the supreme court of
New Mexico and through an investigating committee set up by the
Democratic-controlled legislature. When satisfaction was not
obtained, Chavez petitioned the United States Senate to unseat
Bronson Cutting. While seven charges were made, the petition was
based upon two main counts: the excessive expenditure of funds
in the Cutting campaign and fraudulent voting in San Miguel
county, where approximately 90 per cent of the population was
Spanish-speaking.[2]

The Senate Committee on Privileges and Elections met
on April 10, 1935 and absolved Cutting of the charge of excessive
campaign expenditures, but before its decision on the other charge
had been made, Senator Cutting was killed in an airplane crash.
The governor of New Mexico thereupon appointed Dennis Chavez to
fill the Senate post thus vacated; allegedly it was pressure from
Jim Farley which prompted the governor to make the appointment.[3]

From that time until this, Senator Chavez has been a
national figure, in addition to being the recognized leader of
the Spanish-speaking people of New Mexico. Some would go farther

1. United States Senate, Hearing Before Committee on Privileges
    and Elections, Seventy-fourth Congress, April 10 and June 4,
    1935, p. 3.
2. Ibid., p. 15.
3. "National Affairs," Time, October 31, 1938, p. 11.

and say that the Senator has attempted to manage state political affairs in the grand manner of the patrones of a supposedly by-gone era. Certainly his power centers in the "native" counties of New Mexico. In his Washington office, there is a file of some 52,000 Hispanic voters and potential voters:[1] this forms a mailing list of great importance at election time. And, as a subsequent chapter indicates,[2] throughout his career, Dennis Chavez has influenced both gubernatorial and senatorial elections by playing upon Anglo-Hispano differences in order to maintain his hold on the Spanish-speaking voter. The manner in which this is accomplished was brought out in 1946, when Chavez was last a candidate for reelection to the Senate.

> His victory over Governor Dempsey was indicative of his resourcefulness and astuteness and was equal to that of his political acumen in the campaigns of the past. This was aided quite materially by his pointing out to the native population that they no longer elected governors to office and that to repudiate his leadership at the polls would be to toll the death knell of the last great champion of the Spanish-speaking population. Senator Chavez successfully appeals to the native voters in continuing his position of dominance in New Mexico politics.[3]

But playing upon the theme of inter-group differences is but a minor explanation for the Chavez grip on New Mexico politics. Like the patron whom he succeeded, the Senator has looked after the interests of his followers. True, his personal fortune has not been large enough for him to duplicate the Cutting largesse. Yet he has provided government jobs and he has fought discrimination in private employment. Thus, when a projected highway route

---

1. Interview, David B. Keleher, confidential secretary, United States Senator Dennis Chavez, Albuquerque, December 28, 1949.
2. Cf. Chapter XIV.
3. Walter L. McNutt, An Inquiry into the Operation of the Primary System of New Mexico, p. 51.

threatens to ruin an Hispano's property, he turns to Chavez for
help; when applicants for jobs with the hoof and mouth disease
control program are turned down, they ask the Senator to inves-
tigate; when a young Hispano wants a job--federal, state or
county, he seeks the good services of the Senator.

In looking after the interests of his supporters,
particularly his Hispanic supporters and most particularly members of his own family, Senator Chavez has built up a powerful
political machine. At the same time, he has made himself the
subject of constant and extensive criticism. For example, in
1938 the Hispanic leader became involved in a WPA scandal which
attracted national attention. A federal grand jury indicted 73
people for using WPA as a political machine by giving relief
preference to obedient voters, exacting political contributions
from WPA workers by threats and intimidation, and by organizing
WPA foremen and timekeepers into vote-compelling "social clubs."[1]
Among those indicted was the WPA administrator who owed his office
to Chavez, along with the Senator's son-in-law, sister, cousin,
nephew and secretary. Although all but five of those indicted
eventually were cleared,[2] Senator Chavez thereafter was suspect
in the eyes of many New Mexicans who cataloged him as the latest
edition of the Hispano patron.

In 1948, Senator Chavez intervened in behalf of several
Hispanic-Americans, including his brother-in-law, who aspired to
state office. The Senator's blunt speech and threatening attitude
toward the governor provoked one of the stormiest political tem-

1. "National Affairs," Time, op. cit., p. 11.
2. Current Biography, 1946, p. 110.

pests in the history of New Mexico, and the Anglo-Hispano tension thus induced had repercussions in the subsequent gubernatorial election.[1] Moreover, it was Dennis Chavez' attempt to have his brother elected as the governor of New Mexico (1950) which caused many Anglo Democratic leaders to raise the dread "race" issue by declaring against the union of the two most important elective offices within the one Hispanic family. "Neither would it be good for the state to place the vast power of a Senate seat and the governorship in one family group which leads a political faction that has distinguished itself in this campaign as ruthlessly disdainful of anything that stands in the way of victory."[2]

Opponents of Senator Chavez may call him the last of the patrones; they may describe him as hyper-sensitive, ruthless and guilty of a type of nepotism which seems intent upon placing a large part of the Hispanic-American population on some government pay roll; they even may go so far as to brand his tactics as anti-democratic. But they admit that the Spanish-speaking Senator from New Mexico is astute and that at times he displays amazing courage for a politician. It is this quality which endears him to many Hispanos and wins for him the respect of a good portion of the Anglo community. To illustrate: when Hispanic leaders, backed by labor and liberal Anglo groups, were battling for a state FEPC law, each of the four Congressmen from New Mexico was urged to throw his support behind the measure. Three of the four, including the Spanish-speaking Representative, equivocated, but the senior Senator gave the measure his unqualified support.[3] In

---

1. Cf. Chapter XIV.
2. Editorial, Santa Fe New Mexican, June 1, 1950.
3. Estrella de Taos, Feb. 23, 1949.

fact, it was his alleged behind-the-scenes activity which so
angered the Anglo opponents of the bill.[1] As further indication
of courage, the Senator periodically has taken his political
future into his hands by openly breaking with each state administration. On the national scene, Senator Chavez has received
accolades from liberal newspapers and magazines for his energetic
leadership in repeated battles for FEPC, for his investigation
into Puerto Rican affairs and for his classic denouncement of
Senator McCarthy and Professor Budenz.

Although Dennis Chavez has a powerful hold on New Mexico
politics, particularly on the Hispanic-American voter, it commonly
is said that his day as *patron* is almost at an end.

> The plans for New Mexico's other senate seat now
> held by Sen. Dennis Chavez offer Santa Fe political ob-
> servers their choicest topic of discussion now. Chavez is
> definitely out as far as succeeding himself is concerned.[2]

> Even now U. S. Senator Chavez is fighting for his
> political life, and it appears certain that he or the person
> he names to succeed himself politically can never win another
> election in New Mexico.[3]

The reason for this belief is not hard to find. Perhaps
most important, the Senator supposedly is suffering from an incur-
able malady which will prevent his seeking reelection in 1952.[4]
While Senator Chavez, as a New Deal and Fair Deal stalwart, has
received powerful support from the national administration, he has
made many enemies, particularly among the Anglo politicians of
eastern New Mexico. And since the Senator frequently has cas-

---

1. Interview, John F. Simms, Jr., speaker of the house of representatives, Albuquerque, August 1, 1949.
2. Belen News-Bulletin, May 13, 1949.
3. R. L. Chambers, "The New Mexico Pattern," Common Ground (Summer,
   1949), p. 26.
4. Interview, Thomas J. Mabry, Governor of New Mexico, Santa Fe,
   Dec. 30, 1949.

tigated his erstwhile political allies, he has important enemies
amidst the Albuquerque-Santa Fe clique which has dominated the
Democratic party for many years. His membership on the all-
important Senate Appropriations committee and the patronage-rich
Post-Office committee gives him a following, even among Anglo
businessmen. But in recent years this has been offset by defection in the ranks of Hispanic-American voters. In the 1950 Democratic primary, when the Senator's own brother was a gubernatorial
candidate, "los Chavez" lost a number of predominantly Hispanic
counties, including Valencia and Guadalupe.[1] Despite the fact
that an attempt was made to divide the Anglo vote by entering a
"stooge" candidate, the Chavez forces were trounced in that
historic primary election.

The defection of Hispanic-American voters in the 1950
gubernatorial campaign was indicative of a division in the Hispanic-
American leadership. This was graphically illustrated in the
county conventions which were held between the primary and the
state convention. In three of the most important "native" counties:
Santa Fe, Rio Arriba and Taos, the Democratic conventions were
marked by physical violence when the pro-Chavez and anti-Chavez
forces battled for control.[2] The struggle involved patronage;
in a sense, the controversy hinged on the relative value of federal patronage, as dispensed by Chavez, and state patronage, as
dispensed by the Anglo-dominated machine. Once again Hispanic-
Americans showed their dependence upon state jobs of all descrip-
tions; once again they were forced to choose sides quickly in

1. Will Harrison, "At the Capitol," Santa Fe New Mexican, June
    8, 1950.
2. Santa Fe New Mexican, August 2, 19 and 22, 1950.

order to back the right horse.

Whether the rout of the Chavez forces in the 1950 election and subsequent party warfare indicate that the Hispanic people are deserting the United States Senator is debatable. But the fact that Dennis Chavez is not the patron of New Mexico, in the sense that Bronson Cutting was patron, hardly can be disputed. Cutting's control over the Hispanic vote was as complete as it was undisputed; the rigid character of that control enabled the Anglo patron to deliver the vote of his followers as if it were a commodity, and at will to lead his supporters from party to party. It was a purely personal relationship in the best tradition of the great Spanish dons. In contrast, Chavez' hold on the Spanish-speaking voter never has been complete, and those Hispanos who dispute that leadership have increased with the years. The mastery which Chavez enjoys has been exercised within the party, and it is extremely doubtful if it could transcend party lines.

It is not wishful thinking alone which prompts Chavez' opponents to term him the last of the patrones, the relic of political feudalism. The patron system thrives upon ignorance, economic disadvantage and political adolescence. That the institution presently appears to be tottering is due not so much to the political ineptness of Senator Chavez as to the improved economic and educational status of the Spanish-Americans of New Mexico.

Summary

One of the relics of the feudal past is the continued operation of the patron system in New Mexico. This political

institution involves the complete domination of a village, county
or state by a single individual. The patron's power is derived
from various sources: it may be money, which allows him to
"look after" his dependents; it may be aristocratic birth, which
causes lesser folk to be subservient; it may be political acumen,
which enables him to seize power and to distribute the spoils of
office wisely. In New Mexico, the operation of the patron system
has been characterized by a number of practices commonly regarded
as anti-democratic. Among these has been the tendency for great
landowners and other men of wealth to determine the vote of their
retainers. Another practice has been that of vote-buying, intimidation and bribery.

From the establishment of the first permanent settlement
in 1598 until the present day a series of powerful political leaders
have occupied the center of the stage in New Mexico. Always these
leaders have assumed the role of patron; generally they have sought
and received the unswerving support of the Hispanic people; often
they have led a crusade in their behalf. Thus there always has
been a single political figure who owed his power to an ability to
deliver the Hispanic vote.

During the period of statehood, four men commonly have
been regarded as patrones of New Mexico; of these, three have been
Spanish-Americans. Solomon Luna, key figure at the constitutional
convention of 1910, was content to remain the power behind the
throne. A man of great wealth and varied interests, his political
role was that of the leader who chose candidates, determined policy
and delivered the vote of Hispanic-Americans. He was succeeded
by the brilliant and ambitious O. A. Larrazolo, famed as an orator

and equally famous as the avowed champion of the Spanish-speaking
population of the state. Historians frequently attribute the
acute group consciousness of the people of New Mexico to the
bitter recriminations of this gifted Hispano.

The most powerful patron in the period of statehood was
neither Catholic, native-born nor Spanish in extraction. Bronson
Cutting, wealthy, Episcopalian New Yorker exerted an influence
over the Hispanic people which enabled him to deliver their vote,
almost en bloc, and to lead his devoted followers across party
boundaries when he chose. His position as patron was based upon
his genuine liking for and his sensitivity to the needs of the
disadvantaged Hispanos. The vast wealth which he had at his disposal enabled him to buy newspapers, to give extensive financial
assistance to those in need, and to expend great sums in campaigning. His opponents accused him of buying great blocs of
votes and of bribing those who opposed his political maneuvers.

Cutting's death in an airplane accident brought to the
fore Dennis Chavez, self-acknowledged leader of the Hispanic element, who often is described as the modern patron. In almost
every respect, Chavez was the antithesis of his predecessor. But
like Cutting, Senator Chavez has championed the interests of the
Spanish-speaking population at every turn, and has rendered them
extensive service in the way of jobs, anti-discrimination legislation and aggressive leadership. The control which Chavez
exercised never was as complete as that of Cutting, and in recent
years division in the Hispanic ranks has become apparent. The
Senator's physical condition and the defection of Hispanic voters
in the 1950 election have caused political forecasters to predict

an early end to the Chavez regime. But it is not wishful thinking alone which prompts commentators to declare that Chavez is
the last of the patrones. For the improved educational and
economic status of the Hispanic-Americans of New Mexico has
impaired the foundation of the patron system, based as it is upon
ignorance, economic disadvantage and political adolescence.

CHAPTER XI

GROUP INTERESTS AND POLITICAL CONVENTIONS

The foregoing pages indicate that the political allegiance of the Hispanic population of New Mexico is divided between the two major parties. For that reason, political differences between the Hispanic-American and the Anglo-American
may be exhibited in the context of Democratic party activity or
of Republican affairs. But the political observer may expect to
find the sharpest controversy when one party becomes the self-
professed champion of the Hispano, as opposed to the Anglo.

Political conventions furnish an excellent point of
departure for a study of Anglo-Hispano rivalry. Under somewhat
dramatic conditions and in an atmosphere ordinarily charged with
emotion, men have met to solve the political fate of New Mexico.
The environment has been conducive to the exposure of antagonisms.
Frequently the stakes have been high, and men have not been backward in making their claims.

Of those assemblies, the constitutional convention of
1910 was perhaps the most significant. It came late in the American phase of the history of New Mexico. Some territories had
become states shortly after their acquisition by the United States.
But as Archie McDowell points out,[1] organized opposition to the

_____

1. Opposition to Statehood Within the Territory of New Mexico,
   1838-1903.

admission of New Mexico developed in the territory itself, and
this was reenforced by opposition in the Senate of the United
States. Much of this opposition was based upon the fact that
the territory was distinctly non-Anglo-Saxon. It was felt that
the American minority would be submerged by the Hispanic element,
and that democratic institutions could not develop.

> Native people--which comprise three-fourths of the popula-
> tion--cannot be easily moulded into a free, self-governing
> commonwealth.[1]

> Race prejudice, fostered by the existence of two different
> languages, prevents the voters from selecting the best men
> for public office.[2]

> There is a total population of perhaps 200,000 people in
> New Mexico, and of these not one-fourth are Americans
> thoroughly imbued with the principles of free constitu-
> tional government.[3]

But by 1910 a great influx of Anglo-Americans had
minimized fears of "Mexican" domination, and the rapid development of the territory made statehood desirable in the eyes of the
entrepreneurs. Moreover, Congress was amenable. Accordingly,
the call went out for a constituent convention.

Anglo and Hispano in 1910

Of the 100 delegates who assembled to draft a constitution for the new state, 32 were Spanish-American, and 68 were
Anglo-American.[4] As indicated in the population study in Chapter
II, the Anglo-American population of New Mexico was over-represented
at the constitutional convention, for it was in the minority at

---

1. Ibid., p. 18, quoting New Mexican, March 19, 1888.
2. Ibid., p. 18, quoting New Mexican, March 26, 1888.
3. Ibid., p. 75, quoting Jefferson Reynolds, prominent banker,
   El Paso Herald, Jan. 18, 1900.
4. Blue Book of New Mexico, (1947-48,) p. 28.

this time.

One of the survivors of the convention has described the assembly as "many-sided and colorful, being as it was on the border line where two civilizations had met, fused and developed a society of its own.. . ."[1] Contributing to the many-sided, colorful character of the convention was the fact that ethnic factions quickly formed. Perhaps it might be more correct to say that the Spanish-American delegates quickly formed a faction.

> New Mexico's native sons and daughters inherited a nat-
> ural fear for their security, and justly so, as the his-
> tory of the Anglo-American settler has been that of aggres-
> sion and direct action.. . .They were practically all of
> one religious faith, thus giving them a solidarity not en-
> joyed by the Anglo-American, and all this entered into the
> membership of the convention. Therefore, their united in-
> terests were spontaneous among the Spanish-Americans and
> needed no organization.[2]

Fears that the Hispanic population would be engulfed by a rising tide of Anglo-Americans found expression at the convention. As a result of this fear, provisions affecting the franchise took precedence over all else. The desire to preserve the Spanish language and the "native" culture also caused the Hispanic-American delegates to exhibit great interest in protective clauses. The safeguards which eventually were written into the New Mexico constitution were rigid, and when the document was sent to Congress for approval, provisions protecting the Spanish-American populace met with considerable criticism. The New Mexico delegate was called upon to defend the document before it finally was approved.[3]

---

1. Reuben W. Heflin, "New Mexico Constitutional Convention," p. 61.
2. Ibid., p. 66.
3. Interview, Thomas J. Mabry, member of convention, presently governor of New Mexico, Santa Fe, Dec. 30, 1949.

Constitutional Protection

Examination of the constitution of the State of New Mexico indicates the profound distrust of the Hispanic-American delegates at the convention of 1910.

Article 2, Section 5, guarantees to the people of New Mexico all the rights, privileges and immunities, both civil, political and religious, which had been guaranteed by the treaty of Guadalupe-Hidalgo. Article 7, Section 3, is noteworthy for two reasons. In the first place, it offers extensive protection to any linguistic or racial group:

> The right of any citizen of the state to vote, hold office, or sit upon juries, shall never be restricted, abridged or impaired on account of religion, race, language or color, or inability to speak, read or write the English or Spanish languages except as may be otherwise provided in this constitution;[1]

More important, this proviso was made virtually unamendable by the following provision:

> (It) shall never be amended except upon a vote of the people of this state in an election at which at least three fourths of the electors voting in the whole state, and at least two-thirds of those voting in each county of the state shall vote for such amendment.[2]

Article 12, Section 8, provides for the training of teachers so that they may become proficient in both the English and Spanish languages to qualify them to teach Spanish-speaking students. The following section of the same article stipulates that no religious test shall ever be required as a condition of admission into any public educational institution, either as teacher or student.

---

1. New Mexico Statutes, Annotated 1941, V. I.
2. Loc. cit.

Article 12, Section 10, is even more specific:

Children of Spanish descent in the state of New Mexico
shall never be denied the right and privilege of admission and attendance in the public schools or other public educational institutions of the state, and they
shall never be classed in separate schools, but shall
forever enjoy perfect equality with other children in
all public schools and educational institutions of the
state, and the legislature shall provide penalties for
the violation of this section.[1]

This provision, like that governing the franchise, was made so
difficult to amend that it is unlikely that it ever would be
attempted. For as long as the Spanish-Americans of New Mexico
constitute even a small minority of the total population, they
can prevent any change in this portion of the constitution.

Two minor provisos remain to be noted. Article 16,
Section 1, recognizes and confirms all existing rights to the
use of any waters in the state for useful or beneficial purposes.
The other, Article 20, Section 12, provides for the publication
of all laws in English and Spanish for the first twenty years
after the constitution goes into effect. Thereafter the legislature shall provide for the publication.

As R. L. Chambers recently pointed out in the Belen
News-Bulletin, "The need for a new state constitution is evident
to everyone. But nobody is going to take the responsibility of
pushing a constitutional convention. Too many voters have a firm
belief that the constitution is a sacred thing and shouldn't be
tampered with."[2]

The governor of the state was more specific. Since the
present constitution contains provisos which are not amendable,

---

1. New Mexico Statutes, Annotated 1941, V. I.
2. September 30, 1949.

only a new constitution could impose literacy tests and other
provisions affecting the franchise. "This explains why the
Hispanos of New Mexico are afraid of all talk of a constitutional
convention."[1]

Cooperation and Competition

Attention has been called to the formation of a Spanish-
American bloc in the early days of the convention. This does not
imply that the Hispanic delegates acted as a unit throughout the
deliberations, or that the constitutional protections outlined
above were won after a hard-fought battle with the Anglo-American
delegates.

Accounts of the convention indicate, on the contrary,
that the Hispano Republicans and the Anglo Republicans worked in
harmony. This was particularly evident in the defeat of the Democratic proposals to include constitutional provisions for the
initiative and referendum. As for the protection of ethnic and
linguistic groups, such proposals apparently met with little opposition from the Anglo element, whether Democratic or Republican. Mabry explains this lack of opposition to the Anglo
delegates' realization that the constitution stood no chance at
ratification without them.[2] Heflin, another leading delegate,
offers a somewhat different explanation:

> (The Anglos) held to their common heritage of
> American institutions, and were not alarmed or bound by
> a common fear of some impelling evil as felt by our
> Spanish-American members. Therefore a tolerant view was

---

1. Interview, Thomas J. Mabry, member of convention, presently
   governor of New Mexico, Santa Fe, Dec. 30, 1949.
2. Loc. cit.

taken by those of Anglo extraction, with the thought
that differences because of national origin could be
ironed out somehow.[1]

The secretary of the convention, George W. Armijo, noted that if
anyone could be credited with the inclusion of the famous protective clauses, it would be Solomon Luna and Holm Burson, Republican bosses who "ran the show," but that there was no particular
opposition. Other delegates added the name of Albert Fall to this
pair, but likewise stressed the fact that the writing of this portion of the constitution aroused no angry discussion.[2]

Party Conventions at Work

From its admission into the Union until 1938, New Mexico had no primary election law. It was one of the few states
which continued to use the convention system of selecting candidates for office.

The system was denounced as archaic by many citizens,
but it offered at least one practical advantage. Party politicians exercised great care in balancing the ticket with Anglo and
Hispano candidates. This was possible because party leaders had
full control of the convention machinery. In an effort to prevent the cultural issue from intruding itself into political
campaigns, both Republicans and Democrats arranged the rival
tickets in such fashion that an Anglo candidate rarely was pitted
against an Hispano candidate.[3] Thus if a Democratic convention
named an Anglo-American gubernatorial candidate and selected a
Spanish-American candidate for the lieutenant-governorship, the

1. Reuben W. Heflin, "New Mexico Constitutional Convention," p. 62.
2. Dorothy E. Thomas, The Final Years of New Mexico's Struggle
   for Statehood, 1907-1912, pp. 96-97.
3. Thomas C. Donnelly, Rocky Mountain Politics, p. 238.

Republican convention followed the same procedure. In this
fashion harmony between the two major culture groups ordinarily
was preserved.

As one reads accounts of political conventions in New
Mexico, he concludes tha᷈ ᵤarty leaders made a studied effort to
skirt any issue which ght pit Anglo against Hispano. That this
was practical politics is indicated by the fact that when the issue
did arise on the convention floor, it not only led to angry debate,
but it also armed the rival political party with a very effective
weapon. A brief account of the Democratic convention of 1918 will
illustrate this point.

On the second day of the convention, an Anglo-American
delegate rose to speak in behalf of another Anglo who had been
placed in nomination for governor. The speaker refused the services of the Spanish interpreter, but the latter attempted to
translate the remarks, nevertheless. This irritated the Anglo
speaker. He stopped his address, "and sweeping his left arm
around, backing the interpreter against the wall,--shouted, 'I
don't want to talk to anyone but Americans. I can make my meaning
clear to them.'"[1]

The gravity of the issue thus raised has been underlined by Jonathan R. Cunningham. "To refuse the services of an
interpreter when unable to speak in Spanish is considered a refusal to speak to half of the population of New Mexico and an
unpardonable breach of etiquette."[2] In violating the rule that

---

1. Santa Fe New Mexican, September 28, 1918.
2. Bronson Cutting, a Political Biography, p. 69.

all public meetings be conducted in both Spanish and English,
the Anglo speaker made a grave mistake. But in inferring that
the Spanish-speaking people of New Mexico were not Americans,
the speaker made a major political blunder. It cost his party
dearly.

A few days later, the Republican convention met with
a ready-made issue at its disposal. Octaviano A. Larrazolo,
brilliant orator and acknowledged leader of the Spanish-Americans,
immediately was nominated for governor. One of the most powerful
Republican leaders, Charles A. Spiess, took the platform to de-
nounce "racism." He called upon the people of the state "to ex-
punge from their dictionaries and their vocabularies the hyphenated
Anglo and Spanish terms used in the politics of this state."[1] A
figure of national prominence, Albert B. Fall, paid glowing tribute to the Spanish-speaking people, and a supreme court justice
campaigned for Larrazolo.[2] In short, the appeal to cultural differences made in the Democratic convention, had wide repercussions.
"Race" became a major issue in the ensuing campaign, for Republicans charged the Democratic party with hostility to the native
people and warned the Spanish-Americans that they might expect
discrimination if the Democrats were placed in power. Such charges
contributed to the victory of Larrazolo.

Crisis at the 1926 Convention

Anglo-Hispano differences again rose to plague the Democrats at their 1926 convention. The Hispanic-American delegates,
feeling that their rights had not been respected, let it be known

1. *Santa Fe New Mexican*, Oct. 2, 1918.
2. Jonathan R. Cunningham, op. cit., pp. 70-72.

from the convention floor that they expected one half of all positions on the state ticket. To implement their demand, they announced that a meeting of the Spanish-speaking delegation would be held after the regular convention had adjourned for the evening.

Lorenzo Delgado, "boss" of San Miguel county, addressed the rump convention and repeated the Hispanos' demand for half of the offices to be filled. "Late in the night Delgado met in conference with Democratic leaders and a compromise was worked out. Delgado received the position of lieutenant-governor and the Spanish-Americans were to have three other places on the ticket."[1]

But the Democratic convention was beset by another issue involving Hispano-Anglo differences. This was the Hannett Election Code, a reform which bore the name of the Democratic governor then in office.

> (It) represented a needed reform in New Mexico's election laws. It had been drawn by a non-partisan board, and included such non-controversial issues as personal registration, metal ballot boxes with two dissimilar locks, each requiring its own key, and reform in the procedure relating to election contests. But it also forbade the practice of permitting persons to accompany the voter into the election booth.[2]

The last provision immediately became a burning issue in New Mexico politics. The code was widely discussed at the Democratic convention, and the Spanish-American delegates showed their dissatisfaction. As for the Republicans, they were presented with another ready-made issue. They contended that discontinuance

---

1. Vorley M. Rexroad, The Two Administrations of Governor Richard C. Dillon, p. 35.
2. Charles B. Judah, The Republican Party in New Mexico, p. 16.

of the practice of allowing election officials to accompany voters into the voting booth was aimed at disfranchising a large part of the Spanish-American people. "At a rally in Espanola, Francisco Delgado declared that the Hannett Election Code would disfranchise 25 to 30 per cent of the Spanish-American voters because they could not read or write."[1] A prominent jurist and lieutenant of the Cutting Republicans, Reed Holloman, declared that 20,000 voters would be disfranchised.[2] A former Republican governor, O. A. Larrazolo, campaigned throughout the state explaining to the Hispanic electorate that the election code was a Democratic plot to rob them of their vote.[3] Since the Republican state convention had officially denounced the code in similar terms, campaigners were on safe ground in making such bids for the Hispano vote.

The ensuing campaign resulted in the election of a Republican governor, but that it did not compose differences between Anglo and Hispano is indicated by events at both major party conventions in 1928.

The Democrats met in Albuquerque in early September. Differences between the Anglo and the Hispano delegates developed at once, and they persisted throughout the meeting. Formation of the party ticket was the bone of contention, with the Hispanic-American delegates insisting upon six places. At one point, over 200 Spanish-Americans met in closed session and refused to see the advisory committee. George Armijo, prominent Democratic

1. Vorley M. Rexroad, op. cit., p. 43.
2. Jonathan R. Cunningham, op. cit., pp. 133-4.
3. Vorley M. Rexroad, op. cit., p. 57.

leader, eventually worked out a compromise, and the Hispanic members returned to the convention.[1] Nor had the Hannett Election Code been forgotten, for again the Democratic delegates of Hispanic descent charged their Anglo confreres with race prejudice and discrimination.[2]

When the Republican convention met a short time afterwards, the "race" question intruded. However, differences between Anglo and Hispano were quickly settled in extended conferences. Six places on the state ticket were given Spanish-speaking candidates, and a possible rift was avoided.[3] In the ensuing campaign, two former governors of Spanish descent, Miguel Otero and O. A. Larrazolo, made speaking tours in the "native" counties. And in November, 1928, the Republicans again succeeded in naming the governor of New Mexico.

Study of newspaper accounts of party conventions in New Mexico leads to the conclusion that Anglo-Hispano differences presented themselves on occasion. The record also indicates, however, that major controversies were relatively few in number, and that party chieftains of both ethnic groups exerted themselves to compose differences and promote harmony between the two factions. When New Mexico turned from the convention system, the field of action became the primary election. That becomes the subject for consideration in the following chapter.

Summary

---

1. Santa Fe New Mexican, Sept. 5, 1928.
2. Jonathan R. Cunningham, op. cit., p. 152.
3. Santa Fe New Mexican, Sept. 14, 1928.

At the constitutional convention of 1910 approximately
one third of the delegates were Hispanic-Americans. Roughly
speaking, this was the inverse of the Anglo-Hispano population
ratio. Spanish-speaking delegates formed a faction and showed
great interest in constitutional protections for their group.
A number of rigid guarantees were incorporated, the most important being those which extended the protection of the treaty of
Guadalupe-Hidalgo, protected the franchise, and guaranteed
educational parity for the Hispanic-Americans of New Mexico.
English-speaking delegates did not oppose the incorporation of
such guarantees.

In the period when the state operated under the convention system, both competition and cooperation marked relations
between Anglo-Americans and Spanish-Americans. Under this system of naming candidates for public office, politicians attempted
to promote harmony by balancing the ticket between Anglo and
Hispano contenders. An effort was made to avoid pitting an Anglo
against an Hispano.

On several notable occasions, party conventions became
the scene of strife between ethnic groups. Disparaging remarks
made by an Anglo delegate set off one such battle; on another
occasion, it was an election code, allegedly unfair to the Spanish-
speaking element which touched off an explosion; on yet other
occasions it was the Hispanic delegates' demands for parity on
the party ticket which occasioned strife.

Spectacular as such demonstrations of group differences
may have been, the history of party conventions reveals that

both Spanish-speaking and English-speaking delegates ordinarily
made every effort to prevent rifts between the two groups.

CHAPTER XII

THE DIRECT PRIMARY AND THE HISPANIC-AMERICANS

OF NEW MEXICO

New Mexico was one of the last states to abandon the convention system of naming candidates for public office. The failure to follow other states in adopting some form of primary legislation was based, in part, upon the politicians' unwillingness to surrender an ancient prerogative. To the professional, it seemed both unwise and inexpedient to place into the hands of the masses the right to name their own public officials by direct vote. The role of the party leader as political broker would be weakened.

But an equally compelling reason for the survival of the political convention was the Hispanic-American's opposition to any change in the system. As Donnelly points out, the Spanish-American cultural group feared that its political influence would be lessened if the direct primary were introduced.[1] It was felt that the convention system made possible the "gentlemen's agreement" whereby the state tickets of both parties were ethnically balanced, with the tendency to pit Anglo against Anglo and Hispano against Hispano.

Nevertheless, a campaign to introduce the direct primary was launched in the early 1930's, and in 1933 a bill to effect

---

1. Thomas C. Donnelly, Rocky Mountain Politics, p. 238.

the change was introduced into the legislature. Immediately
the line between Anglo and Hispano was sharply drawn. Representatives from eastern and southern New Mexico, regions of Anglo-
American predominance, supported such legislation, while representatives from northern and central New Mexico, strongholds
of the "native" people opposed primary legislation.[1]

The measure was defeated in 1933, but two years later,
a similar bill was introduced into the legislature. Again the
lines were drawn between Hispanic-American and Anglo-American.
And again the measure was defeated. The "natives" opposed it,
regardless of party affiliation. In the words of a high official,

> The Spanish-American people are opposed to a direct pri-
> mary for the reason that they feel, and are probably
> right, that the primary would result in all natives be-
> ing successful in obtaining the nomination on the Repub-
> lican ticket and all Democrats would be Anglos, which
> would precipitate an open race issue, resulting in the
> eventual elimination of the natives from state offices;
> whereas, by the present system they are in a position to
> wield a balance of power.[2]

Primary legislation received a third defeat in 1937,
again because the Spanish-Americans aligned themselves against
the proposal. It was believed that voting would become complicated, and for that reason the illiterate would be disfranchised.

Political Storm

In 1938 Governor Tingley precipitated a crisis by calling a special session of the legislature to consider direct primary legislation. Leaders of the Spanish-American people were

1. John C. Russell, State Regionalism in New Mexico, p. 196.
2. John C. Russell, "State Regionalism in New Mexico," (Social
   Forces, Dec., 1937), p. 271.

not slow in making their position clear. Representative Concha
Ortiz y Pino, member of one of the most distinguished families
of New Mexico, declared her opposition to a primary system.
United States Senator Dennis Chavez was equally outspoken in
his disapproval. He declared that the enactment of such legislation would be prejudicial to the best interests of the Spanish-
American population.[1] The senator's views in 1938 are of some
interest, for as succeeding pages will indicate, a remarkable
shift in his opinion later occurred.

Organized opposition to the direct primary developed
with the founding of the Good Neighbor League. This bi-partisan
organization based its opposition upon the plea that racial and
religious issues would be injected into New Mexican politics
through the adoption of the direct primary. Soon units of the
Good Neighbor League got under way in all parts of the state.

Proponents of the direct primary promptly made a counter-
attack by establishing the Direct Primary League. To prove that
the proposed legislation was not anti-Hispano, members of the
Direct Primary League pointed to the fact that the head of their
organization was none other than Miguel A. Otero, territorial
governor of New Mexico for nine years.

Otero himself countered the argument that the direct
primary would be prejudicial to the best interests of the
Spanish-Americans of New Mexico by stating that it would not
hurt the native people of New Mexico but that it would hurt

---

1. Walter L. McNutt, An Inquiry into the Operation of the Primary System of New Mexico, p. 14.

only the native politicians of the state. The native people of New Mexico are well qualified by education, their interest in politics and government and by their very tradition to look after themselves. Rather than be hurt by a primary they will be helped, for it will give them an opportunity to express themselves instead of politicians expressing themselves in behalf of their people. I think it is a disgrace for any group of politicians to say that the native population is not ready for a primary.[1]

But the Good Neighbor League had created a political storm. Protest meetings were held, and shortly after the legislature convened in special session, caravans of opponents of the primary arrived at the capital. A parade of demonstrators circled the statehouse amid great fanfare. Senator Dennis Chavez addressed a mass meeting, charging that the primary proposal was conceived in hate and personalities.[2]

The Thirteenth Legislature, which considered the direct primary act, was overwhelmingly Democratic in composition, for 23 of the 24 senators were of that party and 47 of the 49 representatives. Three of the 24 senators were Hispanos and 16 of the 49 representatives.[3] The direct primary bill passed by a vote of 13-11 in the senate and 27-18 in the house.[4] Comparison of the above figures indicates that the voting cut across party and ethnic lines. Closer examination, however, indicates that there was a marked tendency for Anglo senators representing counties in which the "native" population was large to vote against the measure. And the backbone of opposition in the house came from the Hispanic-American members.

---

1. Albuquerque Journal, August 18, 1938.
2. Walter L. McNutt, op. cit., p. 17.
3. Blue Book of New Mexico, (1937-38), pp. 11-12.
4. Walter L. McNutt, op. cit., pp. 18-20.

The Open Primary and Group Affiliation

In general, Hispanic-American political leaders were opposed to the adoption of the direct primary in New Mexico. United States Senator Dennis Chavez, foremost of this group, was particularly bitter in his denunciation of the proposed measure. But it was not long before the majority of the Hispanic political figures were staunch defenders of the primary system. This change of opinion may have arisen from conviction that the open primary was a more democratic system of naming candidates than had been provided by the convention method. On the other hand, the direct primary may have redounded to the advantage of the Hispanic-American political leaders. It is impossible to supply evidence on the first score. It is not difficult to find support for the latter view. For the fact is that high-placed figures in both the Anglo and the Hispano camps believe that the Hispanic-Americans have profited from the operation of the open primary system. Certainly the most strenuous opposition to change has come from Hispanic quarters.

Under the convention system, places on the state ticket were allocated by an assembly of party leaders. A gentlemen's agreement divided posts between Anglo and Hispano. However, as indicated in the previous chapter, the Hispanic-Americans were not always satisfied with the division of spoils. But it was difficult to buck the machine, consequently the activities of any dissenting group were sharply curbed.

The open primary removed most of the restrictions imposed by the convention system. It became possible for any number of Hispanic-Americans to file for every office on the ticket.

This was, of course, equally true of the Anglo-Americans of
New Mexico. It also made possible some highly intricate political maneuvering based upon differences between the two major
cultural groups.

Before describing such maneuvers, it is necessary to
call attention to the fact that voting in New Mexico often
follows ethnic lines. That is, there is a marked tendency for
Anglo voter to cast his ballot for Anglo candidate and for the
Hispano voter to support a candidate of Hispanic descent. This
propensity was underscored by every politically-minded person
who was interviewed in connection with this study, including the
Anglo governor of the state, the Hispano Republican candidate
for governor (1948), the Hispano commissioner of revenue, the
Anglo Democratic state chairman, and a host of lesser political
figures. It was a tendency confirmed by members of the department of government at the state university, such writers as
Erna Fergusson, and by newspaper columnists.

In the most recent primary elections (1948 and 1950),
the ethnic character of the New Mexican vote was described in
both Spanish-language and English-language newspapers. A few
examples will demonstrate the fact that the candidate's ethnic
background is a major concern of many voters.

In this connection, the political careers of Tom
McGrath and Paul Davis are of interest. Their candidacies were
test cases for the charge that voters tend to cast ballots
according to group affiliation. For both McGrath and Davis were
rarities in that they were of Hispanic descent but bore Anglo-
Saxon surnames.

McGrath, candidate for auditor general had another
Hispano, Jerry Trujillo, as a rival in the 1948 Democratic
primary.

> McGrath, in spite of his name, is darker than a reserva-
> tion Indian. And Jerry is more blonde than a Brooklyn
> Irishman. In the last primary election McGrath received
> great majorities in the eastern counties of the state
> where the Texans go by the name.. . .in that campaign
> Jerry went to the eastern counties where the color of the
> skin and hair is of great importance. And McGrath went
> to the northern counties so that he would not be con-
> sidered an "American."[1]

In decrying the type of prejudice which actuates many New Mexican
voters, the chairman of the state Democratic organization stated
that the excellent showing which Tom McGrath made in the eastern
portion of New Mexico was due to the fact that he did no campaigning there. His name was Anglo; if he put in an appearance,
the Little Texans could see that he was Hispano.[2]

McGrath himself called attention to the same quirk,
when he wrote the following letter to the leading Spanish-language
newspaper of New Mexico:

> I was candidate in the last primary election for the same
> post to which I now aspire--state auditor.

> And my full name without doubt was an important factor in
> aiding me to gain votes in the eastern and southern counties
> of the state by being Tom McGrath. But I also am taking
> into account that my name robbed me of many votes in the
> north.[3]

Paul Davis, the other Hispano with an Anglo name, made
an unsuccessful campaign for land commissioner in the 1948 Republican primary, and in 1950 was suggested as a candidate for

---

1. J. E. Medina, "Comentarios Rapidos," El Nuevo Mexicano,
   February 23, 1950.
2. Interview, Bryan Johnson, Albuquerque, December 27, 1949.
3. "Cartas al Editor," El Nuevo Mexicano, March 16, 1950.

governor. Will Harrison, editor of the influential _Santa Fe New Mexican_, and perhaps the most astute political commentator in the state, observed that a Spanish-American with an Anglo name has one of the greatest assets in New Mexico politics.

> It is strange but true that Spanish-American voters always know the racial lineage of such candidates and vote accordingly; the Anglos seldom know, look at the name, and vote accordingly.

> Those registered Republican who can vote in the Republican primary are predominantly of Spanish lineage. Last primary, June 1948, there were 23,596 votes cast for the three major candidates for governor.. . .The two Spanish-American candidates got 91 per cent, the equally prominent (Anglo), 9 per cent.[1]

The manner in which "race" influences voting is indicated in the following letter-to-the-editor, signed "A Native and Proud of It."

> I would like to call to your attention the article of June 7 about natives losing in the primary election. I believe you didn't wait long enough because, thank goodness, Tibo Chavez won the lieutenant governor nomination. There's always the chance the lieutenant governor may succeed to the governorship, and there are natives on both tickets for that office. So you see we are not so far behind.[2]

The Open Primary in Operation

Three skeins in the political fabric of New Mexico now should be drawn together. One is the fact that after 1930 Hispanic-American political leaders became conscious that a shift in power was imminent as a result of the increase in the Anglo-American population. Recognition of the minority status of the Spanish-American population led to a second development: the voter's

---

1. "At the Capitol," _Santa Fe New Mexican_, April 26, 1950.
2. _Santa Fe New Mexican_, June 21, 1950.

increasing sensitivity to "race." The third development was
the introduction of the open primary, placing a weapon in the
hands of those who wished to preserve the status quo.

The combination of these three factors has resulted in
a type of primary election unique in American politics. Its
chief characteristic is the wholesale filing of "stooge" candidates, many of whom are interested in blackmail, whether it be
political or financial. A "stooge" candidate has been defined
as "one who is paid to enter a race with no idea of winning and
for the sole purpose of dividing the voters of another candidate.
Stooge candidates are commonly entered on a racial basis--Anglos
to divide the support of an Anglo candidate and thus help a
Spanish-American, and the other way around."[1]

The device dates from the first primary election (1940),
when a Spanish-American candidate was the victim of Anglo-Hispano
antagonism.

> Filo Sedillo was up for a second term nomination for
> attorney general when Ted Chase slipped in under him
> and won the nomination on an out-and-out racial issue.
> After that the boys learned to employ stooge candi-
> dates, both Anglo and Spanish, to split their opponents'
> votes.[2]

As the above citation indicates, the use of stooge
candidates developed as the result of Anglo-American political
tactics. And it is commonly understood that the device has been
employed by politicians in both ethnic camps. It is perhaps
inevitable, however, that a group which feels itself politically

1. Santa Fe New Mexican, May 4, 1950.
2. Will Harrison, "At the Capitol," Santa Fe New Mexican, March
   1, 1950.

disadvantaged should be more tempted to use such strategy than a group which enjoys ascendancy. Doubtless this is the basis for the popular belief that stooge candidates usually are creatures of Spanish-American politicians.

The manner in which the stooge candidacy operates can best be illustrated with examples from the primary elections of 1948 and 1950. Perhaps the most graphic description was that given by Victor Salazar, strong man of the Mabry administration (1946-50).

> In the open primary, we can pull anything. Last year (1948) I told Dan Sedillo that he would win for four-year corporation commissioner, even though Paul Martinez would get a lot of votes and the Anglos would pull out the east side. So I gave Lester Davis $500.00 and told him to campaign in Eddy County (that's an Anglo county). He did and carried the county with 1,200 votes. He also carried Lea, Roosevelt and the other east side counties by well over 1,000 votes, splitting the Anglo vote and allowing Dan Sedillo to carry native counties and get the organization vote in other counties. If Davis's vote had gone over to any of the other Anglo candidates, the Anglos would have won.[1]

That the Spanish-American candidate sometimes loses by such tactics is shown by another example given by the same political leader.

> In the primary for six-year corporation commissioner we (i. e. the state organization) wanted to get Dan Casados out of there. He hadn't worked with us for years. I told J. O. Garcia that the organization was for him and not to worry as we'd load the ticket. We were worried about Bob Johnston from the east side, so I gave Ingram Pickett $300.00 to campaign on the east side for himself to split Johnston's vote. He did that, but he picked up too many Anglo votes and won by about 900 votes over J. O. Garcia.[2]

As the primary election of 1948 approached, it became

---

1. Interview, Victor Salazar, Santa Fe, Dec. 29, 1949 (Through Melvin Mencher.)
2. Loc. cit.

apparent that opponents of Governor Mabry would attempt to prevent his re-nomination. As political forecasters predicted-- "It would not be surprising to see some Spanish-American. . . file for governor, subject to the Democratic primary. Such a candidate would take more votes from Mabry than any other,"[1]-- an Anglo-Hispano race developed. This diversion, however, did not prevent the incumbent from recapturing the nomination.

Diversionary Tactics in the Open Primary of 1950

As the 1950 primary election neared, representatives of the Democratic party in the northern (Hispanic) counties met to lay plans. The group was commonly believed to be seeking an agreement on a list of Spanish-speaking candidates for the Democratic nomination and of persuading conflicting candidates to withdraw. A member of the informal group explained that its purpose was to attempt "to save for the Spanish people those offices which have customarily gone to Spanish-speaking candidates."[2]

The venture proved unsuccessful, however. The state Democratic machine regarded the move as diversionary in nature, and succeeded in blocking this attempt to consolidate Hispanic-American strength in the approaching primary.

Nevertheless, the 1950 primary was marked by stooge candidacies, particularly in the gubernatorial race. A bitter fight developed between the Chavez and Miles factions of the Democratic party. Federal Judge David Chavez resigned his Puerto Rican post to become candidate for governor of New Mexico; his

1. Albuquerque Journal, April 25, 1948.
2. Santa Fe New Mexican, March 15, 1950.

opponent was John Miles, member of the United States House of Representatives. A close associate of the Chavez forces, Lake Frazier, also entered the primary race, apparently in an effort to divide John Miles's Anglo support. Credence was lent this view by the following statement from a Spanish-language newspaper which gave Chavez full backing:

> Well informed politicians believe that Lake Frazier and the Chavez forces are working in harmony. The Chavez' are concentrating their forces in the northern counties and Frazier in the eastern and southern counties. This system of strategy is being used to take votes from Miles in the sections of the state where his rivals are very well known and popular.[1]

Supporters of Miles not only contended that the Chavez forces entered Frazier in order to divide the Anglo vote, but that another candidate, Henry L. Eager, had been entered in the primary at the last moment as a further diversionary move. Miles's supporters petitioned the state supreme court for a writ of mandamus, charging that Eager did not file his own declaration of candidacy; did not sign his own name to the declaration; and that the filing and signing were done by some person unknown to Eager.[2] The supreme court ordered the removal of Eager as a candidate.

The alleged attempt of the Chavez forces to divide the Anglo vote was widely condemned. An editorial in the leading political organ of the state excused David Chavez from personal complicity in "An elaborate and dangerous plot to defeat the will of the majority of the people,"[3] but accused his partisans of

> A scheme to divide and defeat the majority of the people (revealing) itself scene by scene since the first move-

---

1. *El Nuevo Mexicano*, April 13, 1950.
2. *Santa Fe New Mexican*, May 25, 1950.
3. *Santa Fe New Mexican*, June 1, 1950.

ment by Chavez followers months ago to dupe Lake
Frazier of Roswell into running for governor. It
developed with the filing of Henry Eager of Tucum-
cari as another vote-splitting candidate, extended
to giving secret aid to candidate Ingram Pickett of
Santa Fe and went so far as the filing of a pro-
Chavez candidate in the Republican gubernatorial
primary.[1]

The charges were vehemently denied by the Chavez cam-

paign managers as smear tactics, and the introduction of "racial"

feeling was deplored. Charge and counter-charge were equally

difficult to prove conclusively, yet one fact stood clear: the

open primary provides a very public arena for Anglo-Hispano

rivalries.

Proposed Revision of Primary Legislation

Organized opposition to the open primary system developed

in the period 1940-50. In part, this was based upon the abuses

which became apparent, particularly in the use of stooge candi-

dates. Newspaper editorials called attention to the fact that

such diversionary tactics had resulted in nominees being chosen

with as little as 20 per cent of the vote, or compared the open

primary with the convention system in unfavorable manner.

At their worst the conventions did not equal the common
practices which mark primary elections today.

Take for example the dummy candidates.. . .This abom-
inable practice was not known to nor among the worst
tricks of the politicians of yesterday. In the approaching June election there will be an army of these diversionary candidates.[2]

But it was not newspaper criticism which finally led to

the introduction of legislation to modify the primary system. The

modification was sought by the state administration, and the bill

1. Loc. cit.
2. El Nuevo Mexicano, April 27, 1950.

embodying the changes was pushed through the legislature by
the chairman of the state Democratic organization.

> The pre-primary law is considered a machine-sponsored
> piece of legislation. Everyone within shouting dis-
> tance of the discussion surrounding the bill knows
> that it was invented so that Bryan Johnson, State Demo-
> cratic Party Chief, can run for governor.. . .he and
> right-hand-man Victor Salazar invented the much-discussed
> primary revision.[1]

> The primary revision was sought by Bryan Johnson, as all
> who watched the bill go through both chambers can testify.
> Johnson personally saw to it that his pet bill scooted
> through without trouble.[2]

A brief examination of the provisions of the bill will
reveal why the measure encountered opposition, particularly from
leading Spanish-American political figures. Ostensibly, the revision was in accord with the Colorado primary law and a model
law drafted by Joseph P. Harris of the University of California.
It allowed party conventions to select candidates to run in the
primary. Representation at the convention was to be based on
the number of votes cast for governor in the previous election.

But the New Mexico pre-primary law differed from the
model laws in one important respect. The Colorado and Harris
systems permitted candidates receiving a certain percentage of
the convention vote to run in the primary with party endorsement.
But other candidates could get on the ticket by the petition of
a specified number of voters. The New Mexico law made no such
provision for independent candidates, for it limited the candidates to those who could muster 25 per cent of the delegates in
a party convention.

---

1. R. L. Chambers, "Capitol Views," Belen News-Bulletin, May 31,
   1949.
2. Taos Star, March 23, 1949.

Some critics of the measure pointed out that the plan
was subject to easy rigging. "A controlled convention, such as
most of them are, could drum up 80 per cent or more of the delegates for each of the approved candidates and there would be no
primary contest. Failing that, the convention bosses could
engineer weak opposition for their favorites."[1] Other critics
called attention to the power which would be exercised by the
state machine under the pre-primary system. "It's do-or-die for
the factions within the Democratic party that don't get along
with the administration. Unless they can kill or figure a way
to beat the pre-primary convention system passed by the 19th
legislature, they are dead ducks."[2]

A move to prevent the pre-primary convention system
from supplanting the open primary was made possible by a constitutional provision which permits a referendum if 10 per cent of the
registered voters in at least 24 counties ask for repeal of the
law.[3] Opponents of the proposed system were prompt to take advantage of this proviso. The referendum movement was led by
Dennis Chavez, Jr., son and chief lieutenant of the United States
Senator. That the Chavez forces should take the lead in preserving the open primary was somewhat ironical, since the senator
had vainly attempted to prevent its introduction in 1938.

In ordinary circumstances, a move to block legislation
sponsored by the state organization would have been interpreted
as simple intra-party strife. However, when the opposition was

---

1. Editorial, Santa Fe New Mexican, March 14, 1949.
2. Taos Star, April 27, 1949.
3. R. L. Chambers, "Capitol Views," Belen News Bulletin, July
   15, 1949.

led by the avowed champion of the Hispanic-Americans, the struggle took on an ethnic character. Therefore, the referendum movement led by Dennis Chavez, Jr., was widely interpreted as a desperate effort to preserve the political influence of the Hispanic people.

The necessary signatures were secured, and the pre-primary law was placed into political cold storage until the general election of November, 1950, when it became subject to approval or disapproval by the electorate.

But the manner in which the signatures were secured led to a major political scandal. Charges of wholesale forgery were made by the Albuquerque Tribune, the Santa Fe New Mexican, and other leading newspapers. The grand jury of Santa Fe county

> . . .requested the secretary of state to submit for examination the petitions which had been filed to suspend the operation of the Pre-Primary Law. From our examination of that part of the petitions pertaining to Santa Fe county, it was determined. . .that there are pages of signatures which to the untrained eye are obviously forgeries, and signed by a single person. It is our recommendation that the question of these forgeries be inquired into further under such procedure as may be determined by the court.[1]

Despite demands for court action to invalidate the referendum, the case was not reviewed. The pre-primary law remained in abeyance, and the regular primary election was held in June, 1950. Charges of fraud and corruption were made by those opposed to the Chavez faction, while the latter countered with statements that the pre-primary law was designed to place control of the Democratic party firmly in the hands of the state machine

---

1. Carlsbad Current-Argus, quoted, Santa Fe New Mexican, March 14, 1950.

and its imminent control by the Anglo politicians of the east
and south. The issue was left for the decision of the voter in
the general election of November, 1950.

Summary

New Mexico was one of the last states to abandon the
convention system of naming candidates for public office. Spanish-
American opposition to the open primary was a major factor in the
retention of the convention system. Spanish-American leaders
succeeded in defeating primary legislation at three sessions of
the legislature, but in 1938 a primary law was passed over the
strenuous opposition of leading Hispanic politicians.

Since the primary system came into operation, it has
met with the general approval of Spanish-American political
figures. It is commonly believed that the open primary operates
to the advantage of the Hispanic people.

There is considerable evidence to indicate that the
people of New Mexico tend to vote along ethnic lines. This has
led to the development of a peculiar type of election. Dummy
candidates frequently are entered in order to divert support
from a major candidate. There is a tendency for a strong Anglo
candidate to enter a "stooge" Hispano candidate to divide the
vote of a powerful Hispano opponent, thus making an Anglo victory
more certain. The same device is employed by Hispanic-American
politicians.

This abuse of the primary system, plus the apparent
desire of the state Democratic organization to consolidate its
control, led to the enactment of pre-primary legislation in 1949.

Under this system, party conventions select nominees for primary elections. The legislation met with the opposition of Senator Dennis Chavez and his supporters. A constitutional device which permits a referendum on controversial legislation permitted opponents of the pre-primary system to have the measure shelved temporarily. Fraud was charged in connection with the referendum, but court action was not taken in time to prevent the operation of the open primary in June, 1950. In November, 1950, the electorate passed upon the legislation.

CHAPTER XIII

THE STRUGGLE FOR FAIR EMPLOYMENT LEGISLATION

The history of New Mexico is a record of cooperation, as well as competition, between the two major ethnic groups. If this were not so, the state would not have reached its present state of development. There has been common agreement upon most governmental policies. And as one reads the transactions of the various legislatures, he must conclude that party considerations, more frequently than not, have overridden matters of ancestry and religion.

Yet the history of New Mexico has been punctuated by a series of controversies in which Anglo was pitted against Hispano in unmistakable fashion. To the political scientist these episodes are important because they reveal underlying tensions, tensions which in the ordinary course of affairs are beyond detection. Having learned that individual human beings reveal hidden qualities in time of crisis, the political scientist has reason to suspect that revealing facets of inter-group relationships are displayed when a critical situation presents itself.

Attention already has been called to several intergroup crises in the political history of New Mexico. Consideration of the legislative battle for anti-discrimination measures now is in order, not only because of its recency, but also because of its portent for the future. Certainly the line of de-

marcation between Anglo and Hispano never had been more visible,
and never had spokesmen for the two groups been more outspoken
than they were in this controversy.

The Background of Anti-Discrimination Legislation

The drive for fair employment practices legislation is
intimately connected with changes in the population of New Mexico. Since its organization as a state, each census has reported
population growth. More important as far as this study is concerned, each census has revealed a rather sharp increase in the
population of the most Anglo sections of the state, and a decrease
or very small gain in the population of the most Hispanic counties.
This is underscored in the preliminary returns of the 1950 census
which show that five of the seven most Anglo counties had a considerable increase in population in 1940-50, but that each of the
seven counties having the highest concentration of Hispanic-
Americans lost population.[1]

As indicated in Chapter II of this study, authorities
commonly agree that the rapid increase in population in the eastern
and southern parts of New Mexico has been due, in large part, to
migration from Texas and Oklahoma. In each of the latter states,
the segregation of Negroes is made mandatory by law; in Texas,
those of Hispanic descent are segregated by custom, as the study
of Pauline R. Kibbe[2] proves so conclusively.

In eastern New Mexico, popularly known as "Little Texas"
and "The Bible Belt," the Southerner's attitude toward race is

---

1. Santa Fe New Mexican, July 2, 1950.
2. Latin Americans in Texas.

obvious. It has been noted in Chapter IV of this study, and
its influence in politics has run like a thread through succeeding chapters.

For many years, the people of central and northern New
Mexico, secure in the protection afforded Spanish-Americans by
the state constitution, seemed oblivious to the racial prejudice
exhibited by their eastern neighbors. Spanish-American legislators even allowed a bill providing for the segregation of students of "African descent" to become law in 1923,[1] apparently not
realizing its implications.

But the racism of eastern New Mexico influenced at-
titudes elsewhere. Expansion of irrigation farming brought them
into southern New Mexico; the discovery of gas brought them into
northwestern New Mexico; the war boom brought them into the Albuquerque-Santa Fe region. Wage differentials between Anglo and
Hispano, discrimination in hiring, and other economic manifestations of racism became obvious. And in the capital of the state,
Spanish stronghold for almost four centuries, it became impossible
for Spanish-speaking citizens to purchase property in sections
of the city reserved for Anglos.[2]

These and other types of discrimination brought several
groups into action. Attention has been called to the League of
United Latin American Citizens and its campaign to publicize and
to fight alleged economic, social and political inequality.[3] The
National Association for the Advancement of Colored People con-

---

1. Santa Fe New Mexican, March 4, 1949.
2. R. L. Chambers, "Nuevo Mexico: Tierra de Desencanto," El
   Nuevo Mexicano, Feb. 9, 1950, p. 15.
3. Cf. Chapter VII.

demned the presence of a segregation law in the statutes of a
state outside the South, and fought for economic equality. The
Anti-Defamation League of B'nai B'rith likewise campaigned for
minority rights. Through the ministerial alliances of Albuquerque,
Santa Fe and other large centers in the western half of the state,
the Protestant church joined the attack on what its spokesmen
called a rising tide of discrimination. More potent was the
force which the Roman Catholic church brought to bear. The Archbishop of Santa Fe was outspoken in his criticisms of the economic and social restrictions imposed upon Hispanic-Americans in
most parts of New Mexico. Powerful backing also came from the
New Mexico Federation of Labor and the C. I. O. central organization.

Spokesmen for these groups became increasingly vocal
after the outbreak of World War II. Study of the newspapers of
New Mexico in the decade 1940-50 leads one to conclude, however,
that groups fighting discrimination met with little popular
support. Their activities were reported, but for the most part
such items were notably brief and were tucked away in the back
pages of the newspapers.

If the assertions of anti-discrimination groups met
with an apathetic press, they encountered the opposition of a
number of New Mexicans, both Anglo and Hispano. Some denied that
the Hispanic-Americans of the state were discriminated against;
for that reason, there was no need to organize against it. This
attitude was summarized by a state senator of Spanish-American
ancestry when he said, "We don't need a Fair Employment law here.
There isn't any discrimination. Why should I vote for it? I've

never been told I couldn't do anything because I'm Spanish."[1]

Other New Mexicans frowned upon an organized anti-discrimination drive, not because they denied that discrimination existed, but because they felt that another type of attack was preferable. Theirs was a policy of gradualism, with great emphasis upon education and inter-group activities. The way to attack discrimination, they argued, was on the basis of the injured individual, not the injured ethnic group. The statements of Erna Fergusson, sometimes called the official interpreter of New Mexico, are representative of this point of view.[2]

There were yet others who opposed anti-discrimination legislation because they believed in segregation. The debate on the Fair Employment Practices Act of 1949 revealed this point of view in unmistakable fashion. In the senate, the opposition to the measure was led by a former Texan whose ideas of white supremacy closely resembled those of Southern demagogues. In debate, he said that "Hispanos may be my equals but not niggers, and I call them niggers."[3]

Ethnic organizations, religious groups, and trade unions were aided in their drive for a fair employment practices act by several war and post-war developments. In the first place, the President's Civil Rights Commission fixed the eyes of the nation upon discriminatory practices. To Secure These Rights became a best seller; all over the United States citizens organized

---

1. R. L. Chambers, "The New Mexico Pattern," Common Ground, (Summer, 1949), p. 24.
2. Interview, Albuquerque, Dec. 26, 1949.
3. Senator Burton Roach, Hot Springs; as quoted by Daniel Valdes, Interview, Santa Fe, July 19, 1949.

to correct the abuses pointed out in the Commission report.
Debate on the federal FEPC bill proved a powerful educational
force. Its effects were felt in New Mexico, and the organizations cited above capitalized on this newly aroused interest.

Passage of stringent fair employment practices legislation in New York and New Jersey, and the introduction of such
measures in the legislatures of other states provided the anti-
discrimination groups of New Mexico with further argument. Precedent is a powerful force in a union of states.

Perhaps more important, however, was the return of
thousands of war veterans to their native state. Hispanic-
American soldiers who had been stationed in eastern New Mexico
and in the South remembered the indignities to which they had been
subjected; on the other hand, contact with Hispanic-American troops
had erased ideas of "white" superiority from the minds of some
Anglo-American soldiers. The organization of the liberal American
Veterans Committee provided a vehicle for those desiring to foster
inter-group relations. And of great significance was the fact
that the "G. I. Bill of Rights" provided countless Hispanic-
American veterans with unprecedented educational and economic
opportunity. A reservoir of leadership thus was created.

The Legislative Battlefield

By 1949 the move to secure fair employment practices
legislation had received enough popular support to guarantee the
consideration of New Mexico lawmakers. In the early days of the
nineteenth legislature, Senate Bill No. 45 was introduced, with
Tibo J. Chavez as its chief sponsor. Popularly known as the

FEPC bill, it was officially described as an act:

> Relating to the prevention and elimination of practices
> of discrimination in employment and otherwise against
> persons because of race, creed, color or national origin,
> creating in the executive department of the state a fair
> employment practices commission, defining its functions,
> powers and duties and providing for the appointment and
> compensation of its officers and employees.[1]

That this bill would provoke one of the hardest-fought battles in the history of New Mexico did not become apparent during the transactions of the senate. Upon its introduction in January, the FEP bill was referred to the committee on state and county affairs. It lay buried there, despite all efforts of Senator Tibo Chavez to have it brought to the floor. On March 8, in the closing days of the legislature, Chavez accused the committee of digging a grave for the FEP bill,[2] and succeeded in having the measure transferred to the judiciary committee, of which he was chairman.[3] Chavez promptly brought the bill to the floor of the senate. After a three-hour debate, the measure passed, 13-10.[4] The voting was according to geographical and cultural lines. Geographically, it was the east versus west, with representatives of the western half supporting the measure. From the cultural angle, the great body of support came from Hispanic-American senators or Anglo senators from counties having a high concentration of Hispanic voters. Although the geographical-cultural nature of the voting was obvious, the economic influence should not be forgotten. Two of the affirmative votes were those

---

1. State of New Mexico, Senate Bills--Nineteenth Legislature, 1949.
2. Santa Fe New Mexican, March 9, 1949.
3. Interview, Ebenezer Jones, Assistant Labor Commissioner, July 29, 1949.
4. Santa Fe New Mexican, March 10, 1949.

of senators representing districts where labor was powerful.

It was in the house of representatives, however, where the lines were most closely drawn and where the debate was sharpest. After proponents of the measure succeeded in pushing it through the senate, eyes focused on the house, where it was commonly agreed it would face tougher opposition.

Led by Daniel T. Valdes of the League of United Latin American Citizens, the pro-FEP forces swung into action. The B'nai B'rith's Anti-Defamation League had its Denver representative on hand, Protestant leaders issued statements in support of the measure, and the NAACP had its spokesman in the person of an able minister of the African Methodist Episcopal church. Labor representatives brought pressure to bear on legislators from the coal, oil, potash and copper districts. The Archbishop not only issued a strong appeal for passage of the bill, but he authorized an astute monsignor to lobby on the floor of the house itself.[1]

The League of United Latin American Citizens brought great pressure to bear on Anglo members of the house who represented districts having a large number of Spanish-American voters.[2] One of the most active members of the house, an Anglo who insisted that his name be withheld, told the writer that the lieutenants of United States Senator Dennis Chavez went beyond the exertion of mere pressure. Threats and blackmail tactics were employed, according to this Anglo. The latter also claimed that many non-

---

1. Interview, Monsignor William T. Bradley, Superintendent of Schools, Archdiocese of Santa Fe, Santa Fe, July 21, 1949.
2. Interview, Daniel Valdes, State Governor, Lulac, Santa Fe, December 30, 1949.

Catholic legislators were outraged by Archibishop Byrne's letter
and by the lobbying of Monsignor Bradley.

Proponents of the FEPC bill charged that the measure
was opposed by Governor Mabry and other members of the state
administration. The governor, they accused, had yielded to legislators from Little Texas who were open in their opposition to the
bill. "The state machine, to soothe Little Texas, had promised
a hands-off policy on the bill. Actually it passed word along
that passage of the measure would hurt the machine."[1] Daniel T.
Valdes supported the charge, and stated that the administration's
opposition was made public after the bill passed and the commission
was named. For the governor named as the key member a person who
would negate the very purpose of the FEP bill.[2]

Such accusations were denied by the state administration.
Again corroboration is not lacking. J. E. Medina, editor of El
Nuevo Mexicano, wrote in defense of the governor:

> It is the personal opinion of the author of this
> column that Governor Mabry was not opposed to the enact-
> ment of a FEPC law. Governor Mabry has indicated on all
> occasions that the legislature of the State is an agency
> entirely independent of the executive branch and that it
> has the right to enact projects of law without the inter-
> ference of the governor or of any other state agency.[3]

But whatever the source, the FEPC bill met strong opposition. The last day of the session approached, and Representative
Sixto Leyva, who sponsored the bill in the house, had not succeeded
in getting the measure to the floor. Leyva and six other Hispanic-
American legislators met with their free-lance Anglo counselor

---

1. R. L. Chambers, "New Mexico Pattern," Common Ground, (Summer,
   1949), p. 24.
2. Interview, op. cit.
3. "Comentarios Rapidos," El Nuevo Mexicano, February 2, 1950.

and planned to force the FEPC bill to the floor on the final day,
when representatives would be eager for adjournment. What they
planned was the first filibuster in the history of New Mexico.

Debate on an important appropriations bill was about to
begin when Sixto Leyva was recognized by the speaker of the house,
John F. Simms, Jr. The representative pulled from his pocket a
copy of the report of the President's Civil Rights Commission
and began to read. A murmur ran through the crowded galleries,
where supporters of the FEPC law were very much in evidence.

After Leyva had read for half an hour, the speaker of
the house reminded him that the session was almost at a close
and that much business was on the calendar. Leyva replied that
under the rules of the house he could speak for three hours. It
then dawned upon legislators that the proponents of FEPC were
conducting a filibuster. The speaker called a recess, and house
and administrative leaders held a lengthy conference with Leyva.[1]

Senate Bill 45, the FEPC measure, was brought to the
floor. The atmosphere was electric. The speaker announced that
there was to be no demonstration from the gallery, no talking
through the rail with representatives and no passing of notes
through the rail. He also stated that only friends and relatives
of representatives were welcome on the floor.[2] Nevertheless, in
the course of debate, there was an uproar in the galleries, and
it was necessary to clear them on several occasions.[3] The packed

---

1. R. L. Chambers, "New Mexico Pattern," loc. cit.
   Santa Fe New Mexican, March 13, 1949.
2. State of New Mexico, Journal of the House of Representatives,
   Nineteenth Session, 1949.
3. Interview, John F. Simms, Jr., speaker of the house of representatives, Albuquerque, August 1, 1949.

galleries remained quiet while Representatives Leyva and Valdez spoke for the bill and read statements in its behalf from the archbishop and other Catholic prelates. They burst into applause, however, when the result of the voting became known, clapping and shouting. For the FEPC bill had passed by the narrow margin of 25-24.[1] Shortly afterwards, the governor signed the measure.

The house vote divided Anglo and Hispano into sharply opposing sides. All of the 19 Spanish-American representatives voted for the measure. All of the six Anglo-American representatives who voted for FEPC were from the western half of the state, where the Hispanic influence is strong. Three of them represented districts where the Spanish-American population constitutes more than 50 per cent of the total. It is significant that no representative from the eastern half of the state, even those from the oil, potash and coal sections where labor is a power, cast his vote for FEPC legislation. This reinforces the commonly accepted belief that the measure was "racial" in character.

An interesting and somewhat revealing sidelight on the controversy was offered by the speaker of the house. He indicated to the writer that the crucial vote was cast by Representative Calvin P. Horn of Albuquerque. Horn, a wealthy, devout and self-made man, "had promised the Bible Belt boys that he would vote against FEPC. But he prayed over the matter and then voted as his conscience told him, which was for the bill. Now the eastern boys won't speak to him."[2]

Many politically minded New Mexicans attribute the

1. *Santa Fe New Mexican*, March 13, 1949.
2. Interview, John F. Simms, Jr., *op. cit.*

passage of Fair Employment Practices legislation to a "deal"
between Hispanic-American legislators and their Little Texas
opponents in that body. In return for adoption of FEPC, a reapportionment bill increasing the representation of the East Side
was to be pushed through.

> Some Democrats of the south and east of the
> state actually are in favor of the project (FEPC). They
> realize that if it is not adopted, their favorite project
> of reapportionment will be killed by liberal Democrats
> and those from the north of the state in retaliation.[1]

> Some state senators predicted that action on a
> house-approved reapportionment measure would be held up
> in the senate until the FEPC bill has cleared the house.[2]

But several items appear to contradict the assertion
that a political horse trade made FEPC possible. One is the fact
that the Spanish-American members of the house of representatives
unanimously opposed the reapportionment bill, regardless of party
lines. Spanish-speaking members argued that reapportionment
would reduce their influence in state affairs.

> Sixto Leyva, young firebrand from Domingo,
> made this the big issue. And the Hispano group agreed
> with him. Leyva pointed out that those from the south
> and east sides don't represent the large Spanish-
> speaking group in their areas, so their cry for additional
> representation has a false ring in it.[3]

Equally conclusive is the fact that on the final day of
the nineteenth legislature, representatives from eastern New Mexico unanimously voted against the Fair Employment Practices Act.
In neither case was there evidence of compromise between Anglo
and Hispano.

The words "gentlemen's agreement" and "horse trade"

1. _Estrella de Taos_, Feb. 24, 1949.
2. _Santa Fe New Mexican_, March 10, 1949.
3. _Taos Star_, Feb. 24, 1949.

perhaps may be applied with more accuracy to an alleged understanding concerning the provisions of the bill itself. The
speaker of the house of representatives stated that the tacit
agreement was that the FEPC bill was to be allowed to pass as a
weak measure; it was to be a gesture. The speaker complained
that Tibo Chavez was leading a drive to put teeth into the bill.[1]
Senator Burton Roach, who led the fight against FEPC in the upper
chamber wrote that the bill "was amended to the point that it had
no 'teeth' for enforcement, and no funds to expend."[2] The state
governor of the League of United Latin American Citizens argued
that it was the obvious intention of the state administration to
weaken and restrict the Fair Employment Practices Commission. He
based his claim upon the fact that the bill itself was without
teeth, and that the commission had no funds to expend. Furthermore, the governor had "loaded" the commission by naming two
Hispanos, two Anglos and putting in the key fifth position a
Negro who had publicly fought for segregation in the public schools.[3]

Since the Fair Employment Practices act was pushed through
the legislature with the complete backing of Spanish-American
legislators, the protection it affords merits consideration.

Section one declares that the practice or policy of discrimination against individuals by reason of their race, color,
religion, national origin or ancestry is a matter of state concern, since such discrimination undermines the foundations of a
free democratic state.[4]

---

1. Interview, John F. Simms, Jr., op. cit.
2. Letter to writer, Nov. 4, 1949.
3. Interview, Daniel T. Valdes, Dec. 30, 1949.
4. State of New Mexico, Labor Laws, p. 38.

Section two recognizes and declares the opportunity
to obtain employment without discrimination because of race,
color, religion, national origin or ancestry to be a civil right,
while the following section defines such terms as "employment
agency," "labor organization," "employer" and the like.[1]

Section four enjoins employers, labor organizations
and employment agencies from discriminating on the grounds of
race, color, religious creed, national origin or ancestry, while
section five provides for an anti-discrimination clause in all
state contracts. Section six establishes the state Fair Employment Practices Commission, with the commissioner of labor and the
attorney general as ex-officio members.[2]

Sections seven and eight deal with the policies, powers
and duties of the commission. These include the power to appoint
attorneys and examiners, hold hearings, subpoena witnesses and
take the testimony of any person under oath. Study of the
authority granted leads to the conclusion that the commission is
an agent of the police power of the state.[3]

The FEP commission is given an educational role in
section nine:

> In order to eliminate prejudice among the various
> racial, religious and ethnic groups in this State and to
> further good-will among such groups, the Commission in co-
> operation with other departments of Government is directed
> to prepare a comprehensive educational program, designed
> for the students of the public schools of this State and for
> all other residents thereof, designed to emphasize the origin
> of prejudice against such minority groups, its harmful effects,
> and its incompatibility with American principles of equality
> and fair play.[4]

---

1. Ibid., p. 39.
2. Ibid., pp. 40-41.
3. Ibid., pp. 42-44.
4. Loc. cit.

In section ten the commission is empowered and directed to prevent any person from engaging in unfair employment practices, with the stipulation that informal conciliation is to be attempted before more stringent measures are employed. The procedure is then described. The following section provides for judicial review and enforcement, while section twelve calls for a liberal construction for the terms of the act.[1]

Although members of the commission served without pay and operated with limited funds, they set the state anti-discrimination machinery in operation. One of the first cases heard involved the complaint of two workers at the great Sandia base at Albuquerque who alleged that they had been discharged because they were of Spanish descent. It also heard the contention of B'nai B'rith and the Roman Catholic hierarchy that the application blanks for teachers in the state were possibly discriminatory. Although no direct action was reported in either case, newspapers gave the hearings considerable publicity,[2] and their educative influence was not overlooked. Moreover, the hearings demonstrated that the alliance of ethnic, religious and labor organizations, having secured FEPC, was intent upon implementing it, for representatives of each of these groups were present at the hearing cited above.[3]

Summary

Controversy arising from the passage of Fair Employment Practices legislation is of considerable interest to the political

1. State of New Mexico, Labor Laws, pp. 44-47.
2. Santa Fe New Mexican, Jan. 27, 1950.
3. Loc. cit.

scientist, for it threw into sharp relief Anglo-Hispano differences. Demand for anti-discrimination legislation developed
after a considerable number of Southerners entered the state,
apparently bringing with them deep-seated racial prejudices.
These found expression in economic and social discrimination,
and in the adoption of a measure permitting the segregation of
Negro students.

Ethnic, religious and labor groups fought discriminatory
practices, but made little headway until World War II. Federal
action on civil rights and the impact of returning veterans
strengthened the forces demanding FEP legislation. At the 1949
session of the legislature, a state FEPC bill was introduced.

The measure became the storm center of New Mexico
politics. It passed the senate and was forced to the floor of
the house of representatives by means of the first filibuster in
the history of the state. The FEP bill passed the house by 25-
24 vote and was signed by the governor. Voting in the lower
chamber was strictly according to geographical and cultural lines.
All of the 19 Spanish-American representatives voted for the
measure. All of the six Anglo-American representatives who voted
for FEPC were from the western half of the state, where the
Hispanic influence is strong. Three of them represented districts
where the Spanish-American population constitutes more than 50
per cent of the total. Representatives from the eastern half
of the state, an Anglo stronghold, unanimously voted against the
measure.

Arguments that FEPC legislation was adopted as a result
of a political horse trade in return for a reapportionment bill

favored by eastern New Mexico seem without foundation. The
record shows that Hispanic-American legislators unanimously
opposed the reapportionment bill and the Anglo-American legislators generally opposed the FEPC bill. There is, however, some
evidence to indicate that the anti-discrimination legislation
was intended as a gesture, and that legislators did not envision
a powerful administrative-judicial body.

The New Mexico FEPC bill resembles the proposed federal
measure. The commission set up was denied full police powers,
however, and its funds were greatly restricted. Despite such
limitations, the commission has held hearings, and it has continued to have the full support of those ethnic, religious and
labor organizations which sponsored the legislation.

CHAPTER XIV

GUBERNATORIAL ELECTIONS IN NEW MEXICO,

1912-48

Although the population of New Mexico is small, when
compared with that of most states, the power of the state administration is great. Although the state budget is one of the
smallest in the Union, the administration's control over fiscal
policy suffers no limitations. In short, the state administration of New Mexico plays a dominant role in the lives of its
citizens. Some commentators go further and contend that in no
other state does the government so completely dominate the scene.

R. L. Chambers developed this point when he observed
that political affairs in New Mexico are "conducted along lines
long ago junked in other states. The Democratic Party's powerful
state machine doles out thousands of jobs. It is the largest
single employer in the state. It has become to thousands of
northern and southern Hispanos their sole source of income--
their bread, chili and beans."[1] The role of government as employer was touched upon in Chapter VIII of this study, and reference
was made there to the extraordinary leverage exerted by the power
of patronage. It is because the state administration has so many
jobs at its disposal that it enjoys an unusual hold on the daily

_____

1. "The New Mexico Pattern," Common Ground, (Summer, 1949), pp.
   25-26.

lives of so many New Mexicans. And it is because the governor
is the fountainhead of patronage that he has come to be regarded
as the kingpin in New Mexico politics. Congressmen have been
known to vacate their more lucrative posts in Washington, federal judges to step down from lifetime positions, and chief
justices of the state supreme court to resign from office to
offer themselves as candidates for governor.

Dependent upon patronage though the Hispanic-American
may be, his interest in the governorship goes beyond the need of
a job. The governor, more than any other individual in the state,
determines educational policy, social security benefits and the
enforcement of anti-discrimination legislation. For reasons
pointed out in Chapters IV, V and XIII, each of these matters is
of peculiar importance to the Hispanic population. Such facts,
says Joaquin Ortega,[1] help to explain why at every election the
Spanish-Americans have attempted to place one of their own number in the governor's chair. In every election which has occurred
since United States Senator Dennis Chavez became a power in New
Mexico politics, he has recognized this goal. The hope of
placing an Hispanic-American governor in office periodically is
expressed in the Spanish-language press.

The peculiar importance of the governor's office makes
necessary an examination of gubernatorial elections. For crucial
political campaigns provide yet another proving ground for inter-
group relations. Men speak frankly when the stakes are high.

A statistical interpretation of each of the 19 state

---

1. Interview, formerly director of the School of Inter-American
   Affairs of the University of New Mexico, July 18, 1949.

elections is beyond the scope of this study, which has for its
goal the painting of an entire landscape rather than a single
detail. Therefore, in an effort to picture Anglo-Hispano relations in gubernatorial elections, general comment will be offered
on five such elections. Then a somewhat detailed analysis of
both a recent primary and a general election will be given.

Early Gubernatorial Elections

One gains better understanding of gubernatorial elections during the first decade of statehood if he bears in mind
certain aspects of the constitutional convention of 1910.[1] Of
particular importance were stringent provisions incorporated in
the constitution for the protection of Spanish-American citizens.
As noted in the cited chapter, those provisos had been included
at the request of the Spanish-speaking delegates but with the full
support of the party bosses, among them Solomon Luna. Another
powerful Hispanic-American political figure, although not a member of the convention, wielded tremendous influence. Because
Octaviano Ambrosio Larrazolo later became a leading gubernatorial
candidate, his convention activities must be touched upon here.

An unsuccessful Democratic candidate in several territorial elections, Larrazolo "blamed his defeat on Democratic
defection in so-called Anglo counties, where ordinarily his party
rolled up heavy majorities."[2] Apparently he came to the convention somewhat suspiciously inclined toward Anglo-Americans in
general, for he insisted that the famous protective clauses be

---

1. Cf. Chapter XI.
2. Paul A. F. Walter, "Octaviano Ambrosio Larrazolo," p. 101.

inserted in the constitution. Larrazolo's interest in securing
the rights of the Hispanic-American population caused him to
campaign for the adoption of the constitution, even though the
Democratic party as a whole was opposed to ratification. Eventually the constitutional issue caused him to repudiate the party
of which he had long been a member.

> So dominated was Larrazolo by this race sep-
> aratist idea that he left the Democratic party which had
> thrice honored him by nominating him for congress, and
> espoused the opposition party on the plea that "the
> Democratic party had manifested a decidedly unfriendly
> feeling and disposition toward the Spanish-American
> element in New Mexico to which he belonged."[1]

Larrazolo's campaign had repercussions in the first
state election (1911). Where there was a choice between Spanish-
American and Anglo-American candidates, the Anglo won, regardless
of party affiliation.[2] Examination of the first election returns
leads one to believe that the candidates' cultural affiliations
were of greater consequence than their political affiliations.
This was especially true in eastern New Mexico, where opposition
to the constitutional protection of Spanish-Americans was most
unpopular, and where Larrazolo's tactics had aroused the greatest
antagonism.

The Democrats had placed their Anglo candidate in the
governor's chair in the first state election. In 1916 they nominated a Spanish-speaking gubernatorial candidate and named the
incumbent governor as their candidate for the lieutenant governorship. Immediately the Democratic politicians were accused of an
ulterior motive. Naming De Baca as the Democratic standard

---

1. Ibid., p. 98.
2. Blue Book of New Mexico (1913), p. 96 ff.

bearer was not a concession to the Spanish-speaking element in
the party, said the critics. Rather, it was an effort to perpetuate the tenure of the incumbent governor, McDonald. For De
Baca was very ill when he was nominated, and it was believed
that he did not have long to live. For that reason it was thought
that the Anglo lieutenant governor would succeed the Hispano
governor before his term was out.[1]

The reverses which Hispanic-American candidates received
in the election of 1912 had aroused Larrazolo to an even more
fervent espousal of the Hispano cause. He attempted to secure
the nomination of a Spanish-speaking gubernatorial candidate on
the Republican ticket. That failing, his devotion to the Hispanic
cause led him to support the Democratic nominee, De Baca, even
though he had repudiated that party in no uncertain terms.
Larrazolo, one of the most brilliant orators in the history of
New Mexico, campaigned for De Baca in the northern counties.
Generally he is given considerable credit for the De Baca victory.[2]

The Hispanic-Americans' satisfaction at having one of
their number in the governor's office was short lived, for the
alleged dream of certain Anglo politicians became reality. De
Baca won the election, but he spent the next seven weeks in a
hospital and died there without occupying the governor's chair.[3]
Gubernatorial authority passed to the Republican Anglo lieutenant
governor. Once again Larrazolo felt cheated of the prize he
coveted for his people.

---

1. Jonathan R. Cunningham, Bronson Cutting, pp. 54-5.
2. Paul A. F. Walter, op. cit., p. 102.
3. J. E. Medina, "Comentarios Rapidos," El Nuevo Mexicano, June
   18, 1950.

The gubernatorial election of 1918 presented the
champion of the Hispanic-Americans with his great opportunity.
Larrazolo was regarded by some of his fellow Republicans as a
political turncoat, and others found his racism very distasteful.
It was the powerful support of the native counties and a _faux_
pas of the Democrats which secured Larrazolo's nomination as
Republican candidate for governor.

It will be remembered from Chapter XI   that one of the
delegates to the state Democratic convention of 1918 directly insulted his would-be Spanish interpreter and indirectly insulted
the "native" people of New Mexico. Although the convention
attempted to rectify the mistake by nominating an Hispanic-American
candidate for governor, the damage had been done. The Republicans
promptly named Larrazolo as their gubernatorial candidate and
throughout the campaign posed as the champion of the Hispanic
population. Cultural differences furnished an issue which
Larrazolo had made much of in previous campaigns; now he exploited
it to the full.

In 1918, Larrazolo became the second governor of Hispanic
descent in the period of statehood. But again a victory of the
Spanish-speaking element was robbed of its full worth, as far as
the new governor himself was concerned. For his victory had been
won in competition with another Hispano--not an Anglo.

Moreover, in winning the gubernatorial race, Larrazolo
did not emerge as undisputed leader in the Republican party. Far
from it. He had introduced a divisive element, and many of the
leading party chieftains feared that the Republicans would split
on the "race" issue.

The element of dissatisfaction was subtle in organization, and if carried to its logical conclusion, threatened the very existence of the party.

> This was the Larrazolo native-son propaganda which had been most industriously disseminated for more than a year in certain northern counties. . . .When the time came for putting into effect the doctrine which he had industriously preached, the results were most unwelcome to the Republicans, even to the chief apostle of racial preference, for, put into practice, it had proved a two-edged sword. . . .[1]

That his espousal of the Hispano "cause" was a two-edged sword was proved as the 1920 gubernatorial elections approached. Larrazolo aspired to re-election. But some of the party chieftains determined to prevent his nomination at the convention. This they accomplished by launching a fight against the governor in the county conventions, which were inclined to instruct their delegates for the Spanish-American leader. By obtaining uninstructed delegations, those Republican leaders opposed to Larrazolo successfully blocked a move for his re-nomination.

Some of the charges made against Larrazolo sounded like accusations long made by the Hispanic-American leader himself. This time it was the Anglos who cried racial prejudice. They accused the governor of discriminating against Anglo-Americans in making political appointments. Larrazolo bitterly denied the charges, and indicated that it was the progressive legislation which he sponsored that had brought down the wrath of the Old Guard.[2]

---

1. Ralph E. Twitchell, Leading Facts of New Mexican History (V), pp. 415-17, as quoted by Paul A. F. Walter, op. cit., p. 98.
2. Jonathan R. Cunningham, op. cit., pp. 88-9.

Nevertheless, the party convention denied Larrazolo the gubernatorial nomination in 1920, a fact which further heightened his belief that he had been the victim of Anglo-American hostility. Despite the fact that the Republican party nominated him for a seat on the state supreme court in 1924 and despite his election to the United States Senate in 1928, Larrazolo remained the outspoken champion of the Hispanic-Americans of New Mexico. Until his death in 1930 his influence was felt in each gubernatorial election.

The Second Decade, 1920-30

Gubernatorial elections in the years between World War I and the Great Depression were marked by bitter campaigns in which Anglo-Hispano differences again revealed themselves. Most noteworthy were the elections of 1926, 1928 and 1930, all of which involved cultural differences arising from conflict over the Hannett Election Code.

The proposed reform, which bore the name of the sponsoring Democratic governor, has been considered elsewhere in this study.[1] Here it is sufficient to call attention to the fact that Spanish-American sentiment was aroused by the proviso that election officials could not accompany voters into booths. Since Hispanic-Americans were aligned solidly against the bill and since Anglo-Americans, for the most part, favored it, the gubernatorial campaign of 1926 centered around the proposed election reform. Governor Hannett, re-nominated by the Democrats, campaigned actively and vigorously defended the code. His Republican oppo-

---

1. Cf. Chapter XI.

nent, Dillon, had the backing of the eloquent Larrazolo, who constantly hammered home the alleged injustice which would be done the Spanish-American people if Hannett were re-elected and his code adopted. "In the last days of the campaign, the racial, religious and Klan issues were played up by both sides. In the final week, the accusations that were hurled at each other by the Democrats and Republicans were without precedent in New Mexico political campaign history."[1]

Governor Hannett not only was hampered by the election code which bore his name, but also by the tactics of one of his most important supporters. This was Carl Magee, editor of the Scripps-Howard paper in Albuquerque, and long a stormy petrel in New Mexico politics. Magee already had brought down the wrath of the Spanish-Americans through the contents of an editorial he had written when he was being sued for libel in 1923. When the jury for the trial was drawn, Magee wrote an editorial complaining that eleven of the twelve jurors were Republicans, and that one was a member of the fanatical religious cult, the Penitentes. Furthermore, he charged that all jurors were Spanish-speaking and therefore unfit to make a decision in his case.[2]

In the 1926 gubernatorial election, Magee, still a power in politics, went further. In supporting Governor Hannett's election code, Magee contended "that the Spanish-Americans as a class were illiterate, incapable of understanding the English language, unfamiliar with democratic traditions, and incapable of

1. Vorley M. Rexroad, The Two Administrations of Governor Richard C. Dillon, p. 55.
2. Santa Fe New Mexican, June 20, 1923.

governing themselves."[1]

Governor Hannett received a crushing defeat in the general election of 1926. The election returns indicate that the Republicans were successful in mobilizing Spanish-American voters against the sponsor of the election code. The Democratic gubernatorial candidate received his worst setback in the "native" section. And as John C. Russell points out, Hannett received fewer votes in the Spanish-American counties of Rio Arriba, Sandoval, Santa Fe, Mora and San Miguel than he had polled in 1924.[2] The line between Anglo and Hispano never had been more sharply etched in a gubernatorial election.

The animosity engendered by the struggle over the election code plagued ensuing gubernatorial candidates. The New Mexico Democratic convention of 1928 was rent by dissension between the Anglo and the Hispano delegates. The latter charged the former with race prejudice and held a rump convention. Surface harmony was restored after a compromise was worked out. The Democrats waged a vigorous campaign, and a concerted effort was made to capture the Spanish-American vote by appealing to their Catholicism. Al Smith was the Democratic candidate for President, therefore the devout Hispano was urged to cast his ballot for the entire Democratic ticket.[3] But again the Republicans accused the Democratic party of being the sponsor of "race" legislation and an enemy of the Hispanic people. Again the Republicans succeeded in placing their candidate in the governor's mansion.

But poetic justice was meted out to the Republican

---

1. Jonathan R. Cunningham, Bronson Cutting, p. 125.
2. State Regionalism in New Mexico, p. 186.
3. Jonathan R. Cunningham, op. cit., p. 152.

party in the gubernatorial election of 1930. The Grand Old
Party chose C. H. Botts as its standard bearer. Judge Botts
appeared to be an admirable choice, one who would guarantee
victory. His was a distinguished legal career which had cul-
minated in election to the supreme court; furthermore, he was
popular in eastern New Mexico, that Democratic stronghold.
Confident that they could swing the Spanish-American vote, as
they had in the past two elections, Republican leaders visualized
another victory.

But Judge Botts had served on Governor Hannett's bi-
partisan committee which had drawn up the ill-fated election
code. That fact damned him in the eyes of many Hispanic-American
voters, and thus contributed to his defeat in the ensuing gubernatorial election. He "was defeated because the Spanish-Americans
swung their votes against him and backed the Democratic nominee."[1]
Comparison of election returns in the Spanish-American counties
for the years 1926, 1928 and 1930 underscores the part played by
the defection of Hispano voters in the 1930 Republican debacle.

The Years of the New Deal and Fair Deal

The decade between the great depression and the outbreak
of World War II brought great changes to New Mexico politics.
The population of the state became more Anglo as the result of
migration from Texas and Oklahoma. New Mexico became a one-party
state, as the Republicans were almost completely submerged. The
New Deal policy of the Roosevelt administration, especially the
dispensation of relief, won the allegiance of many disadvantaged

---

1. John C. Russell, op. cit., p. 137.

persons who previously had voted Republican. This accounted for
the defection of a large part of the Spanish-American vote, which
previously had been overwhelmingly Republican. "In the eight
elections of state officers between 1911 and 1929 no predominantly
Hispano county could be classified as Democratic."[1] In 1930 and
1932, most of the native counties went Democratic. "Since 1934
the Republican party has done little better than break even in
the counties where they had previously gained their winning
majorities."[2]

  The decade 1930-1940 saw the death of two of the out-
standing political leaders of New Mexico, leaders whose power
was derived from their influence over the Spanish-American voter.
O. A. Larrazolo died in 1930, Bronson Cutting in 1935. The
mantle of leadership descended to a Democratic leader, Dennis
Chavez. Since that time, Senator Chavez has been the acknowledged
champion of the Hispanic people; not one state election has
occurred in recent years in which "Los Chavez" (the Senator; his
son and administrative assistant, Dennis Chavez, Jr.; and his
brother, Federal Judge David Chavez) have not been active. And
since that time not one election has occurred in which Anglo-
Hispano differences have not been an issue, as the following
editorial comment from leading newspapers indicates.

Tucumcari Daily News

  Every time there is an election year in New
Mexico, Senator Dennis Chavez seems to delight in stirring
up racial intolerance.

  We would like to be a supporter of Sen. Chavez
because he COULD be a great asset in the halls of Congress

---

1. Charles B. Judah, The Republican Party in New Mexico, p. 12.
2. Ibid., p. 13.

because of his background. But his actions make such
a stand for racial intolerance--or intolerance of any
kind, be it racial, religious, or social.[1]

Carlsbad Current-Argus

Senator Dennis Chavez, as usual, has injected
the racial issue into the New Mexico political campaign.
And, as usual, he does this by declaring that someone
else has brought up the issue.[2]

Clovis News Journal

It is a strange thing that the senator always
seems to find some way of getting the (race) issue into
every political campaign whether he is running or not.
If he is a true champion of his people in the fight for
understanding and equality, he would be the last one to
bring this up.. . .The things that the senator is doing,
bringing the racial issue into every campaign, is doing
more to harm his people than anything could.[3]

Springer Tribune

I hope we can see the day when we can have a
political campaign without the injection of the racial
issue. But it seems apparent that the millenium is not
going to arrive so long as Senator Chavez is in the
political picture.

While decrying intolerance, in each and every
campaign during recent years, the Albuquerque solon has
brought in the race issue in one manner or another.. . .[4]

The Chavez forces made repeated efforts to secure the

election of a Spanish-American governor. As each election

approached, Hispanos were reminded that in the entire period of

statehood only two Hispanic-Americans had been elected governor

and that only one of these actually had served. And as each

election approached, Senator Chavez or one of his supporters re-

minded the Hispano that this was their last chance to secure

political equality by electing a Spanish-speaking gubernatorial

1. Quoted, Albuquerque Journal, June 7, 1948.
2. Quoted, Albuquerque Journal, May 31, 1948.
3. Quoted, Albuquerque Journal, June 3, 1948.
4. Quoted, Albuquerque Journal, June 2, 1948.

candidate. Thus in 1942 Chavez bitterly attacked the gubernatorial candidacy of John J. Dempsey. The senator made "a
direct appeal to racial prejudices charging that the Spanish-
speaking voters were about to lose their only chance for
representation in government."[1] He stressed the same theme,
although in a slightly different manner, when he sought re-
election to the Senate in 1946. His campaign

> . . .was aided quite materially by his pointing out to
> the native population that they no longer elected
> governors to office and that to repudiate his leader-
> ship at the polls would be to toll the death knell of
> the last great champion of the Spanish-speaking popula-
> tion. Senator Chavez successfully appeals to the native
> voter in continuing his position of dominance in New
> Mexico politics.[2]

Senator Chavez' subsequent activities belied his
publicly stated belief that the Spanish-speaking people no longer
could elect a governor. As early as 1948, he determined to per-
suade his brother, U. S. Judge David Chavez, to run for governor
in the 1950 election. Accordingly, he sent thousands of letters
to his constituency urging them to support Spanish-American
candidates in the 1948 election in preparation for the 1950 gubernatorial candidacy of David Chavez. An extract from the form
letter indicates the nature of the appeal:

> It is always said that a Spanish-American can-
> not be elected governor or land commissioner in New Mex-
> ico. Let us demonstrate that it is possible to elect
> Joe Gallegos. This office is second in importance to
> that of the governor. If we are successful, I am sure
> that we will be able to elect a Spanish-American as
> governor in two years.[3]

---

1. Walter L. McNutt, An Inquiry into the Operation of the Primary
   System of New Mexico, p. 45.
2. Ibid., p. 51.
3. Albuquerque Journal, June 4, 1948.

Anglo-Hispano Differences in the 1948 Campaign

The 1948 primary and general elections offer an excellent opportunity for a study of Anglo-Hispano political relationships. In the primary campaign, Senator Chavez, acknowledged leader of the Spanish-Americans of New Mexico, was especially active. In both the Democratic and the Republican primaries, Hispano gubernatorial candidates were pitted against Anglo candidates for the governorship. In the general election, an Hispano gubernatorial candidate opposed an Anglo gubernatorial candidate, while a similar situation existed in the lieutenant governor's race. Moreover, the resurgence of the Republican party at the national level gave the moribund party in New Mexico a political "shot in the arm," so that the Democrats and the Republicans were on more equal footing than at any time since 1930.

The incumbent Democratic governor, Thomas J. Mabry, early announced his intention of seeking reelection. He had been elected with Chavez' support, and had worked closely with the senator during his term of office. In fact, sometimes he had been accused of allowing Chavez to dictate appointments and influence policy. According to one of the leading political commentators of the state, "Chavez reportedly named more than half of the Democrats who received lush appointments from Mabry."[1]

Senator Chavez did not oppose Mabry's re-election, but he did interest himself in the candidacies of several Spanish-Americans, including his brother-in-law. As previously indicated,

---

1. Joe M. Clark, "Capitol Slant," Albuquerque Journal, September 24, 1948.

the senator acknowledged that his support of Spanish-speaking
candidates in the 1948 election was an attempt to lay the basis
for his brother's candidacy in the 1950 gubernatorial election.

In May, 1948, Senator Chavez threw a bombshell into the
Democratic ranks when he sent a telegram to Governor Mabry accusing
him of opposing two Democratic candidates for "racial" reasons.
The candidates in question were Gilbert Espinosa, who was offering
himself for state supreme court justice and J. O. Gallegos,
candidate for land commissioner. Senator Chavez telegraphed that
he was "very much disturbed about information that the state
administration is exerting pressure against Gallegos and Espinosa
on ground that these positions should not be filled by native New
Mexicans of Spanish extraction."[1] When he sent his telegram,
Chavez indicated that he would keep the racial issue in the foreground of the campaign, and threatened to come to New Mexico and
participate in the campaign if he did not receive a satisfactory
reply.

The governor's denial of the charge was as complete as
it was prompt.

> I think I need not remind you or any other
> citizen of this state where I have lived for 41 years
> enjoying the respect of our people regardless of racial
> heritage, that I have no prejudice against any man or
> woman because they are of Spanish extraction. I have
> been accused of showing too much favor to our friends
> of that extraction, but never of unfairly opposing them
> for that reason.[2]

Surface harmony was restored when Senator Chavez accepted
the governor's disclaimer. But Anglo-Hispano differences had been

---

1. Albuquerque Journal, May 26, 1948.
2. Loc. cit.

thrown into such sharp relief that they were not to be erased during the primary campaign or the gubernatorial campaign which preceded the general election. In fact, it seemed apparent that Senator Chavez did not intend for the "race" issue to be forgotten. The day after he dropped his bombshell in the governor's office, he mailed 20,000 letters, most of them in Spanish, to his constituency.[1] In the circular letters, Chavez listed his own slate of candidates for several positions on the state ticket. According to newspaper reports, the senator suggested that nine Spanish-Americans be nominated on the thirteen-candidate state ticket.[2]

> At the very moment he was accusing the Governor of anti-Spanish discrimination, Chavez himself was trying to load the Democratic ticket. And that was the considered opinion of scores of Spanish-Americans themselves, many of whom have supported Chavez loyally in the past.
>
> They felt that Chavez' resumption of beating the old "racial discrimination" drum could only harm the party.[3]

Reaction to the Chavez telegram and letters was swift. A rash of editorials, almost all of them condemning the senator, appeared in the newspapers of the state. Congressman A. M. Fernandez, himself a candidate for renomination on the Democratic ticket, hit strongly at Chavez in a state-wide radio broadcast. "Letters in Spanish have been circulated in this campaign, not by candidates but by others, appealing to class sectionalism based on lineage of ancestry and which tend to drive a wedge between the two groups of people who compose the citizenry of our state," the Congressman declared.[4] He then proceeded to

---

1. Pat Monroe, Albuquerque Journal, May 30, 1948.
2. Joe Clark, "Capitol Slant," Albuquerque Journal, May 30, 1948.
3. Loc. cit.
4. Albuquerque Journal, June 4, 1948.

castigate his fellow Hispano, Chavez, although he did not refer
to him by name.

But letter writing was not confined to the Hispanic-
American camp of "Los Chavez." United States Senator Hatch, in
an election speech deploring the injection of the "racial" issue,
first condemned the Chavez circular letter. The Anglo senator
then indicated that an equally vicious missive had come from
opposing Anglo quarters. Hatch said that while in Clovis he was
handed an anonymous letter "which tried to poison the minds of
Democrats in eastern New Mexico against Clinton Anderson and
Governor Mabry by aligning them with honest reputable Spanish-
American citizens and at the same time aligning the opponents
of Mabry and Anderson with a complete slate of candidates of
Anglo names."[1]

Although an Hispanic-American gubernatorial candidate
had entered the Democratic primary, Senator Chavez did not give
him support. In fact, it is probable that the Chavez telegram
to the governor and the form letters he sent out weakened the
candidacy of Ralph Gallegos, candidate for governor. According
to Bryan Johnson, chairman of the state Democratic committee and
close associate of Chavez, the major Anglo contender, Governor
Mabry, benefited from the Chavez blast. "Its effect was to
antagonize the Anglos and shift some of their vote to Mabry as
well as antagonize some Hispanos who don't like to see the race
issue resurrected every election year as Chavez is prone to do."[2]

At all events, the Hispanic-American gubernatorial

---

1. Clovis News Journal, June 8, 1948.
2. Interview, Albuquerque, October 20, 1948 (Through William
   Cunningham).

candidate was snowed under in the Democratic primary of June
8, 1948. The final count gave Mabry 41,991 votes, his Anglo
rival 16,201 and his Hispano rival 12,478.[1] As indicated in
the quotation above, "racial" antagonism may have played some
part in the Hispano's defeat. But the election returns show
that Mabry carried every county in the state, and that he had a
two-to-one lead over his Hispanic rival in all of the "native"
counties but two. Even in the latter two, Taos and Socorro, his
majority was substantial.[2] Governor Mabry had the support of a
powerful state machine and his victory may be attributed to that
fact.

The Republican Primary

Nineteen hundred forty-eight seemed a propitious year
for the Republicans of New Mexico. A resurgence of party strength
had given the Republicans control of the United States House of
Representatives; the Senate seemed destined to follow suit; and
public opinion polls had announced that Dewey would be the next
President. The prospect of patronage quickened the party pulse
in New Mexico, and disheartened politicians forgot their pronouncements of Republican doom and became active.

The announcement that Patrick Hurley, once member of
Hoover's cabinet and later ambassador under Truman, would run for
the United States Senate offered a real challenge to the Democrats.
And when Manuel Lujan, long the popular mayor of Santa Fe,
announced his gubernatorial candidacy, the Republican slate was
strengthened further.

---

1. State of New Mexico, Official Returns of the 1948 Elections, p.
   238.
2. Loc. cit.

In the ensuing primary, the Hispanic tinge of the Republican party became evident. Ten counties predominantly Hispano in population cast 54 per cent of the total vote. In other words, despite the transfer of large numbers of "native" voters to the Democratic party, the stronghold of the Republican party still was in Santa Fe, Rio Arriba, San Miguel, Valencia, Taos, Sandoval, Mora, Guadalupe, Torrance and Socorro counties.[1]

The influence of the Hispanic-American vote was evident in yet another phase of the gubernatorial race. Manuel Lujan had two major rivals, one Anglo, one Hispano. The vote of the three major candidates totaled 23,596, of which the two Hispanic-Americans received 91 per cent.[2] The political commentator, Will Harrison, after calling attention to the fact that the Anglo candidate was equally as prominent as either of his Hispano rivals, concluded that the gubernatorial primary showed the strong pull of cultural affiliation.[3]

It should be borne in mind, however, that the major Hispano gubernatorial candidate, Lujan, carried five of the seven most Anglo counties of New Mexico, tied his Anglo opponent in another Anglo county and lost to him in only one of the seven.[4] Lest too much importance be read into this comparison, it should be noted that in no Anglo county did the total Republican vote reach 500. On the other hand, in none of the "native" counties did the total fall as low as 500.[5]

---

1. Will Harrison, "At the Capitol," Santa Fe New Mexican, April 26, 1950.
2. Loc. cit.
3. Loc. cit.
4. Official Returns of the 1948 Elections, op. cit., p. 238.
5. Loc. cit.

The 1948 Democratic and Republican Campaigns

The defeat of the Chavez-sponsored candidates in the Democratic primary election had repercussions in the Lujan-Mabry gubernatorial campaign. J. O. Gallegos, co-chairman of Mabry's successful campaign in 1946 and long a power in New Mexico politics, swung his support to the Republican nominee, Lujan. Presumably his desertion of the Democratic fold was due to his defeat in the primary,[1] a defeat he attributed to prejudice against his Spanish ancestry.

The state Democratic organization minimized the split brought about by Gallegos, and likewise the hostility of Senator Chavez. The chairman of the state committee predicted that Gallegos would be regarded as a sorehead who left the party because he was defeated. Such opposition was somewhat meaningless, "since most Hispanos are likely to support Lujan anyway. Democratic Hispanos will split their ticket practically straight down the line. However, they won't be able to push Lujan into office because the East Side will go Democratic in the governor's race against him. The Chavez letter was the cause of this situation."[2]

In some quarters, it was expected that Senator Chavez would himself bolt the party and throw his support to the GOP Spanish-American gubernatorial candidate. The state chairman minimized this possibility, however. Instead, he predicted that the senator would remain in the party, even though he might state that he was supporting Lujan over Mabry. The chairman then pointed out that the effect of such a pronouncement would "be similar to

---

1. Clovis News-Journal, September 19, 1948.
2. Interview, Bryan Johnson, Albuquerque, October 20, 1948 (Through William Cunningham).

that of the letter, only more so. Anglos who followed Chavez
would rebel and come out strongly for Mabry, while Hispano support
would shift to Chavez and Lujan."[1] Senator Chavez never made the
expected pronouncement. However, throughout the campaign he was
accused of giving important, though under-cover, support to
Manuel Lujan, Republican nominee.[2]

Despite the fact that Republican party organization was
almost non-existent in many southern and eastern counties, the
GOP gubernatorial candidate, Lujan, did extensive campaigning in
those sections. He invaded his opponent's home territory when he
made a whirlwind tour of eastern New Mexico, pleading for "Return
of honesty rule" and "Return to old idealism," to quote newspaper
headlines.[3] In an area which was almost 100 per cent Anglo and
Democratic the Hispano GOP candidate made a good impression, if
one may judge from newspaper accounts of his speeches. In re-
porting his tour of Roosevelt county, one commentator wrote that
"Deep in the heart of 'Little Texas' this county has shown little
warmth toward most candidates of Latin descent. Yet, Lujan is
known to have made potentially valuable political contacts in
Portales on his several previous visits there."[4]

Although the commentator in question prophesied that
Lujan might cut the expected heavy Democratic majority in eastern
New Mexico, such was not the prediction of most political forecasters. For Republican hopes for victory were pinned on a large
turnout in the "native" counties and Democratic apathy in the

1. Loc. cit.
2. Interview, Bryan Johnson, Albuquerque, Dec. 27, 1949.
3. Clovis News-Journal, Sept. 26-27, 1948.
4. Joe M. Clark, "Capitol Slant," Albuquerque Journal, September 26, 1948.

southern counties. The presence of an Hispano GOP gubernatorial candidate on the ticket was expected to help the Anglo senatorial candidate in those counties where Hispanic-Americans predominated.[1] To what extent Democratic and Republican predictions came true may be determined by an examination of the returns of the general election of November 2, 1948.

Evaluation of the Election Returns

Evaluation of returns in the gubernatorial election of 1948 presents an opportunity to appraise possible Anglo-Hispano differences as revealed in voting. A popular Hispano Republican candidate competed with a popular Anglo Democratic candidate in the race for governor. A well-known Anglo Republican competed with a well-known Hispano Democrat for the position of lieutenant governor. This unusual set of political circumstances makes it possible to cross check and thus prevent a hasty assumption that cultural differences, rather than party affiliations, influenced voting.

Brief examination of Table XI underlines the fact that the Anglo Democratic gubernatorial candidate carried each of the seven most Anglo counties by decisive and sometimes overwhelming majorities. And equally obvious is the fact that the Hispano Republican gubernatorial nominee carried each of the seven most Hispanic counties by decisive majorities. To ascribe this phenomenon to Anglo-Hispano differences would be a hasty assumption, however. Several Anglo Republican candidates for other state offices carried Hispano counties, notably Mora and Socorro,

---

1. R. L. Chambers, "Capitol Views," Belen News-Bulletin, October 29, 1948.

TABLE XI

Standing of Anglo Democratic and Hispano Republican

Gubernatorial Candidates

General Election, 1948

A. **Counties with Greatest Concentration of Hispanic-Americans**

County	Lujan	Mabry	Advantage or Disadvantage of Hispanic Candidate
Guadalupe	1715	1401	# 314
Mora	2144	1309	# 835
Rio Arriba	5216	3901	#1315
Sandoval	1899	1703	# 196
San Miguel	5394	4365	#1029
Socorro	2276	1570	# 706
Taos	3519	2349	#1170

B. **Counties with Greatest Concentration of Anglo-Americans**

County	Lujan	Mabry	Advantage or Disadvantage of Hispanic Candidate
Chaves	2851	5040	-2189
Curry	1794	6303	-4509
De Baca	477	690	- 213
Lea	1209	4849	-3640
Quay	1419	3140	-1721
Roosevelt	770	3445	-2675
Union	1143	1774	- 631

Source of Data: State of New Mexico, Official Returns of the 1948 Elections, p. 10.

TABLE XII

Standing of Hispano Republican Candidate for Governor
and Anglo Republican Candidate for Lieutenant Governor
General Election, 1948

A. Counties with Greatest Concentration of Hispanic-Americans

County	Lujan	Hendrix	Advantage or Disadvantage of Hispanic Candidate
Guadalupe	1715	1533	# 182
Mora	2144	1863	# 281
Rio Arriba	5216	4124	#1092
Sandoval	1899	1526	# 373
San Miguel	5394	4394	#1000
Socorro	2276	2105	# 171
Taos	3519	2761	# 761

B. Counties with Greatest Concentration of Anglo-Americans

County	Lujan	Hendrix	Advantage or Disadvantage of Hispanic Candidate
Chaves	2851	3031	-180
Curry	1794	1868	- 74
De Baca	477	445	# 32
Lea	1209	1103	#106
Quay	1419	1254	#165
Roosevelt	770	846	- 76
Union	1143	1192	- 49

Source of Data: State of New Mexico, Official Returns of the
1948 Elections, p. 10.

TABLE XIII

Standing of Anglo Democratic Candidate for Governor

and Hispano Democratic Candidate for Lieutenant Governor

General Election, 1948

A. Counties with Greatest Concentration of Hispanic-Americans

County	Mabry	Montoya	Advantage or Disadvantage of Hispanic Candidate
Guadalupe	1401	1574	# 173
Mora	1309	1579	# 270
Rio Arriba	3901	4957	#1056
Sandoval	1703	2054	# 351
San Miguel	4365	5248	# 883
Socorro	1570	1704	# 134
Taos	2349	3061	# 712

B. Counties with Greatest Concentration of Anglo-Americans

County	Mabry	Montoya	Advantage or Disadvantage of Hispanic Candidate
Chaves	5040	4649	-571
Curry	6303	6010	-293
De Baca	690	695	# 5
Lea	4849	4828	- 21
Quay	3140	3224	# 84
Roosevelt	3445	3249	-196
Union	1774	1666	-108

Source of Data: State of New Mexico, Official Returns of the
1948 Elections, p. 10.

although no Anglo candidate carried all of the seven. It would
be possible to assume that Lujan, the Republican candidate,
carried each of the seven most Hispanic counties because those
counties have a tradition of Republicanism, and because the GOP
organization is strong in those sections of New Mexico.

It would be equally safe to attribute the Anglo candidate's showing in the seven most Anglo counties to the unbroken
sway of the Democratic party in those counties, and to the support
of a powerful political machine, long entrenched in office.

But the election returns offer proof that many Hispanic-
American Democrats crossed the party line to vote for the Hispano
GOP gubernatorial candidate. To be explicit: analysis of the
returns for each of the eleven state offices indicates that five
of the seven Hispano counties (Guadalupe, Rio Arriba, Sandoval,
San Miguel and Taos) definitely should be classified as Democratic.[1] Yet the Hispano gubernatorial candidate carried each
of these five Democratic counties by a sizeable majority. The
inference is that group affiliation, rather than party affiliation, was the determining factor.

But other comparisons provide a check on Anglo-Hispano
differences as revealed in voting in the 1948 gubernatorial election. Thus purely partisan considerations are ruled out in large
degree by comparing the showing made by the GOP Hispano gubernatorial candidate with the vote cast for the GOP Anglo candidate
for lieutenant governor. (Table XII). As a further check, a
similar comparison may be drawn between the votes cast for the
Anglo gubernatorial candidate and the Democratic Hispano candidate

---

1. State of New Mexico, Official Returns of the 1948 Elections,
   pp. 10-12.

for lieutenant governor. (Table XIII). In each case, the party
organization officially provided equal support to both Anglo and
Hispano; in each case, purely partisan considerations led voters
to cast ballots for Hispano and Anglo alike; a persistent difference between the vote received by Anglo candidate for governor
and Hispano candidate for lieutenant governor therefore may be
ascribed to non-political factors; if Anglo consistently led
Hispano in Anglo counties and Hispano led Anglo in Hispano counties,
the non-political factor may be identifiable as ethnic in nature.
By checking the comparison within the Democratic party and that
within the Republican party a somewhat valid conclusion may be
drawn.

In Table   XII, the vote cast for the Hispano Republican
candidate for governor in the seven most Anglo counties of New
Mexico and the seven most Hispano counties has been placed in
juxtaposition with that cast for the Anglo candidate for lieutenant
governor in the same counties. In the seven most Anglo counties,
the difference between the two tabulations is slight. The fact
that the Hispanic-American candidate actually led his Anglo running
mate in three of the seven counties is noteworthy and would indicate that Anglo-Hispano differences scarcely influenced the
voting.

On the other hand, differences in the tabulation in the
seven Hispanic counties were marked. In several counties, the
margin between the Hispano gubernatorial candidate and his Anglo
running mate approached the difference between the Hispano Republican and Anglo Democrat gubernatorial candidates. However, before suggesting an ethnic explanation for this difference, a

comparison of the equivalent Democratic candidates is in order.

Table XIII indicates that the Anglo gubernatorial candidate led his Hispano running mate in five of the seven most Anglo counties, but in only one instance was the lead substantial. In each of the seven most Hispanic counties the Hispano candidate led his Anglo running mate, in most cases by a substantial margin.

The fact that Anglo and Hispano candidates of both parties made essentially the same showing in the seven counties having the highest concentration of Anglo-Americans leads to the belief that party affiliation was more important than group affiliation in determining the outcome of the gubernatorial elections. On the other hand, the fact that Hispano candidates of both parties had substantial margins over their Anglo running mates in the seven counties having the highest concentration of Hispanic-Americans leads to the conclusion that group differences influenced the voting.

This assumption finds support in other details of the election. Perhaps most important is the fact that even though the Democratic gubernatorial candidate, an Anglo, failed to carry any of the seven most Hispano counties, his Hispano running mate carried five of the seven Hispano counties, as well as the seven most Anglo counties. It was plain that Hispanic-American Republicans split the ticket to vote for a Democratic Hispano. Examination of the third columns of Tables XII and XIII reinforces the statement. In each instance, Section A shows the margin between Anglo and Hispano candidates in the Hispanic counties. A striking balance will be noted. It becomes apparent that Republican voters who cast a ballot for Lujan, but not for Hendrix, voted for the

Democratic Hispano instead.

Judging from the above comparisons, there is a marked tendency for Hispanic-Americans, whether Democratic or Republican, to cross party lines to vote for Hispanic candidates. Data given in the comparative tables above would indicate that Anglo-Americans of both parties are less apt to cross party lines in order to vote for an Anglo candidate.

Summary

When compared with many states, the gubernatorial office in New Mexico is of exceptional importance because of the vast patronage at the governor's disposal. The Hispanic-American's dependence upon state employment causes him to consider the governor as the keystone in state politics. Leaders of the Spanish-speaking people have long urged their supporters to vote for Spanish-American candidates in order to protect their interests.

From the time New Mexico became a state until the present date, gubernatorial elections have brought Anglo-Hispano differences into the foreground. In the early days of statehood, an eloquent Spanish-speaking political leader, Larrazolo, stressed "racial" differences and accused Anglo-Americans of discrimination. Since Larrazolo participated in every state election until 1930, consciousness of group differences became ingrained in state political affairs.

An indiscretion at the Democratic convention of 1918 was interpreted as an insult to the Hispanic-Americans of the state, and group differences became a campaign issue. Espousal of the Spanish-American cause contributed to Larrazolo's re-nomination

as governor in 1920, and further embittered Anglo-Hispano relations. The Hannett election code, which forbade election officials to accompany voters into the voting booth, was interpreted
as anti-Hispano legislation. The proposed code became a campaign
issue in three successive elections and was a factor in the defeat
of candidates favoring the measure.

The period 1930-50 saw the continuance of Anglo-Hispano
recrimination in gubernatorial campaigns. Senator Dennis Chavez,
acknowledged leader of the Spanish-speaking people of New Mexico
and a power in the dominant Democratic party, frequently was
accused of stirring up inter-group differences. The Chavez forces
made repeated efforts to secure the election of a Spanish-American
governor, but without success.

The 1948 gubernatorial election furnishes a suitable
opportunity to study Anglo-Hispano differences as revealed in
voting. In the primary campaign, Senator Chavez was especially
active. In both the Democratic and the Republican primaries,
Hispanic gubernatorial candidates were pitted against Anglo candidates for the governorship. In the general election, an Hispano
gubernatorial candidate opposed an Anglo gubernatorial candidate,
while a comparable situation existed in the lieutenant governor's
race.

In both the Republican and the Democratic primaries
inter-group antagonism was displayed. Senator Chavez' accusations
aroused particular animosity. The Hispanic character of the Republican party was underlined in the primary where ten counties predominantly Hispano in population cast 54 per cent of the total
vote. The defeat of two Chavez-sponsored Hispanic candidates in

the Democratic primary brought a minor split in the party.

Comparative tables based upon returns in the general
election of 1948 indicate that ethnic affiliation was a deter-
minant in voting in the gubernatorial race. Although five of
the seven counties having the highest concentration of Hispanic-
Americans were classified as Democratic, the Hispanic Republican
gubernatorial candidate carried each of the five by a sizeable
majority. On the other hand, his Anglo running mate failed to
carry any of the five counties. Even though the Democratic
gubernatorial candidate, an Anglo, failed to carry any of the
seven most Hispano counties, his Hispanic running mate carried
five of the seven, as well as the seven most Anglo counties.

Election data for 1948 indicate that there is a marked
tendency for Hispanic-Americans to cross party lines to vote for
Hispanic candidates. The data indicate that Anglo-Americans are
less apt to cross party lines in order to vote for an Anglo candidate.

CHAPTER XV
THE ANGLO-HISPANO RATIO IN STATE
AND COUNTY OFFICES

Among politically minded New Mexicans, and especially among those of Spanish descent, it frequently is said that the political influence of the Hispanic-American people has declined steadily since 1910. Some date the decline from 1930, when the Republican party lost its grip on the state government. Others set the date at 1940, when the numerical superiority of the Anglo-American population first became apparent. Yet others draw the line to conform to their own differing explanations for the slump. But in the end, there is basic agreement that the political fortunes of the Spanish-Americans have declined during the period of statehood. The Democratic primary of 1950, in which eight of the nine contested state offices were captured by Anglo candidates,[1] was cited as the final, conclusive proof of the oft-profferred thesis.

Many aspects of Anglo-Hispano political balance have been considered in chapters dealing with party conventions, the controversies arising from direct primary and anti-discrimination legislation, and gubernatorial elections. But the direct approach to the question is to consider the manner in which political power has been shared. If Hispanic-American political influence is

---

1. Santa Fe New Mexican, June 25, 1950.

waning, it will be revealed by a decline in the number of Spanish-
speaking office holders, particularly at the state level. Analysis of the ethnic composition of the executive, legislative and
judicial branches of the state government in the period 1912-1950
therefore is in order.

The "Gentlemen's Agreement"

Editorial comment which followed the defeat of the great
majority of the Spanish-speaking candidates in the 1950 Democratic
primary made frequent reference to the famed "gentlemen's agreement" which had regulated politics in an earlier day. This un-
written political law was somewhat rigidly enforced under the
convention system of 1912-1938. It had two aspects. One rule
was designed to prevent Anglo and Hispano from being pitted against
one another in a race for any office. Thus if the Democrats nominated an Hispanic gubernatorial candidate, the Republican convention followed suit to prevent the dreaded "racial" issue from
arising. The other provision of the "gentlemen's agreement" made
certain state offices the prerogative of Hispanic candidates, with
others being reserved for Anglo candidates.

> In the times of political conventions, what was
> commonly known as a "gentlemen's agreement" was customary
> in both the Republican and the Democratic parties. The
> offices of secretary of state, auditor, a corporation
> commissioner, the lieutenant governor, a Congressman and
> some other post to balance the ticket were conceded to the
> native element.[1]

That this system of "balancing" the ticket between Anglo
and Hispano was recognized by politicians of both culture-groups,

---

1. O. B. Servando, "Dicen Que Se Avecina una Catastrofe Politica
    de Gran Magnitud en N. M.," El Nuevo Mexicano, March 9, 1950.

and that it continued to be more or less binding after the convention system was abandoned for the direct primary was attested in June, 1950, when the defeat of Hispanic candidates in the Democratic primary became known. "It was historic. Never since statehood has either Republican or Democratic party nominated a ticket without balancing between the two predominant races."[1]

Credit for establishing the rule that tickets must be balanced between the two major groups generally is given to O. A. Larrazolo, leader of the Spanish-American people in the first 20 years of statehood. "More than to any other partisan leader it is owing to him that the demand by the Spanish-American group for at least one half of the candidates on the tickets of the two major parties has become a _sine qua non_ in every state campaign."[2] In the period in which Larrazolo dominated politics, he insisted that this rule be followed. Even in the Democratic party, where Spanish-Americans were relatively few in number and Larrazolo was detested, the idea of balancing the ticket prevailed.

During the 1926 state Democratic convention, the _Las Vegas Optic_ reported that "By the time of adjournment for dinner at 6:00 o'clock, it appeared that the Spanish-American delegates were going to cause trouble. They had let it be known from the convention floor that they demanded one-half of the places on the Democratic state ticket."[3] Spanish-American delegates held a protest meeting, and the pressure they brought finally brought concessions from Anglo delegates.

---

1. Will Harrison, "At the Capitol," _Santa Fe New Mexican_, June 7, 1950.
2. Paul A. F. Walter, "Octaviano Ambrosio Larrazolo," p. 97.
3. September 3, 1926.

Two years later, the Democrats again were reminded
of the "gentlemen's agreement." Formation of the state ticket
brought disagreement between Anglo and Hispano delegates. When
the Hispanic-American delegates' demands for six places on the
ticket were not heeded, they again met in closed session. And
again it was necessary to work out a compromise.[1]

A group of Spanish-speaking supporters of Bronson
Cutting organized themselves as the Club Politico Independiente
de Nuevo Mexico. In 1930 they passed a resolution insisting that
both parties give the Spanish-Americans the following places on
the ticket: Congressman, one supreme court justice, lieutenant
governor, state superintendent of public instruction, auditor
and corporation commissioner. Since the club claimed to control
3,000 votes, its pronouncements were highly effective.[2]

The system of balancing the ticket was a political
necessity which operated in the legislative, as well as the executive, branch. Politicians reported that the Anglo-Hispano
alignment in the state senate was due to

> . . .the racial divisions which the party organizations
> made on party tickets. The nomination for the senate is
> usually given to an Anglo; and, if there is a considerable
> Spanish-American element in the constituency, the nomina-
> tion for the House of Representatives is given to a native.
> . . .It has become customary for certain offices to be
> given to Spanish-Americans and for others to be given to
> Anglos.[3]

The abandonment of the convention system of naming candidates did not end the "gentlemen's agreement." On the contrary,

---

1. Vorley M. Rexroad, The Two Administrations of Governor Richard
   C. Dillon, p. 91.
2. Jonathan R. Cunningham, Bronson Cutting, pp. 161-163.
3. John C. Russell, State Regionalism in New Mexico, p. 183.

the necessity of balancing the ticket continued to receive
recognition from politicians. It generally was agreed that
certain offices should be reserved for Hispanic candidates and
other places were to be filled by Anglos. Thus in the period
1940-50, it became a virtual tradition that two of the three
corporation commissioners along with the secretary of state and
the auditor should be Hispanic-Americans.

Concern lest this tradition be broken was expressed
widely as the 1950 Democratic primary approached. Thus the editor
of the Santa Fe New Mexican remarked that "Political observers who
watch the racial balance of the tickets see a possibility of the
Spanish element of the party losing several places in this year's
Democratic nominations."[1] The leading Spanish-language newspaper
carried a lead article in which uneasiness was expressed because
Anglo candidates were seeking posts long reserved for Hispanic-
Americans. "Two Anglo candidates already have announced for the
office of State Auditor.. . . .The same has occurred for the post
of Secretary of State, an office that for many years has been
conceded to a woman of Hispanic ancestry."[2]

One of the most frank and realistic of recent political
figures, Victor Salazar, "second-floor governor" in the Mabry
administration (1946-50), explained the continuing necessity and
procedure for balancing the ticket.

> You have to divide your ticket up racially as
> well as geographically. For example we have an Anglo
> governor, Spanish-speaking lieutenant-governor, Anglo
> land commissioner, Spanish-speaking corporation commis-

1. March 1, 1950.
2. O. B. Servando, "Dicen Que Se Avecina una Catastrofe Politica
   de Gran Magnitud en N. M.," El Nuevo Mexicano, March 9, 1950,
   p. 1.

sioner, and Anglo superintendent of schools. We have one
Anglo and one Spanish-speaking (U. S.) Senator and one
Anglo and one Spanish-speaking Congressman.

You have to see who the officials meet and then
you have to get a man who won't antagonize these people.
For example, since most of the big landowners and oil men
are Anglos, the land commissioner must be an Anglo.[1]

Division of the Spoils

If both Anglo·and Hispano politicians always had abided
by the "gentlemen's agreement," many of the crises already referred
to would not have been precipitated. Nor would preoccupation with
the rise and fall of ethnic fortunes been so marked. For an examination of state election returns during the entire period of
statehood indicates that there never has been an equal division of
political offices.

This is most apparent when one considers the judicial
branch of the government. The Supreme Court of New Mexico represents this category, for the three-member tribunal is the only
judicial body elected by the people of the state. In the 38 years
since New Mexico entered the Union, only one justice of the
supreme court was an Hispanic-American, while 23 were Anglo-
American.[2] Spanish-speaking jurists made strenuous attempts to
secure posts on the bench, notably O. A. Larrazolo in 1924, but
it was not until 1944 that efforts were crowned with success. A
subsequent attempt, made by a Chavez-supported candidate in 1948,
met with crushing failure.[3]

Nine executive officers are elected by the people of

---

1. Interview, Santa Fe, Dec. 29, 1949 (Through Melvin Mencher).
2. State of New Mexico, Blue Books (1913-1949).
3. State of New Mexico, Official Returns of the 1948 Elections.

the state: governor, lieutenant governor, secretary of state,
auditor, treasurer, attorney general, superintendent of public
instruction, land commissioner and corporation commissioner. In
the 19 elections which have been held in the period of statehood,
Anglo gubernatorial candidates have been successful in 17. This
office has become a virtual monopoly of Anglo-American candidates,
since no Spanish-speaking governor has been elected since 1918.[1]

The lieutenant governorship has been more evenly divided
between representatives of the two predominant groups. Twelve
Anglo-Americans have held that office, with seven Hispanic-
Americans appearing on the official roster. The statement that
this post in recent years has been reserved for Hispano candidates
finds little support in election returns. In the last decade, the
office has been occupied by Anglo and Hispano on an almost equal
basis.[2]

Two offices have been held exclusively by representatives
of each of the two great culture-groups. Spanish-American women
have been uniformly successful in capturing the office of secretary
of state, while Anglo-American men have occupied the post of state
treasurer without interruption. The position of state auditor
generally has gone to a Spanish-speaking candidate. Twelve of the
19 state auditors have been Hispano and seven have been Anglo.
The first five auditors were Anglo-American, then an almost unbroken succession of Hispano office holders gave rise to the
popular theory that this position, like that of secretary of state,
was the prerogative of Spanish-speaking candidates.[3]

---

1. Blue Book of New Mexico, (1947-48), pp. 29-31.
   State of New Mexico, Official Returns of the 1948 Elections, pp.
   10-12.
2. Loc. cit.
3. Loc. cit.

The attorney generalship has been captured by Anglo
candidates in 16 of the 19 state elections, while the superintend-
ency of public instruction has gone to an Anglo candidate in all
elections but one. Only two Hispanic-Americans have served as
land commissioner, both of them before 1930. On the other hand,
two of the three members of the corporation commission have been
Hispanic-Americans since that body was established in 1920.[1]

The above survey indicates that Anglo-Americans have
dominated the executive and judicial branches of the state government of New Mexico, as far as their record of elective office-
holding is concerned. Anglo-American preponderance becomes
particularly apparent when one considers that Anglos have enjoyed
a virtual monopoly of the four executive offices which commonly
are considered the most important: governor, commissioner of public lands, superintendent of public instruction and treasurer.

Another approach to the problem of Anglo-Hispano political balance in state government is a tabular comparison of
Hispanic and Anglo candidates who were nominated and elected for
state executive and judicial positions over a period of years.
Such data are given in Table XIV.

Table XIV indicates that the Anglo-Hispano ratio in
elective judicial and executive positions remained fairly constant
in the period under consideration. Statements that there has been
a remarkable decline in Hispano influence, as expressed in the
number of state offices held, find no support in these statistics.
At no time did Hispanic-Americans constitute more than half of
all successful aspirants for state executive and judicial office;

---

1. Loc. cit.

TABLE XIV

Nominations and Elections in State Government,

1916-1948

Year	Elective Offices	Hispanos Nominated	Hispanos Elected	Per Cent
1916	10	6	3	33 1/3
1918	10	8	2	20
1920	10	4	1	10
1922	10	9	5	50
1924	11	6	2	18
1926	10	7	5	50
1928	11	5	5	46
1930	10	10	5	50
1932	12	11	3	25
1934	10	12	4	40
1936	10	12	3	33 1/3
1938	10	8	3	33 1/3
1940	10	7	4	25
1942	10	5	2	20
1944	10	4	2	20
1946	10	6	4	40
1948	11	10	5	46

Sources of Data: Blue Books of New Mexico, 1917-1947.
State of New Mexico, Official Returns of the
1948 Elections.

at no time were they unrepresented in the list of successful
candidates; in the 17 elections Hispanic candidates captured
approximately one third of all elective executive and judicial
posts. However, attention has been called to the fact that there
has been a marked preponderance of Anglo-Americans in those offices
which are considered most important.

In attempting to ascertain the Anglo-Hispano political
balance, consideration of the record of office-holding is not
enough. Administrative officers, largely appointed by the governor,
frequently wield more power than minor elective officers. Analysis of the administrative hierarchy of state government throws
further light on the seat of political power in New Mexico.
Appointive officers who constitute the administrative hierarchy
of the state include the banking commissioner, state comptroller,
budget director, purchasing agent, commissioner of revenue, engineer, director of public welfare, and the directors of a score
of other socio-economic agencies.

The Anglo-Hispano ratio in the upper echelon of state
administration is shown in Table XV. For this purpose, all
appointive offices listed by the Blue Books of New Mexico for the
years 1932-48 have been used.

The figures in Table XV indicate that at no point in
the period did Hispanic-Americans constitute as much as one fourth
of the total administrative corps appointed by the governor. Data
also indicate that there was a relative decline in the number of
Hispanic-American administrative appointees in the period under
study.

Analysis of the group affiliation of the two houses of

TABLE XV

Group Affiliation of Appointive Officers,
1932-48

Year	Appointive Officers	Hispanic Officers	Per Cent
1932	18	4	22
1934	29	7	24
1936	35	8	23
1938	37	7	19
1940	36	6	17
1942	43	8	19
1944	47	7	15
1946	46	5	11
1948	46	6	13

Source of Data: Blue Books of New Mexico, 1931-32 to 1947-48.

the state legislature affords yet another opportunity to examine the Anglo-Hispano political balance. In a democracy, shifts in political power are reflected in the composition of the legislature. Thus the contention that the Hispanic element has lost political power in recent years is correct, a decline in the number of Hispanic-Americans elected to that body should be expected. On the other hand, a gain in the relative number of Spanish-speaking legislators could be interpreted as an indication of increased political power. Data showing the group affiliation of New Mexican legislators in the years of statehood are given in Tables XVI and XVII.

Tables XVI and XVII indicate that the Anglo-Hispano balance in the state senate seldom has reflected the Anglo-Hispano ratio in the total population. Anglo-Americans were greatly over-represented in the upper chamber of the legislature in all sessions except the nineteenth. This disparity, however, has been evident throughout the period of statehood, and there has been no down-ward trend in Hispanic representation. Tables XVI and XVII also indicate that the composition of the state house of representatives generally has reflected the Anglo-Hispano population ratio. In the lower house of the legislature, the number of Hispanic representatives has tended to equal the number of Anglo representatives. Moreover, this legislative balance has been somewhat constant.

One explanation for this constancy of Hispanic representation in both houses of the legislature lies in the fact that the senatorial and representative districts drawn by the constitutional convention in 1910 were not re-drawn to conform to

TABLE XVI

Composition of State Senate,

1912-50

Legislature	Membership	Hispanic-Americans	Per Cent
First	24	5	21
Second	24	5	21
Third	24	7	29
Fourth	24	7	29
Fifth	24	6	25
Sixth	24	6	25
Seventh	24	5	21
Eighth	24	6	25
Ninth	24	5	21
Tenth	24	5	21
Eleventh	24	6	25
Twelfth	24	6	25
Thirteenth	24	3	13
Fourteenth	24	3	13
Fifteenth	24	7	29
Sixteenth	24	7	29
Seventeenth	24	4	17
Eighteenth	24	4	17
Nineteenth	24	9	38

Sources of Data: Blue Books of New Mexico, 1913-14 to 1947-48.
State of New Mexico, Official Returns of the
1948 Elections, pp. 15-228.

TABLE XVII

Composition of State House of Representatives,
1912-50

Legislature	Membership	Hispanic-Americans	Per Cent
First	49	22	45
Second	49	24	49
Third	49	26	53
Fourth	49	22	45
Fifth	49	21	43
Sixth	49	22	45
Seventh	49	21	43
Eighth	49	22	45
Ninth	49	24	49
Tenth	49	25	51
Eleventh	49	19	39
Twelfth	49	20	41
Thirteenth	49	16	33
Fourteenth	49	18	37
Fifteenth	49	21	43
Sixteenth	49	19	39
Seventeenth	49	20	41
Eighteenth	49	20	41
Nineteenth	49	20	41

Sources of Data: Blue Books of New Mexico, 1913-14 to 1947-48.
State of New Mexico, Official Returns of the
1948 Elections, pp. 15-228.

population changes. Thus the rapidly growing Anglo counties of eastern New Mexico continued to send single representatives to the house, while certain Hispanic counties, with static or slowly increasing populations, sent two or more representatives.[1]

Hispanic counties consistently have sent Spanish-speaking senators and representatives to the legislature, while Anglo counties have sent English-speaking legislators. In those counties where the Anglo and the Hispano groups are somewhat balanced, there has been a tendency for senate posts to be occupied by Anglos, with house seats being allocated to Hispano representatives.[2] Thus the fact that the Anglo-Hispano ratio in the legislature has remained virtually unchanged throughout the period of statehood may be attributed to an unchanged system of apportionment, and to the continued operation of the "gentlemen's agreement."

Major change in the Anglo-Hispano ratio in the state legislature was predicted as the result of the passage of a reapportionment bill in 1949. This measure, sought by legislators from the Anglo counties of southern and eastern New Mexico, increased the membership of the senate from 24 to 31 and of the house from 49 to 55.[3] Political commentators were quick to point out that the effect of reapportionment would be to increase Anglo representation in the legislature, while providing no increase in Hispanic representation. In other words, the six additional representatives were to come from Anglo counties, and there was

1. Taos Star, Feb. 10, 1949.
2. John C. Russell, State Regionalism in New Mexico, p. 183.
3. New Mexico Tax Bulletin, May, 1949, pp. 670-71.

to be a corresponding increase in the senate.[1]

Anglo-Hispano Ratio in County Offices

Throughout this study, attention has been focused upon political activities at the state level. In an effort to throw further light upon the Anglo-Hispano political balance as reflected in office-holding, attention now will be centered upon office-holding at the county level. All elective county offices during the entire period of statehood will be considered in this connection.

The data presented in Table XVIII tend to show that there has been no marked downward trend in the total number of Spanish-American officeholders at the county level. The data also indicate that the percentage of Hispano officeholders has been less than the percentage of Hispanic-Americans in the total population. In other words, under-representation generally has existed. This condition was more pronounced in the early days of statehood, when Hispanic-Americans constituted more than 50 per cent of the population, than in recent years, when the Hispanic element has constituted less than half of the total population.

Analysis of the returns by separate county brings out the fact that three of the seven most Anglo counties never have elected a Spanish-speaking officeholder, and that the remaining four very rarely have elected an Hispano to county office. On the other hand, Anglo candidates commonly have been elected to office in the seven most Hispanic counties, although they always

---

1. *Santa Fe New Mexican*, March 13, 1949.

TABLE XVIII

County Officeholders in New Mexico,

1912-50

Year	Total Offices	Hispanos Elected	Per Cent
1912	260	96	37
1914	260	97	37
1916	280	103	37
1918	280	103	37
1920	310	106	34
1922	310	93	30
1924	310	101	33
1926	310	98	32
1928	310	96	31
1930	310	95	31
1932	310	99	32
1934	310	97	31
1936	310	98	32
1938	310	95	31
1940	310	91	29
1942	310	97	31
1944	310	94	30
1946	295	98	33
1948	294	100	34

Sources of Data: Blue Books of New Mexico, 1913-14 to 1947-48. State of New Mexico, Official Returns of the 1948 Elections, pp. 171-228.

have been in a minority.

Anglo-Hispano Balance and the Election of 1950

At first glance, the election statistics assembled in this chapter tend to support the view that the Anglo-Hispano political balance has undergone few changes in the period of statehood. Although the Anglo-American element has been over-represented, both at the state and at the county level, the Hispanic element has not lost ground, when office-holding is the sole criterion. However, attention has been called to the fact that Anglo-Americans generally have secured those state elective offices which afford real power; that the great majority of important state appointive offices likewise have been filled by Anglos; that the state senate always has been dominated by the English-speaking element; and that the same group generally has been in a majority in the house of representatives.

Dissatisfaction of Spanish-American leaders with this arrangement precipitated many of the political crises described in previous sections of this study. That the dissatisfaction mounted as the steady influx of Anglo-Americans into the state caused the Spanish-speaking population to regard itself as an embattled minority also has been indicated in earlier chapters. Finally it became an open issue in the primary election of 1950.

Two developments focused attention upon the Anglo-Hispano balance in politics. One was United States Senator Chavez' determination to bring an end to the unbroken succession of Anglo governors. The other was the bid of Anglo candidates for posts long reserved for those of Hispanic descent. From the outset,

both Anglo and Hispano political leaders recognized the approaching election as one of unusual consequence. Democratic politicos
were most concerned, for New Mexico had become a one-party state,
and nomination in the Democratic primary was tantamount to election. For that reason, Democratic candidates took the center of
the stage.

Several Anglo-American politicians described Senator
Chavez' effort to make his brother the Democratic nominee for
governor as political poaching in the Anglo preserve. Other
Anglo leaders professed alarm at the prospect of uniting the
powerful offices of federal senator and state governor within one
Hispanic family. On the other hand, Spanish-speaking politicos
considered ways of resisting an Anglo invasion of the sacred
Hispano precincts represented in the offices of secretary of state,
lieutenant governor and auditor. The effect of Anglo-Hispano
antagonism on the approaching election caused considerable spec-
ulation, and caused political commentators to observe that "The
campaign will divide old political alliances in a fight that
promises one of the greatest political upheavals this state has
known. It goes further than a mere decision between Miles and
Chavez. This campaign and the general election that follows may
produce the dreaded all-out racial fight that New Mexico has
avoided so long."[1]

While Anglo newspapers decried the ruthless methods of
Senator Chavez and deplored the introduction of "racial" issues,
the only Spanish-language newspaper of consequence placed equal

1. "The Fight Ahead," Editorial, Santa Fe New Mexican, April 25,
   1950.

emphasis upon group differ ..)s. A series of articles presented
the political predicament of the "native" people, and vigorously
argued for more equitable distribution of state offices.

After observing that primary elections had benefited,
rather than harmed, Spanish-speaking candidates in the period
1940-48, O. B. Servando predicted that a major change was in the
offing. He then explained the reason for Hispano misgivings and
fears:

> New Mexico already is a state the majority of
> whose population comes from southern states, particularly
> from the states of Texas and Oklahoma. This element, as
> is well known, is fanatical in its Democratic politics.
> Besides having fixed upon the politics of Jefferson and
> Jackson, they have strong racial prejudices, a combina-
> tion which certainly will lead to their imposing their
> system by force, with grave prejudice to the Spanish-
> speaking element that by general rule is not united.[1]

In March, 1950, a group of Hispanic-American politicians
from the northern counties of New Mexico formed a coalition, in an
effort to preserve what they termed the "rights" of the Spanish-
speaking population. What these leaders had in mind, in particular,
was the continuation of the gentlemen's agreement which virtually
guaranteed Hispanic candidates three places on the state ticket.
The filing of Anglo candidates for each of the three offices in
question was motivation for this Hispanic coalition. Although the
move was doomed to failure because of the powerful opposition of
the state Democratic machine, it was approved by many of the
native people.

> . . . the Spanish-speaking community is in danger
> of losing those posts which they have been conceded as an

---

1. "Dicen Que Se Avecina una Catastrofe Politica de Gran Magnitud
en N. M.," El Nuevo Mexicano, March 9, 1950.

accord between gentlemen, as it is customary to say.
The contributing factor in this political disturbance
is the primary election which was imposed by the demands of political leaders from the southern and
eastern parts of the state.. . .The primary election
law lends itself very well to those who practice discrimination.[1]

Interest in the gubernatorial office was no less marked
than interest in the three minor posts which the Spanish-speaking
people had come to regard as peculiarly their own. The Chavez
forces reminded the Hispanic voters that the 1950 Democratic primary would determine whether or not the Anglo hold on the governor's
office could be broken.

> In this primary election many affairs which
> vitally affect the people of this state will be deter-
> mined. One of these is going to be if the Spanish-
> speaking element counts with sufficient force to nom-
> inate and elect one of its own. This opportunity has
> not been presented in other elections with more fa-
> vorable factors than those which will be put to the
> proof on Tuesday.[2]

As election day neared, J. E. Medina reminded the voters
of New Mexico that for more than half of the period of statehood
Hispanic-Americans constituted a majority of the population. "We
could have elected all the governors in keeping with the phrase
'Charity begins at home' but we did not do this."[3] He contrasts
the Hispanos' attitude with that of the Anglo element which seemed
intent upon exploiting its advantage. The comment concludes with
the statement that "This is not a question of race, it is a
question of 'rights' well deserved."[4]

True to custom, both Anglo and Hispanc aspirants to

---

1. Editorial, El Nuevo Mexicano, March 23, 1950.
2. "Comentarios Rapidos," El Nuevo Mexicano, June 8, 1950.
3. Ibid., May 18, 1950.
4. Loc. cit.

office induced "stooge" candidates to file, thus splitting the
vote of their opponents along ethnic lines. And true to custom,
a number of candidates filed at the last possible moment. When
the official list of candidates in the Democratic primary was
drawn up, it showed 43 contestants for the ten state elective
offices. Nine of the ten offices were contested, and in six of
these races Anglo candidates were pitted against Hispano candidates. Interest centered on the gubernatorial office, where a
prominent Spanish-speaking jurist was attempting to break an Anglo
hold unbroken since 1920, and on the offices of lieutenant governor,
secretary of state and auditor, where Anglo contenders were chal-
lenging Hispano preemption.

　　　　The campaign was regarded as the hardest contested one
in the ten-year history of the primary. "Never before have so
many races been in doubt, and never a campaign that has ex-
perienced the bitterness of the one that closes tonight. A racial
division, generated by the fight between John Miles and David
Chavez for governor, promises to bring a heavier than ordinary
vote to the polls."[1]

　　　　Political forecasters freely predicted that the outcome
of the election would depend upon the turnout of voters in eastern
New Mexico, the Anglo stronghold. It was generally assumed that
the northern counties would give a traditionally heavy vote to
the Hispanic candidates. The Democratic primary in New Mexico
attracted national attention when Drew Pearson predicted that
David Chavez would vanquish his Anglo rival, John E. Miles - a

---

1. Santa Fe New Mexican, June 5, 1950.

prediction that ran contrary to local betting.[1]

The 1950 primary was unprecedented as far as the total vote cast was concerned, but it was historic for yet another reason: the clean sweep of Anglo candidates. John E. Miles piled up a commanding lead over his Hispanic gubernatorial rival, David Chavez. "The result came after David Chavez and his brother Senator Dennis Chavez had toured the state telling that a Chavez defeat would mean the end of Spanish-American influence in New Mexico politics."[2] An Hispanic candidate for lieutenant governor eked out a victory over his Anglo rivals, but this was the only contested office gained by a Spanish-speaking candidate. Sixteen of the 17 Hispanic candidates who ran against Anglos met defeat. The Hispanic defeat was underscored by the capture by Anglos of the two posts long considered the prerogative of the "native" people: the offices of secretary of state and auditor.[3]

The outcome of the election made a profound impression on Hispanic-Americans. "Wherever two persons who speak Spanish meet, and more if they are politically minded, the first question which one asks the other is, 'What is the meaning of the Tuesday election?'. . .Above all, there seems to be an agreement that it has established a bad political precedent."[4]

Hispanic reversals in the Democratic primary left several courses of action open to Spanish-speaking political leaders. One

1. Loc. cit.
2. Will Harrison, "At the Capitol," Santa Fe New Mexican, June 7, 1950.
3. Santa Fe New Mexican, June 23, 1950. (Canvass Board's Primary Finals)
4. J. E. Medina, "Comentarios Rapidos," El Nuevo Mexicano, June 22, 1950.

was to bolt the party and swing their support to Republican
nominees, in an attempt to capture several state posts in the
general election. But Senator Chavez discouraged such tactics,
officially at least, when he promised the successful Anglo Democratic gubernatorial nominee his "full-hearted support."[1]

A second course of action was to secure the abolition
of the primary election system which in 1950 had proved so disas-
trous to Hispanic interests. Return to a modified convention
system, provided for by legislative act, was halted in 1949 by
referendum proceedings instituted by the Chavez forces. The 1950
primary, however, provided strong argument for Spanish-speaking
leaders who urged their supporters to ratify the measure in-
stituting a pre-primary convention at the general election of 1950.

A third course of action was the exaction of reprisals.
In other words, the Anglos having exploited their numerical advantage by placing their candidates in state offices, the Hispanos
could exploit their similar advantage in the northern counties.

> . . .racial hatred or call it what you will, is an instru-
> ment that cuts with two edges.. . .It has been the very
> common practice in the northern counties to give representa-
> tion to the Anglos on the county ticket. A representative
> to the legislature, a senator and a commissioner.. . .In
> view of what occurred last Tuesday, the Spanish-speaking
> will not easily forget, in the five months until general
> election, the disregard which they have suffered, and will
> pay the guilty parties.[2]

Other Spanish-American leaders minimized the role which
"race" played in the 1950 Democratic primary. In particular, they
attributed the defeat of Judge David Chavez to the fact that he
vigorously supported civil rights legislation, received the

---

1. Santa Fe New Mexican, June 8, 1950.
2. J. E. Medina, op. cit.

blessing of the Truman administration as a staunch Fair Dealer,
and that he was opposed by the powerful state Democratic machine.[1]
If the native people were to secure the rights which they felt had
been denied, their only chance of success lay in an alliance with
labor and liberal Anglos, most of whom lived in the Albuquerque-
Santa Fe area.

But whatever course of action the Spanish-Americans of
New Mexico decided upon, as a result of the Democratic primary
of 1950, that contest was recognized as a boundary line. Whether
the Hispanos would become a dwindling and increasingly belligerent
minority, or the nucleus of a powerful political coalition remained
a question for Spanish-speaking leaders to decide.

Summary

One of the chief characteristics of politics in New
Mexico has been the operation of a "gentlemen's agreement." In
its original form, it had two aspects. One rule was designed to
prevent Anglo and Hispano from being pitted against one another
in a race for any office. The other provision made certain state
offices the prerogative of Hispanic candidates, with others
being reserved for Anglo candidates.

Credit for establishing the rule that tickets must be
balanced between the two major groups generally is given to O. A.
Larrazolo, leader of the Spanish-American people in the first 20
years of statehood. In this period, party conventions frequently
were marked by inter-group clashes based upon an alleged failure

---

1. Letter, Molvin Mencher, Republican publicity chairman, July
   6, 1950; also Editorial, Santa Fe New Mexican, June 5, 1950,
   and news article, same paper, June 8, 1950.

to observe the gentlemen's agreement.

The increase of the Anglo population has caused Hispanic leaders to fear that this tradition will be broken. Frequently assertions are made to the effect that the Spanish-speaking people are "losing out" politically. Generally such remarks are based upon a belief that the number of Hispanic-American officeholders has declined in recent years.

Examination of state election returns for the entire period of statehood indicates that there never has been an equal division of political offices. This is most apparent in the judicial branch of government, where only one Hispanic judge has been a justice of the supreme court, the only elective position in the state judiciary.

The governorship has become a virtual monopoly of the Anglo-Americans, since no Spanish-speaking governor has been elected since 1918. The lieutenant governorship has been more evenly divided between the two predominant groups, for 12 Anglo-Americans have held that office, with seven Hispanic-Americans appearing on the official roster. Two offices have been held exclusively by representatives of each of the two great culture-groups. Spanish-American women have been uniformly successful in capturing the office of secretary of state, while Anglo-American men have occupied the post of state treasurer without interruption. The position of auditor generally has gone to a Spanish-speaking candidate. Of the other state elective posts, most have been in Anglo hands more often than not. In state appointive offices, Anglo-Americans have been in overwhelming majority. The Anglo-Hispano balance, first evident in 1912, has remained relatively unchanged throughout the period of statehood.

The same statement applies to the legislative branch of government. Anglo-Americans always have enjoyed a decisive majority in the state senate, and generally have had at least a bare majority in the house of representatives. There has been no notable downward trend in Hispanic representation in either house. Major change in the Anglo-Hispano ratio in the state legislature was predicted as a result of the passage of a reapportionment bill in 1949. This measure increases representation from eastern New Mexico, where the Anglo population predominates.

The Anglo-Hispano ratio in county offices resembles that which characterizes state offices. When the total of elective offices is considered, it becomes evident that Anglo-Americans have predominated in the period of statehood, roughly 2:1. There apparently has been no downward trend in the total number of offices held by Hispanic-Americans.

The primary election of 1950 had as one of its major issues the preservation of the gentlemen's agreement and the continued balancing of the ticket. Attention focused on the Democratic race, since nomination by that party is tantamount to election in New Mexico. Hispanic-American political leaders attempted to break the Anglo monopoly of the governorship, while Anglo-American candidates competed for state posts long held by Hispanos.

With one exception, all Hispanic candidates who took part in contested elections went down in defeat. An Anglo candidate was successful in the gubernatorial race, and Anglo candidates captured positions as secretary of state and auditor, both of which traditionally had been held by Hispanic-Americans.

The election of 1950 was called historic, and was recognized as marking the boundary of a political era.

CHAPTER XVI

THE POLITICAL ROLE OF THE HISPANIC-AMERICAN

One of the most notable advances in education came when the teacher resolved to view the child as the total product of his environment, rather than the mere output of an isolated classroom. For then it became obvious that the child could be seen in true perspective only against a background encompassing hereditary factors, parental care, economic status and many other factors. A similar advance occurred in medicine through the efforts of the psychosomatic physicians. For in assuming that illness has interrelated physical and mental causation, the psychosomatic school went beyond mere clinical examination to psychic and social examination. Illness became understandable only in terms of the total background of the patient.

The social scientist for many years has attempted to employ the techniques more recently popularized by educators and physicians. Thus long before Marx, historians were interpreting the course of human events in terms of economics; and long before Toynbee, the psychological and philosophical overtones of historical events had been noted. When political science became a recognized subdivision of the social sciences, its exponents likewise subscribed to the thesis that man, the political animal, is understandable only in terms of man, the physical, the social and the economic animal.

Throughout this study an attempt has been made to view
the politics of New Mexico against a background of geography,
sociology, anthropology, religion and economics, as well as that
of government. The various threads which compose the fabric of
New Mexico politics have been examined, sometimes in considerable
detail. Particular attention has been focused on strands which
have passed through the hands of the Spanish-American people. It
now becomes necessary to bring these threads together in the com-
pass of a few pages, in order that the pattern of New Mexico
politics may emerge.

The background of the pattern is supplied by geography.
New Mexico is a hostile land, hostile because the sun-baked earth
is rough and water so precious that it must be hoarded. In the
fourth largest state in the Union, fewer people live than in the
city of Pittsburgh. The population not only is sparse but a
large part of it is isolated. In the ranch section, neighbors
live miles apart; those who live in villages often are hemmed in
by lofty mountains or the sheer walls of deep canyons.

Moreover, geography produced a type of land settlement
which further isolated the people of New Mexico by causing Anglos
and Hispanos to live apart. Spanish colonists followed the Rio
Grande to its headwaters, settling wherever fields could be
irrigated. Today their descendants till the same small fields,
resisting the encroachment of the Anglo commercial farmer. On
the other hand, the great plains of eastern New Mexico were
settled by Anglo ranchers from Texas and Oklahoma, and some of
these were succeeded by the dry-land farmers with their endless
fields of wheat. Thus geography created barriers which led to

different patterns of land settlement and differing types of
agriculture. In New Mexico the age-old conflict between cattle-
man and sheepman, between dry-land farmer and irrigationist,
between mountaineer and plainsman, between rancher and villager,
easily translated itself into Anglo-Hispano differences.

Geography placed a major barrier between the Anglo-
American and the Hispanic-American. Language imposed another,
for in a democracy, the free exchange of ideas is imperative, and
any inhibition of that interchange imposes great strain on government. Difference in religion was but another manifestation of the
conflicting cultures of the Anglo and the Hispano. The numerically
superior Hispanic-Americans could not absorb the Anglo minority,
possibly because the Spanish culture was static. Yet the aggressive Anglo-Americans could not impose their culture on the Spanish-
speaking people; it was as if two great currents of water filled
the banks of a stream without commingling.

Despite geographical, linguistic, religious and general
cultural differences, Anglos and Hispanos inevitably were brought
into juxtaposition. The pages of this study show rather plainly
that whenever the two major groups came into contact, the Hispanic-
Americans of New Mexico appeared at a disadvantage. Economically
they were subordinate because use, rather than money value, was
their criterion. Lacking the Anglo-Saxon urge to acquire money
for its own sake, the Hispanic-American was quickly disinherited.

A stronger race came and took away their
inheritance. . .the Mexican, sharing neither in the pater-
nalism of the government nor in the natural resources of
field, forest, or mine, is in his own country an outcast,
a poor relation. Lacking capital, he is shut out from all

participation in their development, except as a laborer.[1]

Although the federal government made tremendous efforts
in the direction of educating the American Indian and in intro-
ducing English as the basic language in Puerto Rico and the
Philippines, that policy was not pursued in New Mexico when that
alien land was annexed. Apparently it was felt that the Spanish-
speaking people of New Mexico would be absorbed as readily as
overseas immigrants, and that English quickly would be substituted
for Spanish as the common idiom. Such was not the case. Despite
the tireless and sometimes dedicated efforts of New Mexican educators, both Anglo and Hispano, to rectify the damage done in early
territorial days, the fact remains that the average Hispano today
is handicapped both because he does not speak English fluently
and because he has not been trained to compete with his Anglo
neighbors. This view finds expression in the works of Tireman,[2]
Sanchez,[3] and other educators; it often has been expressed by
Bronson Cutting, Dennis Chavez and other political figures;[4] it
is a common theme in the publications of Hispanic-American organizations,[5] and is implicit in the creed of the League of United Latin
American Citizens.

> The acquisition of the English language, which
> is the official language of our country, being necessary
> for the enjoyment of our rights and privileges, we
> declare it to be the official language of this Organiza-
> tion, and we pledge ourselves to learn, and speak, and

1. Ross Calvin, Sky Determines, pp. 215-16.
2. Loyd S. Tireman, Teaching Spanish-Speaking Children and A
   Community School in a Spanish-Speaking Village.
3. George I. Sanchez, Forgotten People.
4. Cf. Chapter X.
5. Cf. Chapter VII.

teach same to our children.[1]

The failure of the Hispanic-Americans to acquire educational status as a group cannot be attributed to Anglo hostility. While many, if not most, of the latter group have been indifferent to the educational needs of the Spanish-speaking people, some have made strenuous efforts to provide the necessary facilities. A truer explanation would lie in a combination of Anglo neglect and Hispano indifference to the opportunities presented by education. For all too frequently, the Spanish-speaking people because of inertia have failed to take advantage of the educational opportunities afforded them.

But whatever the reason for the educational disadvantage of the Hispanic-Americans of New Mexico, their inadequacies have proved a grave handicap. Their role in the business and professional life of the state is highly restricted, and their activities in government likewise have been circumscribed by lack of education. Hispanic leaders often have contended that Spanish-speaking candidates are discriminated against when appointments are to be made in the upper echelons of government. But frequently Hispanic-Americans are barred from such offices, not because of discriminatory practices, but because of their lack of training. The younger Hispanos recognize this fact, which explains their insistence upon widened educational opportunity for Spanish-speaking youth. It also explains their efforts to awaken the Hispanic population to the educational opportunities it now possesses.

---

1. "What Lulac Stands For" (1949 revision).

Literature in the field of the social sciences is in itself a commentary on the general disparity between the Anglo-Americans and the Hispanic-Americans of New Mexico. The investigator is struck by the fact that of the countless books, articles and other publications dealing with the Spanish-speaking population, only a minute fraction are written in Spanish. Much more revealing, however, is the fact that Spanish-American authors are so few in number as to be conspicuous. It is the Anglo social scientist who describes the Hispanic people and their culture.

It is the Anglo social scientist who concerns himself with inter-group relations.

Educational disadvantage is both the cause of and the effect of economic and social discrimination. The Hispano speaks English not at all or with a decided accent--therefore he is a "foreigner." An alien in his native land, he has immigrant status as regards wages, housing and recreational facilities. The aggressive, materialistic culture of the Anglo offers almost irresistible attraction for the Hispano. But when he attempts to become part of it, he often meets with rebuff. Hyper-sensitive, he draws inward, finds protection in his own group, and further accentuates the gulf between Anglo and Hispano. Examples of the operation of this defense mechanism are numerous in the field of government. The manner in which Spanish-speaking legislators invariably unite when any matter pertaining to their ethnic group arises is but one such example.

The disparity between the two principal cultural groups has caused many Hispanic-Americans to acquire an inferiority complex, to accept subordination as their role in life, to resign

themselves to economic and social discrimination. On the other
hand, the disparity has led other Hispanic-Americans to combat
all types of discrimination in an aggressive, and sometimes ruthless manner. The organization of the League of United Latin
American Citizens, the National Association of Mexican-Americans
and the Association for the Advancement of Spanish-Americans may
be traced to this determination to bring an end to discrimination.
The Hispanic-American drive for Fair Employment Practices legislation is another example from the realm of politics.

Shadows of the Future

Efforts of the Hispanic people to preserve their culture
have had continuous repercussions in the field of government.
Perhaps the most noteworthy case was the incorporation of those
rigid constitutional guarantees so often referred to in the pages
of this study. In their attempt to preserve an island of Spanish
culture in an Anglo-Saxon sea, the "native" people of New Mexico
have been amazingly successful. With the exception of the Pueblo
Indians, perhaps no minority in American history has been more
successful in preserving its entity. More than a century after
their incorporation into the United States, the Hispanic people
have retained their identity.

But it now seems apparent that this identity soon will
be lost. Great modification of the Hispanic culture pattern, or
its disappearance, would produce profound change in the politics
of New Mexico. Some of the consequences already are visible on
the horizon.

From the standpoint of population alone, the pressure

against the Hispanic culture has become difficult to withstand.
At the time of the American occupation, the English-speaking
residents of New Mexico constituted less than two per cent of
the total population. A century later, they constituted approximately 60 per cent.[1] Study of census returns during the period
of statehood indicates that the Anglo: Hispano ratio will contin
ue to become more disparate. The implications for the Hispanic
culture are obvious; the political ramifications have been indicated
on numerous occasions in this report.

Census returns reveal another, and more important, reason for the steady decline of the Hispanic culture. That is the
trend toward urbanization. The Hispanic culture is essentially a
rural culture, with agricultural villages as its seat. The numerous case studies cited in this investigation show that the
number and the importance of these villages have decreased in recent years. There has been a corresponding increase in the number
and in the importance of urban centers. Preliminary returns in
the 1950 census indicate that each of the seven most Hispanic
counties lost population in the 1940-50 decade.[2] Since the birth
rate remained high, the inference was that the "native" people
were moving from their rural villages. The inference received
factual support from the 1950 census which showed that 20 of the
leading cities and towns of the state showed an approximate 85
per cent gain in population over the 1940 figures.[3] The Hispanic
trek to the cities received further verification from public
welfare reports.

1. Cf. Chapter II.
2. Santa Fe New Mexican, July 2, 1950.
3. Santa Fe New Mexican, June 21, 1950.

There are many other factors indicative of
social disorganization. In the peripheral low-rent
areas around the cities, migrants from New Mexico
villages swarm the already overcrowded hovels of their
poor urban relatives. Driven from the infinitesimal
land holdings of their fathers by the pressure of poverty they come to the city to get jobs.[1]

The Spanish-American culture is rooted in the soil and

centered in the home. Urbanization thus destroys the very founda-

tion of the culture, and by weakening family ties makes the perpet-

uation of the pattern almost impossible. Moreover, when the

"native" moves to town, he becomes subject to a thousand alien

currents which his rural isolation once deflected. The motion

picture, newspaper, radio, school and pool room exert an influence

once supplied by his family and his church. Even the patron is

lacking, and the newcomer finds it hard to get his political

bearings because of a seeming absence of leadership.

Even those Hispanos who remain in their villages have

become subject to great pressure from the Anglo-American culture.

A brief visit to Los Alamos, the federal atomic city with its

$18,000,000.00 annual pay roll,[2] or to one of the vast installa-

tions near Albuquerque or Alamogordo will give the reason. Thou-

sands of Hispanic-Americans commute to these great military

establishments each day. There they come into contact with one

of the most advanced, if most artificial, phases of Anglo-American

culture. Equally important, they earn enough to buy all the

trappings which in the popular eye represent that culture: automo-

biles, radios, sleek clothes, plumbing and tinned foods. Economic

independence breeds political independence, along with independ-

---

1. Helen H. Ellis, Public Welfare Problems in New Mexico, p. 7.
2. Taos Star, June 30, 1949.

ence from family and church controls.

The relaxation of the strong family and religious ties
which have bound the Hispanic-Americans into a significant culture
group is no less marked than the weakening of linguistic ties.
Those who have lived in New Mexico for a period of years frequently have remarked that the Spanish language is on its way out.
It is employed less in the legislature and in the printed acts of
government; the use of court interpreters is declining; more often
than not, political gatherings are conducted exclusively in English. Such facts are verifiable only by observation, for there
are no statistics dealing with the subject. However, the decline
of the Spanish-language press is a matter of record, and it lends
credence to the statement that the Hispanic people are abandoning
their native language. In 1915 there were 22 Spanish-language
periodicals having a combined circulation of approximately 15,000.
In 1938 the number of periodicals printed entirely in Spanish had
dropped to four with a combined circulation estimated at 5,000.
In 1948 the Ayers directory showed only two Spanish-language
publications in New Mexico, one having a circulation of 5,500, the
other a circulation of 725.[2] The editorial columns of the only
remaining Spanish-language newspaper of consequence recently have
been filled with letters-to-the-editor deploring the abandonment
of Spanish as the language of the "native" people.

The marked changes which have taken place in the Hispanic
culture pattern in recent years have presented educators and

1. Paul A. F. Walter, Jr., A Study of Isolation and Social Change
   in Three Spanish Speaking Villages of New Mexico, p. 62.
2. Ayers Directory of Newspapers and Periodicals, 1948, pp. 617-
   21.

political leaders with problems of the first magnitude. Small
wonder that confusion and conflicting policies have resulted.
On the one hand, there has been an attempt to preserve the
Spanish culture in order to effect a fusion between the Hispanic
and Anglo-Saxon civilizations. Evidence of this effort may be
found in legislation calling for the teaching of Spanish in the
elementary schools of the state; it shows itself in the preoccupation of Anglo artists and scholars with the Spanish heritage,
and the preservation by municipal authorities of the outward expression of this heritage as manifested in architecture, music
and dancing. In its extreme form, this effort to preserve the
Hispanic culture aims to maintain New Mexico as a museum piece,
with the "native" people providing the quaintness which tourists
find so attractive. As a prominent Hispanic leader wryly remarked,
the extremists close their eyes to the open privies of the "native"
sections of Santa Fe and lavish their attention on the great
September fiesta.

Attempts to preserve the Hispanic culture meet with the
opposition of other educators and political leaders. While fully
aware of the many desirable characteristics of the "native" culture, they believe that it cannot survive.

> We must concede that the Spanish-American culture
> pattern, unless radical land reforms are put into effect
> and the national competitive system changed from the prevail-
> ing income economy to an economy of use, is of doubtful
> value. It may only serve to keep the Spanish-Americans in
> an economically depressed condition, continuing as isolated
> subsistence farmers cultivating their tiny plots of land in
> traditional fashion. If they are to enter the Anglo econ-
> omy and become participating members of the Anglo society,
> the larger part of their culture heritage would become a

liability rather than an asset.[1]

Those who subscribe to this point of view have been responsible for educational and governmental policies aimed at incorporating the Hispanic-Americans of New Mexico into the Anglo culture as quickly and as painlessly as possible. Officials of the New Mexico Education Association and of the state department of public instruction have worked, with considerable success, for a curriculum which will prepare Spanish-speaking youth to fit into an Anglo economy. This has been accompanied by a drive to equalize educational opportunity, as represented by financial support of schools in various parts of the state. No longer can it be said that Hispanic youth are illiterate in two languages.

Apart from the determination of educational policy and the provision of financial support, government agencies also have been active in the incorporation of the Hispanic people into the body politic. The stress has been upon economic rehabilitation as a prerequisite to active participation in an Anglo-dominated community. The work of the county and home demonstration agents has been aimed in this direction. Likewise the Soil Conservation Service and Reclamation Bureau have been active in promoting the economic welfare of the Hispano to permit his absorption into the prevailing culture. The proposed Rio Grande Authority would be the culmination of governmental efforts to integrate a people through integrating an economy. The difficulties are enormous; from the geographical point of view the great handicap is lack of

---

1. School of Inter-American Affairs, University of New Mexico, Conference on the Problems of Education Among the Spanish-Speaking Populations of Our Southwest, p. 6.

water; from the human point of view, the great handicap is lack
of skilled labor, especially among the Hispanic-Americans; from
the financial point of view the great handicap is the poverty of
the state and the necessity of securing federal support. But as
it becomes increasingly clear that the social and political
subordination of the Hispanic population is derived from their
poverty, pressure for governmental intervention will mount.

The necessity of raising the economic status of the
Hispanic-Americans is recognized by those who believe that the
presence of an economically disadvantaged minority undermines
democratic government. It also is recognized by those leaders
who take a long-range view of economics. This point of view was
expressed at the second seminar on the Spanish-speaking of the
Southwest and West sponsored by the National Catholic Welfare
Conference.

> To hold this large segment of our population in
> poverty is false economy. To pay miserable wages to our
> Spanish-speaking workers is a luxury which our business
> man can hardly afford. If the purchasing power of this
> great group of people were equal to their capacity to con-
> sume, our business men would enjoy the greatest prosperity
> that they have ever known.[1]

The necessity of improving the economic position of the
Hispanic-American as a prerequisite to his participation in the
community has been a tenet of the League of United Latin American
Citizens, National Association of Mexican-Americans, the Association for the Advancement of Spanish-Americans and other ethnic
organizations from the outset. Through lobbying and other forms
of pressure they have secured governmental intervention in behalf
of the Hispano, notably in the passage of Fair Employment Practices

---

1. Proceedings, Denver, 1944, p. 44.

legislation. It is too early to predict the success of this
form of governmental activity, but Hispanic leaders already have
expressed a determination to strengthen the law and provide its
enforcing agency with real power.

Politics in Retrospect

Unlike most disadvantaged cultural groups, the Spanish-
Americans of New Mexico have been very active in politics.
Throughout the period of statehood, practical politicians and
social scientists alike have remarked upon the unusual interest
which the average Hispano takes in all forms of political activity.
This exhibits itself in attendance at political meetings; participation in speech-making, canvassing and other forms of elec-
tioneering; and concern with the distribution of the spoils of
office. Perhaps the most noteworthy deviation from the political
inertia which characterizes many disadvantaged culture groups is
the voting record of the Hispanic people of New Mexico. The
percentage of registered voters who actually cast ballots in the
most Hispanic counties is almost double that of the state as a
whole.[1] When predominantly Anglo counties are compared with
Hispanic counties on this basis, the political importance of the
Spanish-speaking voter becomes obvious. The Hispanos of New
Mexico consistently go to the polls on election day, while only
an issue of crucial importance will bring more than a third of
the potential Anglo voters to the polls.

The average Hispano not only goes to the polls, but he
also tends to vote for candidates having a Spanish name. In this

----

1. Supra.

respect, he resembles his Anglo neighbor, who tends to vote for candidates bearing Nordic names. This voting habit has been characteristic throughout the period of statehood, with some evidence pointing to an increased emphasis on ethnic affiliation in recent years. The tendency may be traced to the well known antipathy which the "native" New Mexican has borne for the Texan since the Civil War period, when armed forays were made by Confederate troops. As Texans have poured into eastern and southern New Mexico, they have reciprocated the "natives'" antipathy with an ill-concealed dislike for people whom they consider colored and a somewhat suppressed contempt for Mexicans, whom they remember in connection with the struggle for Texas independence.

Far more important than the mutual dislike of Hispanic New Mexican and Anglo Texan in influencing voting habits, has been the Hispano's growing conviction that he is a member of a beleaguered minority which must cling together for mutual protection. Expressed in terms of politics, this means that the Hispanic voter believes that a Spanish-speaking officeholder will be inclined to prevent an Anglo usurpation of privilege and power. To a degree, this attitude is but a projection of the intense feeling for family which is so evident in the Hispanic culture. The alleged discrimination of one cultural group against another inevitably leads to reprisal, and eventually it becomes very difficult for any candidate for office to win support from both groups.

The Hispanos' belief that they are members of an out-maneuvered minority has been strengthened by the manner in which political offices have been distributed. Throughout the period

of statehood, Anglo-Americans have had the lion's share of the
more important elective and appointive offices. Despite the
fact that the Hispanic population exceeded the Anglo population
during much of the period, most of the political plums fell into
the hands of Anglo-Americans. And despite the fact that the
Hispanic voter was far more loyal than the Anglo in exercising
the franchise, the latter furnished most of the top executives of
the major parties.

This failure to gain political power commensurate with
numbers, party loyalty, exercise of the franchise and other
considerations which generally bring advantage, may spring from
the conscious subordination of one culture group by another. On
the other hand, the failure may be attributable to characteristics
of the disadvantaged group itself. Thus one of the most prominent
Anglo political leaders in the state recently forswore further
cooperation with Hispanic politicos on the grounds that they
neither understood the English language nor the principles of
democracy. To state it otherwise, Hispanic-Americans have not
enjoyed their share of political power because they have constituted a cultural enclave which has defied incorporation. Since
political authority is generated more by economic and educational
status than by mere numbers, the Spanish-speaking people have
been forced into a subordinate role in the affairs of government.
Only in those counties having a large preponderance of Hispanic-
Americans has that group enjoyed political domination.

Politics in Prospect

There is considerable evidence to support the thesis

that the Hispanic culture pattern is breaking down, and that the
"native" people are being absorbed into the Anglo-Saxon culture
in the same manner that immigrants from eastern and southern
Europe were amalgamated into the population of the United States.
The analogy breaks down at one vital point, however, for unlike
European immigrants, the Hispanic people of New Mexico are deeply
rooted in the American soil. They are the old settlers and the
Anglos are the immigrants. However dynamic the Anglo-American
culture, however great the pressure it brings to bear, the
Hispanos of New Mexico will persist as a group for many years.
Their culture is the end product of an evolutionary process which
brought man into harmony with his land, his fellows and his god.
A culture which satisfies such needs is relinquished but slowly.

The astrophysicists predict that the temperature of the
universe eventually will reach equilibrium as the heat of the
tropics modifies the cold of the arctic and as suns cool to warm
the ether. Anthropologists predict that one human race will
emerge as endless intermarriage mixes human genes. By the same
token, political scientists predict one world government and
sociologists one world culture. On a greatly reduced scale, it
is safe to predict that New Mexico will be characterized by a
highly homogeneous population: one race of people living in a
state having a common political and social climate. But that this
is a remote prospect, all would agree. Man speculates upon the
distant future, but is truly concerned only with the immediate
future. Thus concern for the political future of New Mexico is
in terms of 1960 and not 2960. What then is the immediate political future of the Hispanic-Americans of New Mexico?

Resentful of the economic, social and political disadvantage of the "native" people, and goaded to action by the
rout of Spanish-speaking candidates in the 1950 primary, Hispanic-
American leaders may attempt to form a third party. This is the
most radical of the political routes open to the group and therefore the one least likely to be taken. But it has been suggested
often enough to merit consideration.

In theory, the organization of a third party based upon
cultural affiliation has much to recommend it. The formation of
such a party would kindle enthusiasm, provide unity of purpose,
and offer the possibility of capturing control of the state government. Political domination would lie in the grasp of the Hispanic
party because it would hold the balance of power--as between
Democratic and Republican parties and as between the eastern and
the western sections of New Mexico. The Hispanic party would be
strengthened further if it gained the support of the newly enfranchised Indians, some 20,000 of whom were entitled to vote in
1948.[1] As underprivileged groups, the Hispanos and the Indians
have common interests; in a state where the total vote cast rarely
exceeds 100,000 the combined vote of the two groups would be
conclusive. Furthermore, since each group is predominantly
Catholic, the Church would provide cohesion and leadership.

Attractive though such a political grouping may be to
some Hispanic-American politicos, it would be almost impossible
to effectuate. As often indicated in this essay, the Hispano is
highly dependent upon government assistance, whether provided by

---

1. R. L. Chambers, "Capitol Views," Belen News-Bulletin, September 14, 1948.

state or local employment, unemployment relief or other forms
of economic support. However anxious he may be to launch a
third-party movement, the Hispano does not enjoy the economic
independence which makes that possible. When display of political independence means loss of employment, the Hispanic-American,
like the Anglo-American, ordinarily remains quiescent or renders
at least lip service to the party which supplies him with bread.

      While the economic block is perhaps the greatest ob-
stacle to the formation of an Hispanic party, there are other
great hindrances. The caste system, which Myrdal found in American
Negro society, is no less present in the Spanish-American community
of New Mexico. The gulf which separates the illiterate, poverty
stricken Negro who has removed from the Deep South to inner
Harlem from his highly cultivated colored brother who occupies
a penthouse on upper Lexington is no wider, no deeper than the
gulf which separates the lowly Hispanic occupant of a hovel in
Carlsbad from his aristocratic brother who lives on a great
hacienda. In other words, the class distinctions of American
society, as limned in Elmtown's Youth and the study of Jonesville,
are a powerful force in New Mexico. Among the Hispanos, as among
the Anglos, class affiliation frequently overrides ethnic
affiliation.

      And to speak of a political alliance between Indian and
Hispano is equally visionary. The Indians themselves are divided
sharply, with the Pueblos representing the intelligent, literate
citizen enjoying a high degree of economic independence and the
Navajo representing the backward, illiterate citizen having the
highest death rate and the lowest per capita income of any group

in the United States.[1] Between such Indian groups there can be
no community of interest; to speak of an alliance with the Hispanos
is therefore out of the question.

Only the most visionary of Hispanic-American leaders
would contemplate the formation of an Hispanic party for yet
another reason. The appearance of such a political grouping would
produce instant retaliation which would undermine the very government itself. For the Anglo-Americans, now as disunited as the
Spanish-speaking people, would coalesce if faced with the danger
which an Hispanic party would represent. In any such political
struggle, the advantage definitely would lie with the Anglo-
American group.

Several of the factors which mitigate against the formation of an Hispanic or Hispanic-Indian party also operate against
the revival of the Republican party and its use as the vehicle
of Spanish-American aspirations. Of these, the Hispanos' dependence upon patronage is perhaps the chief obstacle. However
aroused he may become at the alleged discrimination of Anglo Democrats, the Hispano hesitates to leave the dominant party because
he is economically dependent upon it. While it may be true that
the Hispanic people might fare better in a Republican administration, the switch involves a gamble which the Spanish-speaking
voter cannot now afford.

Furthermore, the leadership of the Republican party
remains in the hands of a group opposed to policies which would
serve the Hispanic-American group. Albert K. Mitchell, Patrick
Hurley, Ed Springer and other men of great wealth continue to

---

1. Helen H. Ellis, Public Welfare Problems in New Mexico, p. 5.

dominate the higher echelon of Republican leadership. In many
respects, their statements resemble those of ex-President Hoover.
Certainly the Republican party in New Mexico is far from progressive, and its policy frequently is labeled reactionary. The
Hispanic-American quite naturally is reluctant to support a party
which is opposed to the very measures which would serve his interests: the creation of a Rio Grande Authority, a vast re-
housing program, and increased expenditures in the field of public
health, education and social security.

Should the Republican party gain control of the national
administration, the political climate in New Mexico would undergo
an immediate change, however. The hard core of Hispanic voters
who have kept the Republican party alive, although not furnishing
its leadership, would come into its own when patronage was dispensed. And those Hispanos who deserted the Republican ship as
it floundered in the seas of the Great Depression again would be
forced to review their party allegiance. The difficulty would be
twofold, since it would be necessary to compare the merits of
federal Republican patronage and state Democratic patronage and
at the same time attempt to predict whether the Republican victory
at the national level would lead to a similar victory at the state
level.

At this point, the dilemma shows no sign of presenting
itself, for there is no indication of a Republican revival. For
all intents and purposes, New Mexico is a one-party state, which
means that from the purely practical point of view, the Hispano's
political problems lie within the orbit of the Democratic party.
This does not mean that politics in New Mexico are analogous to

those of the Democratic South. To the economic, social and
historical factors which so complicate politics in those states
a further complexity has been added in New Mexico. This is the
presence of a minority, in some respects akin to the submerged
Negro minority of the southern states, but unlike that ethnic
group, enjoying civil rights which entitle it to full participation in government.

Yet despite its claim to complete equality, the Hispanic-
Americans never have enjoyed political parity. Thus for the past
20 years the major reins of government have been grasped by Democratic officeholders and party leaders of Anglo descent. Attempts
to dispute that control frequently have been made by Hispano
leaders, but even when successful they have been short-lived.
The continued success of the Democratic party at the polls and
its continued domination by Anglo leaders, confronts the Hispanic-
American politician with several unhappy choices.

He may follow the path of least resistance and let
things ride. This implies recognition of the fact that numerical
superiority, economic superiority and better educational status
entitle Anglo-Americans to continue, and perhaps extend, their
control of the state government. The Spanish-speaking leaders
would be content to control the governments of the few predominantly Hispanic counties and to occupy whatever state elective
and appointive offices might be assigned to them in return for
their support. This tactic would place a premium upon an Hispanic
leader's attaching himself to a successful Anglo politician, thus
placing his personal fortunes above those of the Hispanic community. While this policy has been pursued by individual Hispanic-

Americans throughout the period of statehood, undoubtedly it
will be increasingly practiced as politicians reflect upon the
unprecedented and portentous rout of Hispanic candidates in the
election of 1950. The tactic has much to recommend it, both
from the standpoint of short-term advantage to the individual
Hispano and from the standpoint of long-term advantage to the
Spanish-speaking people as a whole. Incentive is given to personal advancement: the young Hispano knows that education,
initiative and personality bring their political reward, regardless of cultural background. The Anglo and Hispanic cultures
thus become fused through a mingling of their leadership over a
period of many years.

Another course of action open to Hispanic-American
political leaders is the formation of a Spanish-speaking bloc
within the Democratic party. Certain conditions favor this
development. One is the inter-group hostility engendered by the
FEPC fight of 1949 and the wholesale defeat of Hispanic candidates
in the Democratic primary of 1950. In each instance, the need for
intra-group solidarity became almost painfully obvious; the struggle for FEPC legislation in particular laid the groundwork for an
Hispanic bloc.

A second factor favoring the development of a Democratic
bloc based upon ethnic affiliation is the conflicting interests of
the Anglo politicians of the Albuquerque-Santa Fe region and the
eastern or Bible Belt. As far as voting strength is concerned,
the two sections are rather evenly balanced, as Judah recently
pointed out.[1] The record shows, however, that throughout the two

---

1. Charles B. Judah, The Republican Party in New Mexico, p. 21.

decades of undisputed Democratic control, the party has been
dominated by a small group from Albuquerque and Santa Fe. The
creation of Los Alamos county, with its almost 100 per cent
Anglo population, should strengthen the hands of the party ol-
igarchy. But numerous references have been made in this study
to the growing restiveness of the eastern Democratic leaders.
Thus one of the most astute observers of the New Mexico political scene recently wrote that "The Bible Belt has been slow to
wake up to its political power. That awakening is now taking
place.. . .By 1960 at the latest the East and South sides will
have taken over control of the Democratic party and consequently
will run New Mexico political affairs."[1]

An East-West struggle for control of the Democratic
party would furnish Hispanic-American politicians the opportunity
to exercise the balance of power. The creation of a Spanish-
speaking bloc for this purpose offers several attractions. Certainly the bloc could exact promise of patronage and the passage
of desired legislation as the price of its support. And the
formation of such a political grouping would encourage a feeling
of self-respect and group pride among the Spanish-speaking population.

But the same considerations which inhibit the formation
of a third party based on ethnic affiliation, discourage the
formation of an Hispanic bloc within the Democratic party. The
formation and operation of such a political bloc demands group
solidarity, along with a high degree of discipline. That neither

1. R. L. Chambers, "Capitol Views," Belen News-Bulletin, September 30, 1949.

of these factors is now present in the Spanish-speaking community of New Mexico is only too apparent.[1] Even if such cohesion characterized the Hispanic group, its leaders would hesitate to operate as a political bloc for fear of Anglo reprisal. While English-speaking Democrats from central and western New Mexico now may be engaged in a struggle with English-speaking Democrats from eastern and southern New Mexico, they would quickly form a coalition to dispose of any Hispanic bloc which might emerge from the welter of politics. The outcome of that struggle would reduce the Hispanic people to a type of political vassalage which they are not willing to contemplate.

A third route open to the Spanish-American leaders is the formation, within the Democratic party, of a liberal faction which not only would seek the support of Anglo voters, but also would elicit the support of the progressive wing of the Republican party. A number of considerations may encourage embarkation on this route. Poverty breeds the desire for drastic change--and no one questions the extent of poverty in New Mexico. In the base year 1939, more than 31 per cent of the total labor force in the state had annual incomes of less than $100.00. Sixty-two per cent of the urban population had incomes of less than $1,000.00, while almost 87 per cent of the rural farm population fell into this low-income group.[2] Thus it will be seen that poverty cuts across ethnic boundaries. Hispanic politicians who demand vigorous governmental intervention in behalf of the disadvantaged New Mexican speak for the poverty-stricken Anglo and win his

---

1. Cf. Chapter X.
2. Helen H. Ellis, Public Welfare Problems in New Mexico, p. 4.

support.

    While labor has become a force in New Mexico politics
only in recent years, it must be reckoned with. It is significant
to note that it was the C. I. O. which backed the formation of the
Asociacion Nacional Mexicana-Americana[1] and that the State Federation of Labor joined forces with the League of United Latin American Citizens to force the passage of the Fair Employment Practices Act.[2] The basis for powerful labor support of Hispanic
economic and social goals thus exists; the two groups might well
form the nucleus of a liberal bloc within the Democratic party.

    Should they attempt such a grouping, Hispanic-American
leaders could expect to receive support from yet another quarter:
the independent voters of Los Alamos, Albuquerque, Alamogordo and
other war-boom cities. Here the population is largely Anglo,
but in large part it is made up of people from the East and Midwest, rather than from the South.[3] That this new voting population is not influenced by ethnic considerations is demonstrated
by the fact that the Hispanic gubernatorial candidate carried
Los Alamos and the exclusive Anglo section of Albuquerque in the
1948 election.[4] The independent character of this new vote, along
with the absence of "racial" considerations, should make it recep-

---

1. Cf. Chapter VII.
2. Cf. Chapter XIII.
3. Interviews, David Keleher, confidential secretary, United States
   Senator, Dennis Chavez, Albuquerque, Dec. 28, 1949; Thomas
   Mabry, Governor of New Mexico, Santa Fe, Dec. 30, 1949; Manuel
   Lujan, Republican gubernatorial candidate, 1948, Santa Fe, Dec.
   29, 1949; Daniel Valdes, State governor, Lulac, Santa Fe, Dec.
   30, 1949; Bryan Johnson, Chairman, State Democratic Committee,
   Albuquerque, Dec. 27, 1949.
4. Estrella de Taos, November 11, 1948.
   Official Returns of the 1948 Elections, pp. 51-52.

tive to the proposals of liberal Hispanic politicians. This belief is augmented by the fact that a large portion of the "new"
New Mexicans are federal employees who owe their positions to
the New Deal and Fair Deal. It would be logical to expect that
a similar program at the state level would meet with their support.
In a sense, this group of "new" New Mexicans holds the future of
the state in its hands. As a group, it is highly intelligent,
economically independent and therefore politically independent,
and removed from inter-group conflict.

Hispanic-American leaders who envisage a liberal political grouping have yet another source of support. This is the
great reservoir of good will which is present in certain segments
of the Anglo community. Acts of discrimination against Hispanos
have been numerous, as this study has brought out in many instances. But the number of Anglo-Americans who are anxious to
bring an end to such practices is large, and there is evidence
that the number of sympathetic Anglos is rowing.[1] In the great
cultural centers of Taos and Santa Fe, the metropolis and
Albuquerque and the college and university towns this spirit is
most in evidence. But among professional and religious leaders
and among veterans the desire to effect a democratic modus
vivendi is evident. This may be observed even in eastern New
Mexico. The recently founded New Mexico Council on Human Relations includes not only the organizations which represent the

1. Thus Harper, Cordova and Oberg, in their exhaustive study,
    Man and Resources in the Middle Rio Grande, observe that
    "Fortunately there are many signs that the number of Anglo-
    Americans who appreciate the special obligations of a tri-
    cultural society is steadily increasing." (p. 117)

Hispanic, Negro and Jewish minorities, but it also has representation from the Ministerial Alliances and other Anglo
groups. The Council was an effective force in the struggle for
FEPC legislation, and it remains a potential nucleus for a liberal grouping within the Democratic party.

These are several of the avenues open to the Hispanic-Americans of New Mexico. It is simple to describe these political
routes, but difficult to predict which will be taken. For in
New Mexico, as elsewhere, politics does not operate in a vacuum.
An election in a remote mountain village is affected by debate
in the United Nations or by the mobilization of a Balkan nation,
no less than by the petty ambitions of a local politician. More
obviously, the village election is determined by the price of
chili and beans, which in turn is determined by the economic pulse
of the entire nation. Likewise, the extent to which civil rights
and economic opportunity are extended in New Mexico will be no
less determined by national policy.

Thus the politics of New Mexico is but one barometer of
many which register the sudden changes in the economic and social
climate of the world. Yet barring catastrophe, and attempting
to apply cold logic, it is difficult to contemplate any marked
change in New Mexico politics in the next few decades. A series
of loose and transitory alliances between Hispano and Anglo politicians, in which personal preferment outweighs group loyalty, will
continue to dominate the political scene. The Hispano politician
will persist in manipulating the Spanish-speaking minority in
order to achieve power, but having reached his goal, he will not
concern himself unduly with the grave problems of his culture

group. Under this system, the ambitious Hispano will fight his way to the political surface and gain his individual reward, leaving behind the great mass of his underprivileged people. Periodic political crises which exacerbate Anglo-Hispano relations will continue to develop, but they will become more widely spaced as the Spanish-speaking minority declines in numerical importance, and its leaders recognize the personal advantage of cooperation with politicians from the Anglo majority.

No one could doubt the accuracy of this picture were it not for the presence in the body politic of a new yeast. This is a handful of young men, both Anglo and Hispano, who not only believe in change, but, more important, that change is possible. Working through the American Veterans Committee, in the ethnic organizations, in the Protestant and Catholic churches, as well as in labor unions and in the Young Democrat and Young Republican clubs, this group already has made its presence felt. The political future of New Mexico may be determined by how quickly the idealistic young become the realistic old. To that degree, the problem of New Mexico is the central problem of the human race.

A SELECT BIBLIOGRAPHY

BOOKS

Abousleman, Michel D., Who's Who in New Mexico. Albuquerque: Abousleman Company, 1937. Pp. 254.

Bancroft, H. H., Arizona and New Mexico. San Francisco: The History Company, 1888. Pp. 829.

Bolton, Herbert E., The Spanish Borderlands. New Haven, Connecticut: Yale University Press, 1921. Pp. 320.

Bogardus, Emory S., The Mexican in the United States. Los Angeles: The University of California Press, 1934.

Bright, Robert, The Life and Death of Little Jo. Garden City, New York: Doubleday, Doran, & Company, Inc., 1944. Pp. 216.

Calvin, Ross, Sky Determines. Albuquerque: University of New Mexico Press, 1948. Pp. 333.

Coan, Charles F., History of New Mexico. Chicago and New York: American Historical Society, 1925. 3 vol.

Courtright, William H., (comp.), New Mexico Statutes, Annotated. Denver: W. H. Courtright Publishing Company, 1949. Pp. 2068.

Crichton, Kyle S., (Robert Forsythe, pseud.), Proud People. New York: Charles Scribner's Sons, 1944. Pp. 368.

Davis, Ellis Arthur, (ed.), Historical Encyclopaedia of New Mexico. Albuquerque: New Mexico Historical Association, 1945. Pp. 2079.

Davis, W. W. H., El Gringo. New York: Harper, 1857. Pp. 432.

Donnelly, Thomas C., The Government of New Mexico. Albuquerque: University of New Mexico Press, 1947. Pp. 330.

Donnelly, Thomas C., Rocky Mountain Politics. Albuquerque: University of New Mexico Press, 1940. Pp. 304.

Fergusson, Erna, Our Southwest. New York: A. A. Knopf, 1940. Pp. 396.

Fergusson, Harvey, The Blood of the Conquerors. New York: A. A. Knopf, 1921. Pp. 265.

Fergusson, Harvey, Rio Grande. New York: A. A. Knopf, 1933. Pp. 296.

Fulton, Maurice G., and Horgan, Paul, New Mexico's Own Chronicle. Dallas, Texas: Banks Upshaw & Company, 1937. Pp. 372.

Gamio, Manuel, Mexican Immigration to the United States: A Study of Human Migration and Adjustment. Chicago: University of Chicago Press, 1930. Pp. 262.

Garner, Claud, Wetback. New York: Coward-McCann, Inc., 1947. Pp. 216.

George Peabody College, Division of Surveys and Field Services, Public Education in New Mexico. Nashville, Tennessee, 1949. Pp. 420.

Haines, Helen, History of New Mexico. New York: New Mexico Historical Publishing Company, 1891. Pp. 631.

Hammond, George P., and Donnelly, Thomas C., Story of New Mexico. Albuquerque: University of New Mexico Press, 1936. Pp. 331.

Harper, Allan G., et al., Man and Resources in the Middle Rio Grande Valley. Albuquerque: The University of New Mexico Press, 1943. Pp. 156.

Johansen, Sigurd, Population of New Mexico: Its Composition and Change. State College, New Mexico: Experiment Station Press, 1940. Pp. 56.

Keleher, William A., Maxwell Land Grant. Santa Fe: Rydal Press, 1942. Pp. 168.

Kibbe, Pauline R., Latin-Americans in Texas. Albuquerque: The University of New Mexico Press, 1946. Pp. 279.

Lange, Dorothea, and Taylor, Paul S., An American Exodus. New York: Reynal & Hitchcock, 1939. Pp. 158.

Long, Haniel, Piñon Country. (American Folkways Series.) New York: Duell, Sloan & Pearce, Inc., 1941. Pp. 327.

McWilliams, Carey, Brothers Under the Skin. Boston: Little, Brown, 1943. Pp. 325.

McWilliams, Carey, North From Mexico. Philadelphia: J. B. Lippincott, 1949. Pp. 324.

Otero, Nina, Old Spain in Our Southwest. New York: Harcourt, Brace, 1936. Pp. 192.

Prince, LeBaron B., _A Concise History of New Mexico_. Cedar Rapids, Iowa: Torch Press, 1912. Pp. 272.

Sanchez, George I., _Forgotten People_. Albuquerque: University of New Mexico Press, 1940. Pp. 98.

Saunders, Lyle, _A Guide to Materials Bearing on Cultural Relations in New Mexico_. Albuquerque: The University of New Mexico Press, 1944. Pp. 528.

Soil Conservation Service, Division of Economic Surveys, _Tewa Basin Study_ (Vol. II). Albuquerque, 1939. Pp. 209.

State of New Mexico, _Blue Book_. Santa Fe: Secretary of State, (1913-1950).

Stillwell, Hart, _Border City_. Garden City, New York: Doubleday, Doran & Company, Inc., 1945. Pp. 276.

Stowell, Jay Samuel, _The Near Side of the Mexican Question_. New York: George A. Doran Company, 1921. Pp. 123.

Taylor, Paul S., _An American-Mexican Frontier_. Chapel Hill: The University of North Carolina Press, 1932. Pp. 337.

Teja Zabre, Alfonso, _Guide to the History of Mexico_. Mexico, D. F.: Press of the Ministry of Foreign Affairs, 1935. Pp. 375.

Thoma, Francisco, _Historia Popular de Nuevo Mexico_. New York: American Book Company. Pp. 185.

Tireman, Loyd S., _Teaching Spanish-Speaking Children_. Albuquerque: University of New Mexico Press, 1948. Pp. 218.

Tireman, Loyd S., and Watson, Mary, _A Community School in a Spanish-Speaking Village_. Albuquerque: University of New Mexico Press, 1948. Pp. 169.

Tuck, Ruth D., _Not With the Fist_ (A Study of Mexican-Americans in a Southwest City). New York: Harcourt, Brace and Company, 1946. Pp. 231.

Twitchell, Ralph Emerson, _The Leading Facts of New Mexican History_. Cedar Rapids, Iowa: Torch Press, 1911. (2 Vol.).

United States Department of Agriculture, _Climate and Man_. Washington: United States Government Printing Office, 1941. Pp. 1248.

University of New Mexico, _New Mexico State Business Directory and Economic Handbook_, (1946-47). Albuquerque: Bureau of Business Research, 1947.

Vaughn, John H., History and Government of New Mexico. State College, New Mexico: The Author, 1925. Pp. 369.

Villagra, Gaspar de, Historia de La Nuevo Mexico. Mexico City: Imprenta del Museo Nacional, 1900. 2 vol.

Works Progress Administration, New Mexico Historical Records Survey, Directory of Churches and Religious Organizations. Albuquerque, 1940. Pp. 385.

ARTICLES

Austin, Mary, "Mexicans and New Mexico." The Survey, Vol. 66 (May 1, 1931), pp. 141-144; 187-190.

Austin, Mary, "Rural Education in New Mexico." University of New Mexico Bulletin, Experimental School Series, Vol. 2, No. 1. Albuquerque: University of New Mexico Press, 1931.

Barker, S. Omar, "La Politica." New Mexico Quarterly, (February, 1934), pp. 3-13.

Campa, A. L., "Manana is Today." New Mexico Quarterly Review, (February, 1939), pp. 3-11.

Castañeda, Carlos E., "Some Facts on Our Racial Minority." The Pan-American, Vol. I (October, 1944), pp. 4-5.

"New Census Returns and Education of Our Spanish-Speaking Population." Education for Victory, Vol. I (July 15, 1942), pp. 7-8.

Chambers, R. L., "The New Mexico Pattern." Common Ground, (Summer, 1949), pp. 20-27.

Chambers, R. L., "Nuevo Mexico, Tierra de Desencanto." El Nuevo Mexicano, (February 9, 1950), p. 15.

Coers, W. C., "Comparative Achievement of White and Mexican Junior High School Pupils." Peabody Journal of Education, Vol. 12 (January, 1935), pp. 157-162.

Conway, T. F., "Bilingual Problem in the Schools of New Mexico." Alianza, (February, 1943), pp. 13-17.

Culbert, James I., "Distribution of Spanish-American Population in New Mexico." Economic Geography, Vol. 19 (April, 1943), pp. 171-176.

Davenport, Everard Lee, "The Intelligence Quotients of Mexican and Non-Mexican Siblings." School and Society, Vol. 36 (September, 1932), pp. 304-306.

Eyring, Edward, "Spanish for the Spanish-Speaking Students in the United States." Modern Language Forum, Vol. 22 (May, 1937), pp. 138-145.

Fergusson, Erna, "New Mexicans All." New Mexico School Review, (January, 1944), pp. 1-2.

Fisher, Reginald, "Hispanic People of the Rio Grande." El Palacio, (August, 1942), pp. 157-62.

Gonzalez, Jennie M., "Shall Spanish Be Taught in the Elementary Schools of New Mexico?" Lulac News, (October, 1940), p. 6.

Guiterrez, Edward A., "Darkness Lifts to the Dawn." Lulac News, (April, 1939), pp. 10-13.

Hamilton, Arthur W., "Rio Grande Death Watch." New Mexico Quarterly, (Spring, 1948), pp. 67-79.

Haught, B. F., "The Language Difficulty of Spanish-American Children." Journal of Applied Psychology, (February, 1931), pp. 92-95.

Heflin, Reuben, "New Mexico Constitutional Convention." New Mexico Historical Review, (January, 1946), pp. 60-68.

Johansen, Sigurd, "Social Organization of Spanish-American Villages." Southwestern Social Science Quarterly, (September, 1942), pp. 151-9.

Keleher, William A., "Law of the New Mexico Land Grant." New Mexico Historical Review, (October, 1929), pp. 350-371.

Krich, Aron, and Garoffolo, Vincent, "Regionalism and Politics." New Mexico Quarterly, (November, 1937), pp. 261-9.

Laughlin, Ruth, "Coronado's Country and Its Children." Survey Graphic, Vol. 29 (May 1, 1940), pp. 276-282.

Loomis, Charles P., "Wartime Migration from the Rural Spanish-Speaking Villages of New Mexico." Rural Sociology, Vol. 7 (December, 1942), pp. 384-395.

Ludi, Phillip, "Radio Programs to Improve Spanish-American Minority Status." New Mexico School Review, (October, 1943), p. 12.

Lynn, K., "Bilingualism in the Southwest." Quarterly Journal of Speech, Vol. 31 (April, 1945), pp. 175-180.

Manuel, H. T., "The Educational Problem Presented by the Spanish-Speaking Child of the Southwest." School and Society, Vol. 40 (November 24, 1934), pp. 692-695.

Martinez, Filemon T., "Conservation and Purification of the Spanish Language." Lulac News, (November, 1938), pp. 13-18.

Martinez, Paul G., "Teaching English to Spanish-Speaking American Children in New Mexico." New Mexico School Review, (September, 1933), pp. 22-23.

McWilliams, Carey, "Mexican Bundle of Myths." Saturday
    Review of Literature, (December 25, 1948), p. 13.

Montalbo, Philip J., "Our Rights." Lulac News, (February,
    1938), pp. 3-5.

Mullins, R. J., "The Dixon Ruling." New Mexico School Re-
    view, (May, 1949), p. 14.

Mullins, R. J., "Where Did They Go? And Why?" New Mexico
    School Review, (May, 1949), (Reprint).

Otero, Adelina, "My People." The Survey, Vol. 66 (May 1,
    1931), pp. 145-148.

Rebolledo, Antonio, "Lo Que Nos Toca Hacer." Lulac News,
    (September, 1940), p. 19.

Russell, John C., "Racial Groups in the New Mexico Legislature,"
    Annals American Academy Political and Social Sciences,
    V. 195, pp. 62-71.

Russell, John C., "State Regionalism in New Mexico." Social
    Forces, Vol. 16, 1937. Pp. 268-72.

Salinas, Ezequiel D., "Las Aspiraciones de los Lulacs."
    Lulac News, (October, 1938), pp. 25-6.

Sanchez, George I., "New Mexico Acculturation." New Mexico
    Quarterly, Vol. II (February, 1941), pp. 61-68.

Sandoval, Benjamin, "Adelante Lulacs." Lulac News, (October,
    1940), p. 23.

Servando, O. B., "Dicen que se Avecina una Catastrofe
    Politica de Gran Magnitud en N. M." El Nuevo Mexicano,
    (March 9, 1950), pp. 1-13.

Speiss, Jan, "Feudalism and Senator Cutting." American
    Mercury, (November, 1934), pp. 371-74.

Strickland, V. E., and Sanchez, G. I., "Spanish Name Spells
    Discrimination." The Nation's Schools, (January, 1948),
    pp. 22-24.

Taylor, Paul S., "Mexicans North of the Rio Grande." The
    Survey, Vol. 66 (May 1, 1931), pp. 135-140; 197; 200-202.

Tittman, Edward D., "The First Irrigation Lawsuit." New
    Mexico Historical Review, (October, 1927), pp. 363-68.

Valencia, F., "March Onward Lulac Soldiers." Lulac News,
    (February, 1938), pp. 7-8.

Walter, Paul A. F., "Octaviano Ambrosio Larrazolo." New Mexico Historical Review, (April, 1932), pp. 97-104.

Walter, Paul A. F., Jr., "The Spanish-Speaking Community in New Mexico." Sociology and Social Research, Vol. 24 (November 10, 1938), pp. 150-157.

Weeks, O. D., "The League of United Latin-American Citizens." Southwestern Political and Social Science Quarterly, (December, 1929), pp. 257-278.

MONOGRAPHS, BULLETINS, AND PAMPHLETS

Alpenfels, Ethel J., Sense and Nonsense About Race. New York: Friendship Press, 1946. Pp. 48.

Asplund, Rupert, and Nohl, Albert K., New Mexico's Tax Structure. Albuquerque: Division of Research, Department of Government, University of New Mexico, 1946. Pp. 31.

Beckett, Paul, and McNutt, Walter L., The Direct Primary in New Mexico. Albuquerque: Division of Research, Department of Government, University of New Mexico, 1947. Pp. 34.

Buck, Carl Edward, Health Survey of the State of New Mexico. Santa Fe: New Mexican Publishing Company, 1935. Pp. 35.

Catholic Welfare Conference, "The Spanish-Speaking of the Southwest and West." (Reports of the Conferences held at San Antonio, Texas, July 20-23, 1943, and at Denver, October 7-20, 1944). Washington, D. C., National Catholic Welfare Conference, 1944.

Donnelly, Thomas C., The State Educational System. Albuquerque: Division of Research, Department of Government, University of New Mexico, 1946. Pp. 35.

Ellis, Helen H., Public Welfare Problems in New Mexico. Albuquerque: Division of Research, Department of Government, University of New Mexico, 1949. Pp. 35.

Judah, Charles B., Governor Richard C. Dillon. Albuquerque: Division of Research, Department of Government, University of New Mexico, 1948. Pp. 40.

Judah, Charles B., The Republican Party in New Mexico. Albuquerque: Division of Research, Department of Government, University of New Mexico, 1949. Pp. 37.

Leonard, Olen, and Loomis, C. P., "Culture of a Contemporary Rural Community, El Cerrito, New Mexico." Rural Life Series, No. 1. Washington, D. C.: United States Department of Agriculture, Bureau of Agricultural Economics, 1941.

Mullins, R. J., and Fixley, E. H., Public School Attendance and School Costs in New Mexico. Albuquerque: Division of Research, Department of Government, University of New Mexico, 1946. Pp. 26.

National Catholic Welfare Conference, Proceedings, Second Seminar on Spanish-Speaking of Southwest and West, Denver, 1944. Pp. 45.

New Mexico State Federation of Labor, Official Yearbook. Albuquerque: Ward Anderson Printing Company, 1947. Pp. 77.

Parish, William J., The New Mexico State Budget System. Albuquerque: Division of Research, Department of Government, University of New Mexico, 1946. Pp. 24.

Reeve, Frank D., New Mexico: Yesterday and Today. Albuquerque: Division of Research, Department of Government, University of New Mexico, 1946. Pp. 20.

Reynolds, Annie, "The Education of Spanish-Speaking Children in Five Southwestern States." Bulletin No. 11. Washington, D. C.: United States Department of the Interior, Office of Education, 1933. Pp. 64.

Rusinow, Irving, "A Camera Report on El Cerrito, A Typical Spanish-American Community in New Mexico." Washington, D. C.: United States Department of Agriculture, Bureau of Agricultural Economics, Misc. Pub. No. 479, GPO, 1942.

Saunders, Lyle, Spanish-Speaking Americans and Mexican-Americans in the United States. New York: Bureau for Intercultural Education, 1944. Pp. 14.

Seyfried, J. E., Illiteracy Trends in New Mexico, Bulletin, V. 8, No. 1. Albuquerque: University of New Mexico, 1934. Pp. 38.

State of New Mexico, Child Health Services in New Mexico. Santa Fe: Department of Public Health, (September, 1947), pp. 64.

State of New Mexico, Labor Laws. Santa Fe: State Labor and Industrial Commission, 1949. Pp. 130.

State of New Mexico, New Mexico Educational Directory. Santa Fe: State Department of Education, 1949. Pp. 104.

State of New Mexico, New Mexico Public School Code, 1941 Supplement, 1938 Compilation. Santa Fe: State Department of Education, 1941. Pp. 78.

State of New Mexico, Official Returns of the 1948 Elections. Santa Fe: Secretary of State, 1949. Pp. 526.

State of New Mexico, A Survey of Illiteracy in New Mexico. Santa Fe: New Mexico State Planning Board, 1936. Pp. 48.

Taxpayers Association of New Mexico, This Is How Public Schools Are Financed in New Mexico. Santa Fe: The Association, 1949. Pp. 29.

Twitchell, Ralph E., *Spanish Colonization in New Mexico*,
    Publication No. 22. Santa Fe: Historical Society of
    New Mexico, 1919. Pp. 39.

University of New Mexico, *Conference on the Problems of
    Education Among Spanish-Speaking Populations of Our
    Southwest*. Albuquerque: School of Inter-American
    Affairs, 1943. Pp. 6.

Valdez, Daniel T., "The Spanish-Speaking People of the
    Southwest." WPA *Program of Education and Recreation*,
    Bulletin WE-4. Denver: Colorado State Department of
    Education, (June 25, 1938).

Walter, Paul, Jr., and Calvin, Ross, *The Population of New
    Mexico*. Albuquerque: Division of Research, Depart-
    ment of Government, University of New Mexico, 1947.
    Pp. 38.

UNPUBLISHED THESES

Chavez, A. B., Use of the Personal Interview to Study the
Subjective Impact of Culture Contacts. Albuquerque:
University of New Mexico, 1948. Pp. 132.

Cunningham, Jonathan R., Bronson Cutting, A Political Biography. Albuquerque: University of New Mexico, 1940,
Pp. 243.

Harper, William Lee, A History of New Mexico Election Laws.
Albuquerque: University of New Mexico, 1927. Pp. 87.

Johansen, Sigurd, Rural Social Organization in a Spanish-
American Culture Area. Madison: University of Wisconsin,
1941. Pp. 254.

Johnson, Claudia L., The Re-Organization of an Elementary
School for Spanish-Speaking Children. Austin: University
of Texas, 1946. Pp. 140.

Kluckhohn, Florence, Los Atarqueños. Cambridge, Massachusetts:
Radcliffe College, 1941. 2 Vol.

McDowell, Archie M., Opposition to Statehood Within the
Territory of New Mexico, 1888-1903. Albuquerque: University of New Mexico, 1939. Pp. 103.

McNutt, Walter L., An Inquiry into the Operation of the Primary System of New Mexico. Albuquerque: University of
New Mexico, 1946. Pp. 98.

Rexroad, Vorley M., The Two Administrations of Governor
Richard C. Dillon. Albuquerque: University of New
Mexico, 1947. Pp. 128.

Russell, John C., State Regionalism in New Mexico. Palo Alto,
California: Stanford University, 1938. Pp. 284.

Sanchez, George I., The Education of Bilinguals in A State
School System. Berkeley: University of California,
1934. Pp. 154.

Stumph, Roy C., The History of the Referendum in New Mexico.
Albuquerque: University of New Mexico, 1941. Pp. 87.

Swayne, James B., A Survey of the Economic, Political and
Legal Aspects of the Labor Problem in New Mexico. Albuquerque: University of New Mexico, 1936. Pp. 121.

Thomas, Dorothy, The Final Years of New Mexico's Struggle for
Statehood, 1907-1912. Albuquerque: University of New
Mexico, 1939. Pp. 141.

Walter, Paul A. F., Jr., *A Study of Isolation and Social Change in Three Spanish Speaking Villages of New Mexico*. Palo Alto, California: Stanford University, 1938. Pp. 343.

The Mexican American

An Arno Press Collection